Unity
Apprentice

By Matt Larson, Ben MacKinnon & Eric Van de Kerckhove

Unity Apprentice

Matt Larson, Ben MacKinnon & Eric Van de Kerckhove

Copyright ©2022 Razeware LLC.

Notice of Rights

All rights reserved. No part of this book or corresponding materials (such as text, images, or source code) may be reproduced or distributed by any means without prior written permission of the copyright owner.

Notice of Liability

This book and all corresponding materials (such as source code) are provided on an "as is" basis, without warranty of any kind, express of implied, including but not limited to the warranties of merchantability, fitness for a particular purpose, and noninfringement. In no event shall the authors or copyright holders be liable for any claim, damages or other liability, whether in action of contract, tort or otherwise, arising from, out of or in connection with the software or the use of other dealing in the software.

Trademarks

All trademarks and registered trademarks appearing in this book are the property of their own respective owners.

ISBN: 978-1-950325-59-7

Table of Contents

Book License 7
Before You Begin **9**
   What You Need 11
   Book Source Code & Forums 13
      About the Authors 16
      About the Editors 16
      About the Artists 17
Section I: Creating Your First Game **19**
   Chapter 1: Getting Started 21
      What is Unity? 22
      Why use Unity? 22
      Requirements and expectations 23
      What's ahead 23
      Key points 24
      Where to go from here? 24
   Chapter 2: Installing & Using the Unity Editor 25
      Introduction 25
      Installing the Unity Hub 26
      Start a new project 27
      Unity Editor 29
      Publishing a game 34
      Key points 38
   Chapter 3: GameObjects & Prefabs 39
      Getting started 40
      GameObjects 41
      Components 46

    Prefabs.. 51
    Making it all come together................................ 55
    Key points.. 61

Chapter 4: Creating & Using Scripts With C# 63
    Scripting with C# 64
    Scripting fundamentals 66
    Your first script 71
    Using scripts with other components......................... 73
    Key points.. 76

Section II: Now You're Building With Components 77

Chapter 5: Setting Up a Scene 79
    Getting started 80
    Camera.. 82
    Lighting a scene 87
    Adding characters 100
    Key points 106

Chapter 6: Input & Collisions................................ 107
    Input systems... 108
    Setting up the new input system 110
    Linking input to movement..................................... 120
    Physics... 133
    Key points 138

Chapter 7: User Interfaces 139
    Title screen overview... 140
    Canvas.. 141
    Adding UI elements 145
    Interaction system 156
    Key points 166

Chapter 8: Scriptable Objects 167

Dialogue user interface 168
Dialogue manager overview........................... 169
Creating a dialogue system............................ 170
Lines of dialogue.. 172
Conversations 173
Dialogue starter component 176
Improving the dialogue manager 180
Handling questions..................................... 186
Key points 197

Section III: Smart Enemies & the Bigger Picture .. 199

Chapter 9: Basic AI & Navigation........................... 201
Introduction to the Arena 201
Game logic... 207
Game state 213
Common pitfalls with NavMesh Agents............... 216
Key points 217
Where to go from here?............................... 217

Chapter 10: Advanced Camera Controls With Cinemachine.. 219
Introduction 220
Cinemachine Components 220
Challenges... 231
Key points 231

Chapter 11: Asynchronous Functions, Coroutines & Object Pooling... 233
Introduction 233
Timed destruction of GameObjects................... 234
Synchronous and asynchronous functions 234
Understanding coroutines 235
Object pooling... 238

How to implement object pooling 239
Complete the ObjectPool 240
Creating an object pool for projectiles 242
Updating the projectile launch 244
Creating an object pool for the enemies 245
Key points 248

Section IV: Cooking Up Animations 249

Chapter 12: Basic Animation Principles 251
Introduction to Unity animation types 252
Introducing the kitchen 252
Deciding on how to animate your GameObjects 254
Building a tween library 255
Setting up a basic animation 264
Key points 274

Chapter 13: Advanced Animation Principles 275
Animator component 276
Importing the animations as states 279
Animator transitions 282
Animator parameters 287
Animator triggers 295
Challenge 302
Key points 302

Chapter 14: Advanced Scriptable Objects 303
Scriptable objects as data containers 304
Scriptable Objects as events 309
Expanding Chef's repertoire 316
Challenge 325
Key points 326

Conclusion 327

Book License

By purchasing *Unity Apprentice*, you have the following license:

- You are allowed to use and/or modify the source code in *Unity Apprentice* in as many apps as you want, with no attribution required.

- You are allowed to use and/or modify all art, images and designs that are included in *Unity Apprentice* in as many apps as you want, but must include this attribution line somewhere inside your app: "Artwork/images/designs: from *Unity Apprentice*, available at www.raywenderlich.com".

- The source code included in *Unity Apprentice* is for your personal use only. You are NOT allowed to distribute or sell the source code in *Unity Apprentice* without prior authorization.

- This book is for your personal use only. You are NOT allowed to sell this book without prior authorization, or distribute it to friends, coworkers or students; they would need to purchase their own copies.

All materials provided with this book are provided on an "as is" basis, without warranty of any kind, express or implied, including but not limited to the warranties of merchantability, fitness for a particular purpose and noninfringement. In no event shall the authors or copyright holders be liable for any claim, damages or other liability, whether in an action of contract, tort or otherwise, arising from, out of or in connection with the software or the use or other dealings in the software.

All trademarks and registered trademarks appearing in this guide are the properties of their respective owners.

Before You Begin

This section tells you a few things you need to know before you get started, such as what hardware and software you'll need to get the most out of this book, where to find the project files for this book, and more.

What You Need

To follow along with this book, you'll need the following:

- **The Unity Hub**: The latest version will work. At the time of writing, this was version 3.0.0.

- **The Unity Editor**: Choose to install the latest 2020.3.x LTS Release. All the sample projects will work with this version.

- **Any Code Editor or IDE**: Ideally, this should be able to understand and format C#. Since C# was originally written by Microsoft, a good choice would be Visual Studio Community (if you're using Windows) or Visual Studio Code (if you're using macOS or Linux). But, you can use whatever editor you're most comfortable with if you prefer!

Book Source Code & Forums

Where to download the materials for this book

The materials for this book can be cloned or downloaded from the GitHub book materials repository:

- https://github.com/raywenderlich/uapp-materials/tree/editions/1.0

Forums

We've also set up an official forum for the book at https://forums.raywenderlich.com/c/books/unity-apprentice. This is a great place to ask questions about the book or to submit any errors you may find.

"To Bonnie, Merlijn and Harvey. Thanks for all the support and the laughs. This wouldn't be possible without you."

— *Eric Van de Kerckhove*

"To my two sons, Felix and Leif, and all the games we will play together."

— *Matt Larson*

"In memory of Ian Quin, who taught me better English long before I would ever write a page worth reading. You will be missed, Grampa."

— *Ben MacKinnon*

About the Authors

Eric Van de Kerckhove is a hobbyist game developer and 3D printing enthusiast from Belgium. Most days, you can find him at his desk while tinkering on scripts to automate tasks and creating 3D models to use in games or to print.

Matt Larson is a software developer for the life sciences and scientific visualization. He was an author on Unity AR & VR by Tutorials and is a believer in new technologies for engaging with 3D content. When he is not working on software, you'll find him fixing up old synthesizers, kayaking and spending time with his wife and kids.

Ben MacKinnon has been a Unity Developer for as long as he has been a father, with both playing a huge part in his life. He spent a large part of his career Augmenting Architecture, but more recently has focussed on VR in development of the virtual communications platform ENGAGE.

About the Editors

Toby Flint is a tech editor of this book. Toby is a software developer inspired by a love of games. When he's not programming or otherwise staring at a screen, you can find him exploring the backcountry, tasting a new crispy beverage, poking at a piano, or staring at a wall, absent-mindedly absorbed in his own thoughts.

Srikar Mutnuri is a tech editor of this book. Srikar is a software developer who loves building things. When the git commits are done, you can mostly find him reading a book, practicing music, or simply bingeing that new series.

Megan Mallicoat is the editor of this book. She's a university journalism instructor and has professional experience in communications management, web design and graphic design — but she's most devoted to pointing out grammar and spelling errors. In her "free time," you'll most likely find her on the sidelines of some kind of kids sports practice, holding a book.

Adrian Strahan is the final pass editor for this book. Adrian is a lead iOS developer working for a leading UK bank. When he's not sat in front of a computer building apps or playing games, he enjoys long walks, streaming movies, building Lego models, listening to music and trying to keep fit and healthy.

About the Artists

Jake Nolt is a 3D artist, indie game developer and game development professor. When not developing or teaching, Jake enjoys spending time with family, gaming and being outdoors.

Section I: Creating Your First Game

Unity provides two applications to help you manage your game assets: the Unity Hub and the Unity Editor. This section will introduce you to both and show you how to start building your first game.

You'll learn all about the Unity Editor's user interface and gain a solid understanding of how everything is organized. Then, you'll learn about GameObjects and Prefabs. You'll go on to write some basic C# scripts to enhance the gameplay and add some interactivity to your first game - a very strange weapon-manufacturing machine!

Chapter 1: Getting Started

By Eric Van de Kerckhove

Welcome to the start of your game development journey with the help of *Unity Apprentice*!

By opening this book, you're already on your way to becoming a game developer. The four sections within these pages will teach you how to create games using the Unity game engine. From navigating the editor and adding objects to a scene to creating complex animations and using advanced scripting, it's all in here for you to discover.

This book assumes you have no experience with Unity or the programming language C#. That means if you're completely new to Unity, you'll feel right at home. Even if you're a veteran, this book is full of useful tips and techniques the authors have learned over the years.

What is Unity?

Unity is a cross-platform **game engine**, which is a software framework designed for creating video games with a lot of tools geared toward making the process easier and more comfortable. It's developed by *Unity Technologies* and has been regularly updated since its introduction in 2005. There's a good chance you've played at least one game developed using Unity — some of the more popular titles include *Among Us*, *Cities: Skylines*, *Hearthstone*, *Hollow Knight* and *Cuphead*.

Why use Unity?

Unity is the most popular game engine to date and loved by beginners and experts alike for a lot of reasons. Here are some reasons why Unity is great:

- Unity is free to use for hobbyists and small game studios.

- Unity's editor runs on Windows, macOS and Linux — making it a true cross-platform tool.

- The Unity editor is easy to use and navigate, and the way you manipulate objects in a scene is intuitive.

- Unity uses the "create once, deploy anywhere" principle. This means you can create a game and distribute it to all standalone platforms, mobile devices, consoles and the web without needing to maintain multiple projects or code bases.

- The scripting language driving Unity games is C#, which is one of the most-used programming languages around the globe. This makes it easy to learn the language because the web is full of articles and tutorials on the subject.

- There's a helpful community spread across the forums, Unity Answers and its Discord server that are friendly toward beginners.

- Most parts of Unity are well-documented with clear explanations and examples.

If you're still not convinced, check out some of the stories (https://unity.com/madewith) by game studios that use Unity for their development. Some of these stories offer unique behind-the-scenes perspectives that are worth a read.

Requirements and expectations

Getting into making games nowadays is easier than ever! All you need to follow along with this book is a computer, an internet connection and some time. Unity and the tools used throughout the book — like Visual Studio (Code) — are free.

This book covers some mechanics and ideas used in popular indie games like *Night In The Woods* and *Overcooked*. The resulting games provide basic gameplay and artwork to complete a concept and get important ideas across. They aren't full-featured games like you would buy from Steam or the Epic Games Store. Each of the final projects provides a great starting point to learn from and build upon to create something truly unique yourself.

What's ahead

This book is divided into four sections:

- **Section 1** covers **why and how you should use Unity**. The goal of this section is to give you a broad overview of the Unity editor. You'll build a sample project to learn all about GameObjects, Prefabs and even some C# scripting.

- **Section 2** goes over **Unity's essential features**. This includes setting up a scene and its lighting, handling input and user interfaces. At the end of it, you'll have a charming game with an easily extendable conversation system.

- **Section 3** is all about **pathfinding and AI**. This section will teach you how to make AI-controlled characters find their way around an arena and use advanced camera techniques. This section concludes with a fun shooting game to use as a base.

- **Section 4** shows you the ropes when it comes to **animations**. From lerps to tweens, this section teaches you how to make your games more dynamic and lively by using Unity's scripting API and animation system. As a cherry on top, it shows you how to use scriptable objects in interesting ways. At the end you'll have a cooking game that's ready for you to expand upon.

By the end of this book, you'll be able to create your own games and make them run on Windows, macOS and Linux!

Key points

- You don't need any experience with Unity or C# to follow along with this book.
- Unity is a **free cross-platform game engine**.
- The documentation for Unity and its scripting API can be found online.
- With Unity, you can create games for a lot of different platforms — including Windows, macOS, iOS, Android and even the web.
- Scripting is done with **C#**, a popular programming language.
- The projects in this book are **starting points** to create your own games.

Where to go from here?

It's easy to get overwhelmed by the amount of windows, components and settings Unity provides. If you're unsure what something does or how to use it, you can take a look at Unity's manual (https://docs.unity3d.com/Manual/index.html). And, you can take a peek at the scripting reference (https://docs.unity3d.com/ScriptReference) when you want more information about a certain class or method while scripting.

In case you can't find what you're looking for in the sources above, there's the forums (https://forum.unity.com/) and Unity Answers (https://answers.unity.com/index.html), both of which contain a treasure trove of information and give you a place to ask your own questions. There's also Unity's Discord server (https://discord.com/invite/unity), where you can share your creations and ask for feedback and help.

Finally, there's the raywenderlich.com website, which is full of articles about game development (https://www.raywenderlich.com/gametech) for Unity and tools to help you on your journey.

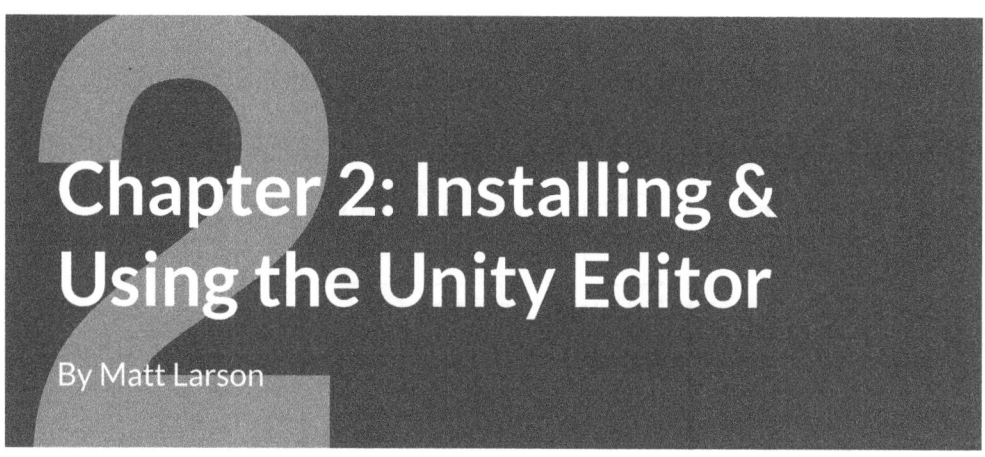

Chapter 2: Installing & Using the Unity Editor

By Matt Larson

Introduction

It's time to develop your first Unity game! The **Unity Hub** is your gateway to install the **Unity Editor**, manage all your projects and find tutorial resources.

Be aware there are different versions of the Unity Editor as updates and improvements are continually released. However, the Unity Hub will help you install and manage editor versions. It acts as a single overall manager for downloading the latest Unity Editors, keeping track of your projects and launching the Unity Editor.

Installing the Unity Hub

Start by downloading the Unity Hub installer for either Windows or Mac from https://unity.com/download:

1. Download the Unity Hub

Follow the instructions onscreen for guidance through the installation process and setup.

Download for Windows
Download for Mac
Instructions for Linux

You should install the latest version of the Unity Hub (3.0.0 at the time of writing) to have an up-to-date listing of sample starter content. After installation, start the Unity Hub and you'll see this:

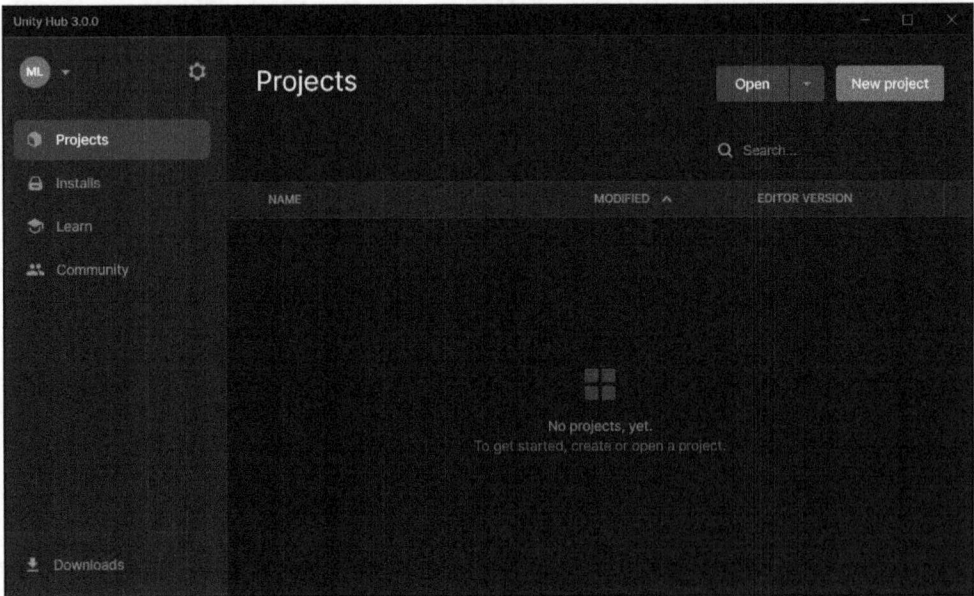

On the left side of the Unity Hub, select **Installs**, then click **Install Editor** in the top right of the hub.

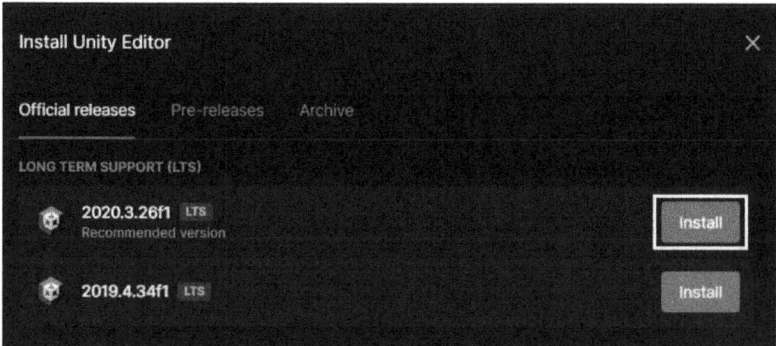

Choose to install the latest **2020.3.x LTS** release. For reference, all of this book's sample projects were built with **2020.3.26f1**, but any 2020.3 release should be compatible.

Start a new project

Once the install has finished, switch back to the **Projects** tab and click **New project**.

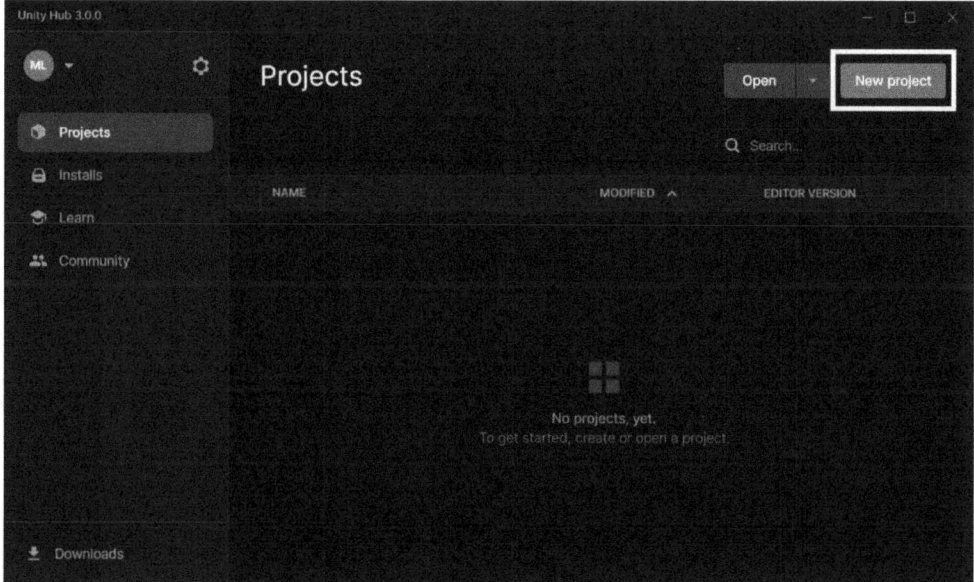

With the 2020.3 LTS Unity Editor as the default, the Unity Hub will provide a variety of templates. Find the **Third Person Template** under the **Core** tab on the left.

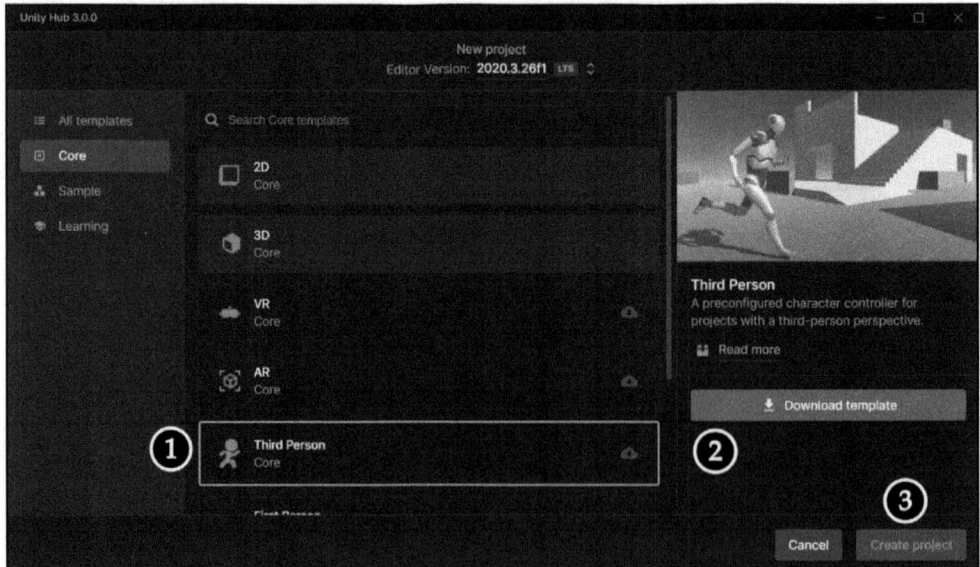

Click **Download template** to download the required assets for this template.

When this has downloaded, look under **Project Settings** and set **Project name** to **ThirdPerson**, then specify a location on your local disk drive. Finally, click **Create project**.

This template provides an over-the-shoulder view of the player's character — called a third-person view — which can often be a great starting place to develop a variety of games. And, this example project already has simple controls to move the character and generated level content. You'll use this simple game to tour some of the main features of the Unity Editor.

Unity Editor

After creating the third-person template project, the Unity Editor will open.

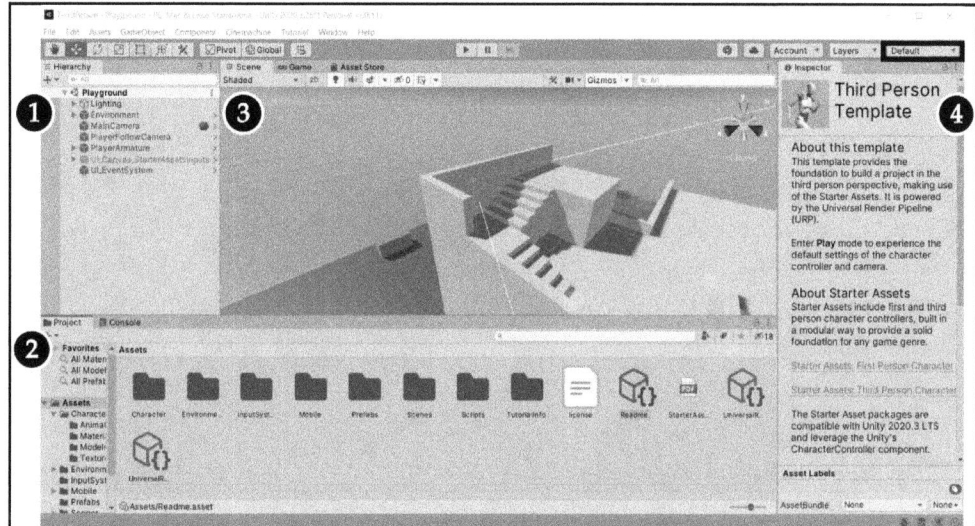

Initially, you'll see several panes within the Unity Editor:

1. The **Hierarchy Window**: Provides a listing of the components that make up a scene.

2. The **Project Window**: Lists the assets in your project that you can add to a scene.

3. The **Scene View**: Shows the level of the scene.

4. The **Inspector Window**: Shows the details about a selected object.

> **Note**: If your layout is different, you can reset the panel layout as shown above by choosing the **Layout** menu in the upper-right of the window and selecting the **Default** option.

Scene View

The most visually striking of the set of panes is the **Scene View** that shows the current level of the game.

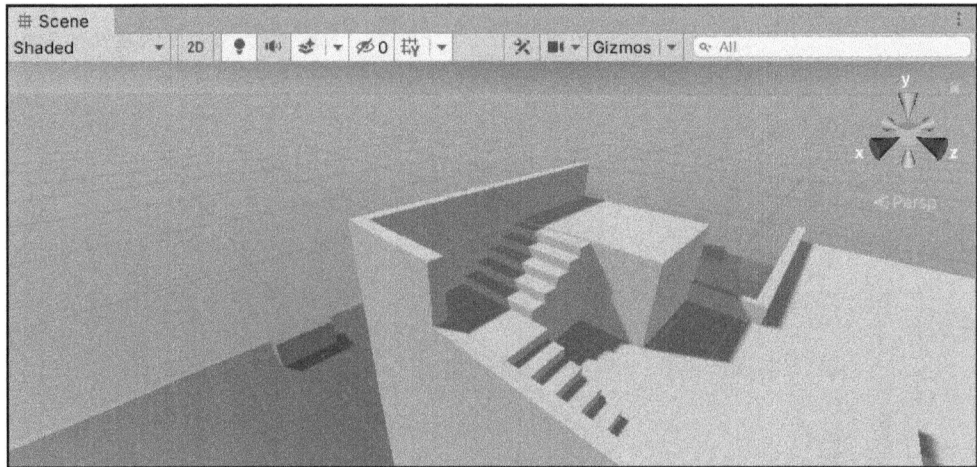

Look to the upper-right in the view and find the **Scene Gizmo** — the axis showing the X, Y and Z directions in the 3D world. This shows your current orientation in the environment. You can change this at any time by interacting with it, together with the move, orbit and zoom tools as described in Scene view navigation (https://docs.unity3d.com/Manual/SceneViewNavigation.html).

The top toolbar of the Scene View includes different tools that control how the environment of the level is displayed.

The **Draw Mode** drop-down is set as **Shaded**, but it can be changed to different rendering modes in the Scene View. Next, notice the toggles for a 2D camera, lighting and sound. Then, there's a drop-down menu with controls enabling various effects like fog and particle systems. Finally, the last category worth mentioning is **Gizmos**, which are visual aids that show in the Scene View and can help annotate a scene.

Game View

Choose the tab next to the **Scene View** to switch to show the **Game View**. Now the camera is behind a robotic character in the game.

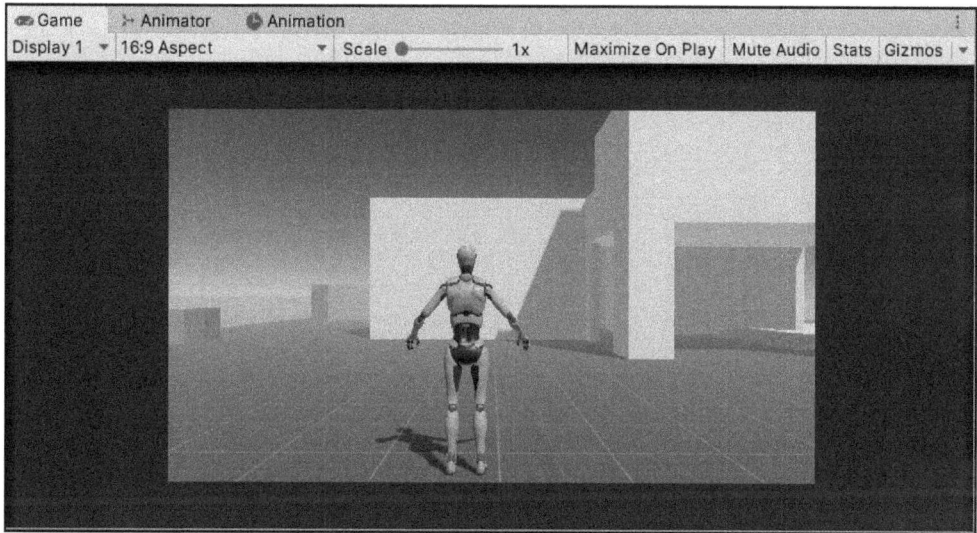

The toolbar of the Game View controls the behavior of the view and what happens when you begin playing the game. The **Maximize On Play** toolbar item can be enabled to make the Game View take up the entire Unity Editor view when playing a scene.

Running the game

Look at the top of the editor and find the game controls.

Press the Play button on the left to activate the game view. The mouse now controls the in-game camera, and the keyboard's a, s, d and w keys move the character around the scene. You can press the **Escape** key at any time to release the mouse from the focus of the Game View, and click the **Play** button again to end gameplay. The **Pause** button in the middle halts execution of the game, and the button on the right allows you to step forward a single frame at a time - great for carefully inspecting small details.

Hierarchy window

The **Hierarchy** window shows a list of items that are within the scene. In Unity, these are called GameObjects, which are essential units for building a game. Chapter 3 will provide a more detailed description of GameObjects and how you can use them to build your first game.

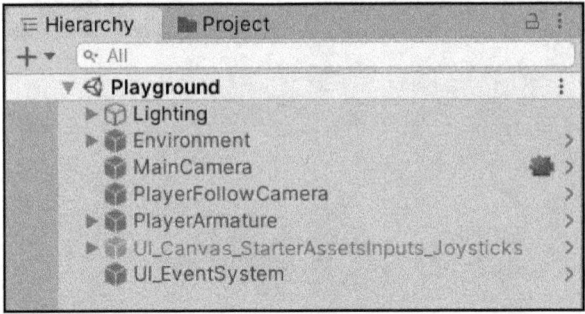

Project window

The **Project** window is in the lower left of the default layout. What you see in this view is a listing of the **Assets** of the game. These include all the 3D models, images, sounds, animations and other generated artwork that can be used to assemble and define your game.

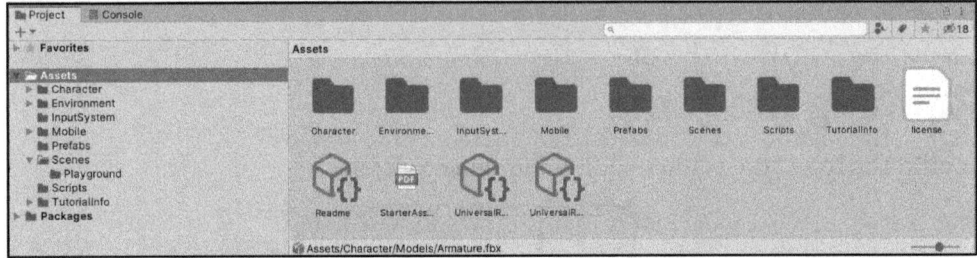

Expand the **Character** folder in the Project window and select the subfolder called **Models**. Click the **Armature** item to select it.

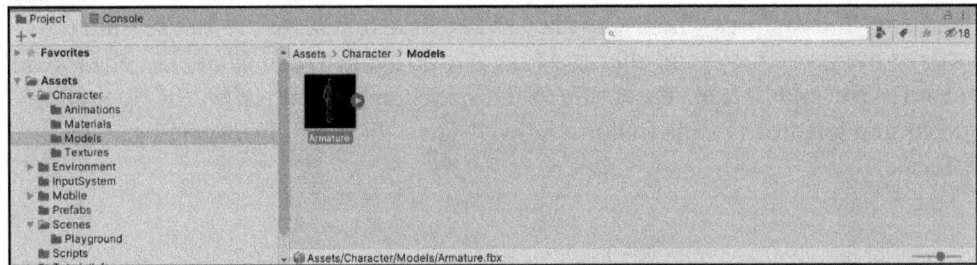

Inspector window

Upon selecting a different item in the Project, the **Inspector** window updates to display new details. It's also where you can see the details of any GameObject or asset in your project or scene. Additionally, this is the primary location to make changes to parameters that configure how the GameObject or asset will behave in the game.

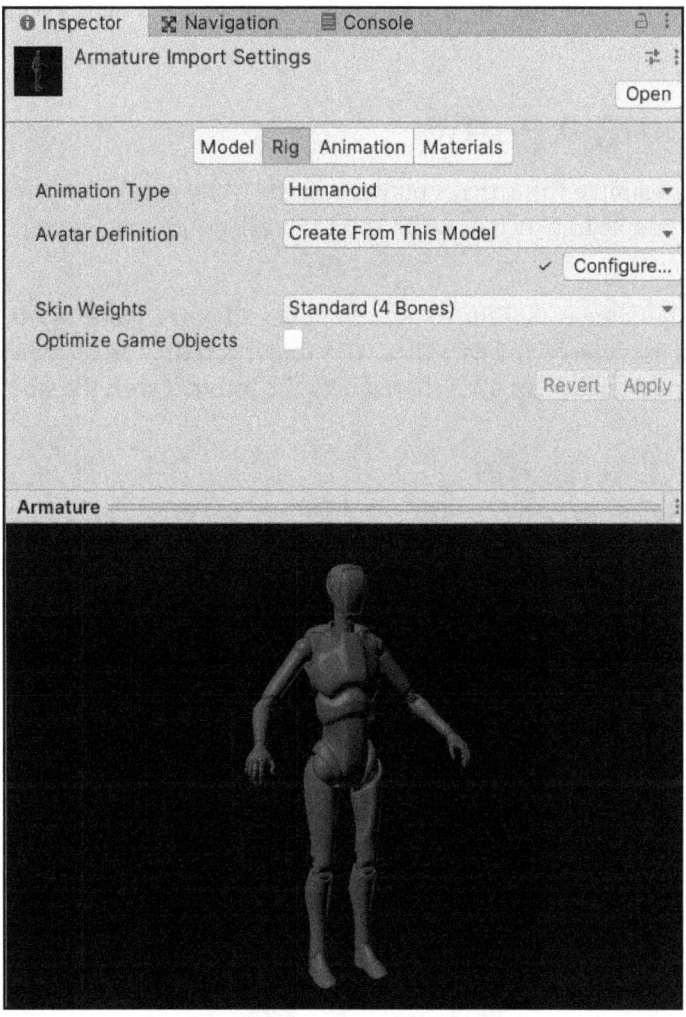

In this instance you can see details about the 3D model that's the main character shown in the Game view. This is the character controlled by the player in the third-person game template.

Other windows

Additional Unity windows will be covered later in the book, including:

- The **Navigation Window**. This is covered in depth in Chapter 9 as you build a project using the Unity NavMesh Agents.

- The **Animator Window**. This is introduced during Chapter 12 when different mechanisms of animating content in Unity will be integrated into a game.

Publishing a game

You now have a simple game that's playable in the Unity editor. But what if you wanted other people to play it as well? You can't ask everyone to install Unity and open your project.

This is where building comes in — which compiles all of the game assets into a single folder with an executable and data files. This folder can then be archived and sent to your family and friends — or even shared over the internet with the whole world.

Adding platforms

Unity supports a lot of platforms for building your game — including Windows, macOS, Linux, Android and iOS. The default Unity installation only includes the platform you installed the editor on, but you can easily add more platforms. To check out what platforms you have installed, open the **Unity Hub** application and click **Installs**.

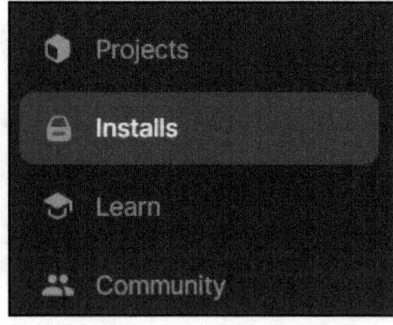

Open the **Add Modules** screen for your version of Unity by clicking the gear menu for an installed editor version and selecting **Add Modules**.

Check all the platforms you want to add to your Unity installation and click **Continue**.

Add modules	Required: 5.11 GB	Available: 214.2 GB
OpenJDK	67.2 MB	145.91 MB
iOS Build Support	377.13 MB	1.72 GB
tvOS Build Support	374 MB	1.71 GB
☑ Linux Build Support (IL2CPP)	98.15 MB	408.39 MB
☑ Linux Build Support (Mono)	97.58 MB	402.12 MB
☑ Mac Build Support (Mono)	304.79 MB	1.66 GB
Universal Windows Platform Build Support	270.12 MB	1.91 GB
☑ WebGL Build Support	304.28 MB	1.07 GB
☑ Windows Build Support (IL2CPP)	69.75 MB	353.18 MB

Now return to the Unity editor. It's time to set up everything and create a build.

Creating a build

Open the **Build Settings** window by clicking **File ▸ Build Settings…** or by pressing **Control-Shift-B** on Windows or **Command-Shift-B** on Mac.

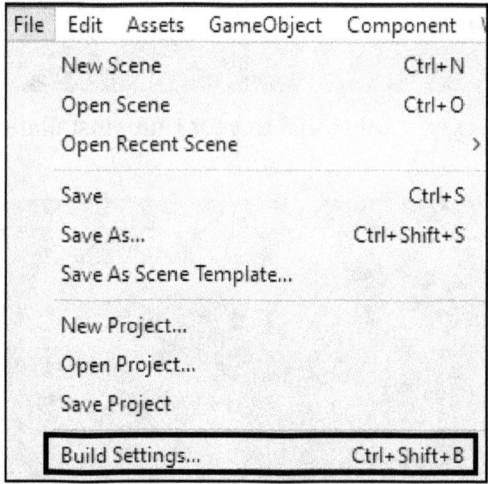

The **Build Settings** window consists of three main parts:

- At the top is a list with included scenes. This is empty at the moment.
- On the left is the list with all available platforms, even those you haven't installed.
- On the right are the build settings for the selected platform.

To start, you'll want to add the **Playground** scene that's open in the editor, so click the **Add Open Scenes** button below the scene list to quickly add it. Another way to add a scene to this list is dragging the scene asset from the **Project** view into the scene list.

In the end, the scene should be visible in the scene list:

Any scenes in the list will be added to the final build in the same order. This means the first scene will be shown first, so it's a good idea to make this your title screen.

Now, select the very first platform in the list on the left: **PC, Mac & Linux Standalone**. Next, select your preferred platform on the right in the **Target Platform** drop-down. Selecting a different platform in this drop-down will trigger Unity to reload all assets and optimize them for the target platform. You can leave the rest of the parameters as-is.

Finally, click the **Build** button at the bottom right and select a name and location for the build. Unity will now build the player executable. After a short while, the folder will be opened in your system's file explorer.

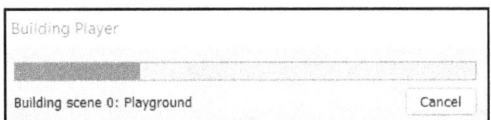

While it builds, as an aside, should you prefer customizing certain properties for the build, Unity's Player Settings (https://docs.unity3d.com/Manual/class-PlayerSettings.html#general) and the more general Project Settings (https://docs.unity3d.com/Manual/comp-ManagerGroup.html) will come in really handy.

Congratulations on making your first build! At this point, you have all the tools ready to start working on the projects of this book. The next chapter will introduce you to the building blocks of Unity, the GameObjects and how to create your own playable projects.

Key points

1. The **Unity Hub** is a one-stop gateway to Unity Editor versions, projects and learning resources.

2. Everything happens within the **Unity Editor**, where you can build levels, script your gameplay and test your game.

3. The **Scene View** is where you'll build your game levels and organize your 3D content.

4. The **Game View** shows a preview of the camera view. After pressing play, it becomes the active gameplay of your scene.

5. A scene is composed of GameObjects. All of the GameObjects of your scene are shown in the **Hierarchy Window**.

6. All the assets of your game are shown in the **Project Window** and the details of an individual asset can be viewed in the **Inspector Window**.

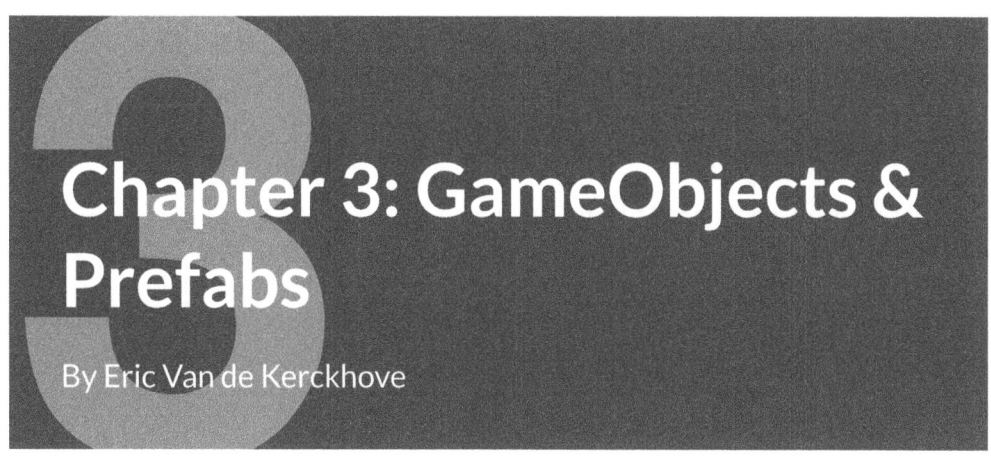

Chapter 3: GameObjects & Prefabs

By Eric Van de Kerckhove

In the previous chapter, you learned about the windows and views you'll use throughout this book. This chapter will focus on the **Hierarchy**, the **Project window** and the **Inspector** — and how to use them together to create a game. Now that you've learned how to install Unity and navigate around the editor, you're ready to create something of your own.

In this chapter and the next, you'll create your first playable project — a small clicker game — from the ground up! In this game, you'll construct forks and skewers using an ammunition machine for the tank to use in one of the later chapters.

While creating the game, you'll learn all about **GameObjects**, the building blocks that can represent just about anything from lights and scenery to NPCs by attaching **components** to them. These components add logic and functionality to your objects. You'll also learn the basics of **prefabs**, which act as GameObject templates and allow you to effortlessly spawn instances of a GameObject into a scene.

Getting started

To kick things off, you'll need to know how to open an existing Unity project. The easiest way to do this is to start up the **Unity Hub** application first. With Unity Hub opened, click the white **Add** button at the top right, navigate to the **projects** folder for this chapter and select the **Chapter 3 Starter** folder. This will add the project to the top of the list.

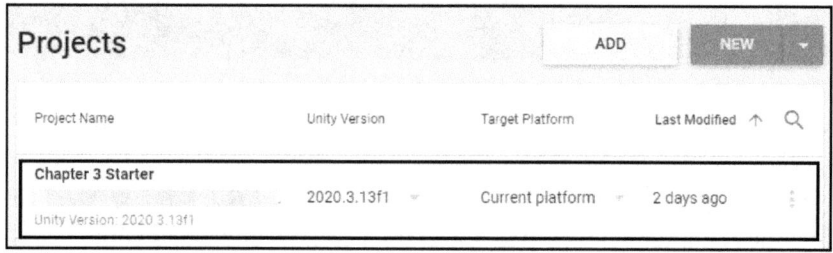

Now, click the name of the project to open it in Unity. The project should load up in less than a minute.

> **Note**: You may get a warning that you don't have a particular version of Unity installed on your machine. This is because every project is tied to a specific version of Unity. To fix this, select an available version using the **Unity Version** drop-down on the right side of the project name. For this book, any recent version of Unity LTS 2020.X will work.

The starter project comes packed with several assets for you to use. These assets are categorized per type in a folder called **RW**. You can look at them in the **Project view**.

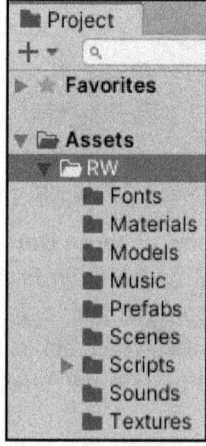

Here's an overview of what's included:

- **Fonts**: This contains the font used throughout the book for UI elements.
- **Materials**: A folder containing the material files that hold the data for what a 3D model should look like.
- **Models**: This folder contains all 3D models used in this chapter.
- **Music**: A music track used for the background music lives in here.
- **Prefabs**: This folder holds all the prefabs for the scenery and pre-assembled GameObjects. More on prefabs later in this chapter.
- **Scenes**: A single scene sits in here — the **Weapon-Forge** scene, which you'll be working in.
- **Scripts**: A folder containing a few scripts to get started. The next chapter covers scripting in more detail.
- **Sounds**: This folder holds the sound effect used when creating ammunition.
- **Textures**: A folder containing image files that are used as the textures for the 3D models.

Double-click the **Weapon-Forge** scene file in **RW / Scenes** to open that scene in the Unity editor. If you take a look at the **Game view**, you'll notice there's nothing there except for a dark gray background. A perfect starting place!

GameObjects

GameObjects are the fundamental building blocks of every Unity project. Every single object in the Hierarchy is a GameObject!

Take a look at the Hierarchy — there are two GameObjects already present. Any newly created Unity scene comes supplied with a **Main Camera** and a **Directional Light**, as these provide you with a way to view the game world — the light shines on all models and provides shadows while the camera renders a 2D image to your screen.

Go ahead and add a new empty GameObject to the scene by clicking the **Plus** icon at the top left of the Hierarchy and selecting **Create Empty**.

Name this new GameObject **Managers**. The default name of a newly created GameObject is simply "GameObject", but you can rename GameObjects by slowly double-clicking it in the Hierarchy or by pressing **F2** on your keyboard. Select your new GameObject in the Hierarchy and take a look at the Inspector.

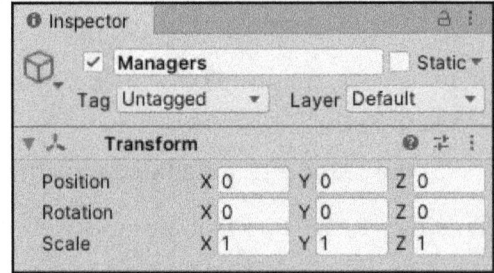

Every GameObject has two things in common:

- Attributes like a name, tag and layer

- A **Transform** component

You can see and edit the attributes at the very top of the Inspector.

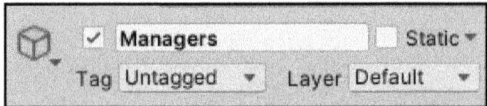

From the top left to the bottom right, these are:

Icon

You can assign an icon to GameObjects to make it easier to find them in the **Scene** view.

Try assigning Managers a blue icon from the top row by clicking on the cube icon and selecting the second icon in the list.

If you look at the **Scene view**, you'll see a blue label with "Managers" written inside it. If you don't see the label immediately, select **Managers** in the Hierarchy and press **F**. This will move the camera in the scene view to focus on the selected GameObject.

Besides the built-in icons, you can use your own by clicking the **Other...** button and selecting an image from the assets. You might have noticed that the **Main Camera** and **Directional Light** have an icon in the **Scene view** even though their GameObject doesn't. Some components, like **Camera** and **Light**, draw an icon themselves; you can see and toggle these by opening the **Gizmos** drop-down in the top right of the **Scene** view. More on components later on in this chapter.

Active checkbox

The little checkbox next to the name of the GameObject allows you to temporarily activate or deactivate a GameObject and all of the components attached to it. Deactivating a parent GameObject deactivates all of its children as well. The names of inactive GameObjects turn gray in the Hierarchy.

Name

This is simply the name of the GameObject. Make sure to give GameObjects distinct and clear names so you can easily find what you're looking for, even in a crowded Hierarchy.

Static checkbox and drop-down

This checkbox marks a GameObject as **static** — meaning it won't move while running the game. Static GameObjects save on performance since a lot of Unity's under-the-hood systems skip or simplify certain calculations for these GameObjects. A few examples of objects that might be marked static are walls, non-moving props and other pieces of scenery like mountains. By default, GameObjects are **dynamic** so they are able to move freely.

The static drop-down menu allows you to specify in detail what systems should perceive the GameObject as static. Most of the time, you'll simply want to check the static checkbox for maximum performance.

Tag

The **Tag** drop-down allows you to assign a tag to a GameObject. A tag is a keyword to put a GameObject together with the rest of its kind in a group. For example, Unity comes with a built-in tag named **Player**. You can assign this tag to the main character you control. Now, when an enemy is looking around for a hero to attack, it might look for all GameObjects with the **Player** tag. You can also add your own tags by clicking the **Add Tag…** list entry. This way, you can add any word or short sentence as a custom tag.

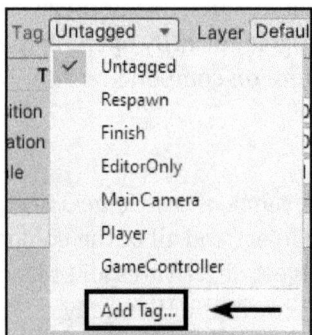

You can use this to add a **Healing** tag, for example, and whenever the player walks into an area marked with this tag, they regenerate their health. Tags are extremely powerful when used with scripting. One thing to watch out for is that a GameObject can only have a single tag assigned to it.

Layer

The **Layer** drop-down lets you assign a layer to a GameObject. Layers are keywords used for filtering collisions, lights and camera rendering. Similarly to tags, you can add custom layers with the **Add Layer...** list entry. For collisions, layers can be used to specify which GameObjects collide with others and which don't. For example, you could add a **Ghost** layer that doesn't collide with the scenery but can get hit by the player's magical projectiles. The same **Ghost** layer can be used for filtering out light of ghostly entities.

As for using layers for camera filtering, certain effects — like showing a minimap to the player — benefit from using their own layers. For example, you could add red-colored cubes above the heads of enemies and add a **Minimap** layer to those cubes. You could then add a camera that looks down from above, restrict it to only see the Minimap layer, and show what it sees in a corner of the screen. Like tags, layers are powerful and versatile!

GameObjects for organization

Empty GameObjects can be used as dividers and even folders in the Hierarchy. Any GameObject can be parented to another GameObject, making it a child. Click the **Plus** button at the top left of the Hierarchy and select **Create Empty** again like you did for **Managers**. Name this new GameObject **Ammunition Spawner**. Make this GameObject a child of **Managers** by dragging it on top of **Managers** in the Hierarchy.

Ammunition Spawner is now offset in the Hierarchy. You'll see a little arrow to the left of **Managers**.

As you can see, Managers is used like a folder in this case, holding a single manager GameObject for now that will soon have some logic added to it.

Components

As mentioned before, GameObjects are the basic building blocks, but they're also containers for **components**. A component is what gives a GameObject its features, its functionality and some visuals in the Scene view, like the icons. Even an "empty" GameObject has a **Transform** component, which gives the GameObject a position, rotation and scale in the scene. A GameObject can have multiple components attached to it to make layers of functionality. This is known as an **Entity Component System** (ECS). In Unity, the entities are the GameObjects and the components are… the components. :]

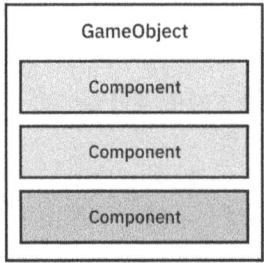

Unity comes with a lot of components built in. Here are some often-used examples with their intended uses:

- **Audio Source**: Play music and sound effects.
- **Light**: Shine light on objects in the scene.
- **Camera**: Render the scene to the Game view.
- **Mesh Filter**: Loads 3D geometry from an asset.
- **Mesh Renderer**: Render a 3D mesh from a **Mesh Filter** component at the position of the **Transform** component.
- **Particle System**: Emit particles to create visual effects like fire and smoke.
- **Box Collider**: Add a cube-shaped collision area to a GameObject.
- **Rigidbody**: Add physics to a GameObject that has a collider attached.

You can also create your own components by writing scripts. This is where things get interesting as you can implement just about any logic yourself by going this route. Writing scripts will be covered in the next chapter; for now, it's important to understand what components are and how you can add them to GameObjects.

Adding components

Time to add a component and take a look at what makes it tick! Select **Ammunition Spawner** in the Hierarchy and, in the Inspector, click the **Add Component** button below the **Transform** component. Next, start typing "ammunition" until **Ammunition Spawner** shows up in the list. Click the entry to add it as a component.

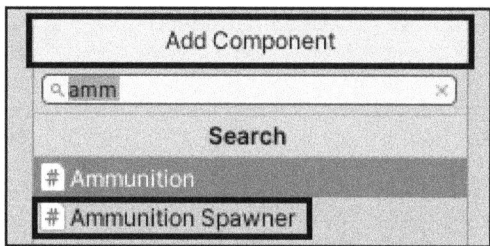

The **Ammunition Spawner** component is now added to the GameObject of the same name. This component was created by writing a script, denoted by the "(Script)" tag after its name. Before delving into this specific component, you'll want to know about a few pieces that are shared among all components.

From left to right these are:

Active checkbox

Like GameObjects, individual components can be enabled and disabled using a checkbox.

Component name

Every component has a distinct name. When writing a script, you can choose this name yourself.

Reference button

Clicking this little help button opens Unity's documentation for any built-in component. You can add a URL to your own documentation via scripting. If you're unsure what a certain component or its attributes do, make sure to remember this useful button.

Presets

The **Presets** button allows you to store the currently filled in attributes as a preset asset and load existing presets. For example, you might have set up the light for a torch just the way you like it and you want to easily apply the same settings to others of its kind. Simply press the **Presets** button, click the **Save current to…** button and save the preset somewhere with your other assets. From now on, the preset you saved will appear in the Presets list after pressing the **Presets** button — allowing you to instantly apply your carefully tweaked parameters. This is another useful tool to be aware of!

Commands button

> **Note**: Random trivia time! Did you know a button with three vertical dots like this one is called a **kebab menu**?

This final button opens up the commands menu, which you can also access by simply right clicking on a component. It shows even more options to play with.

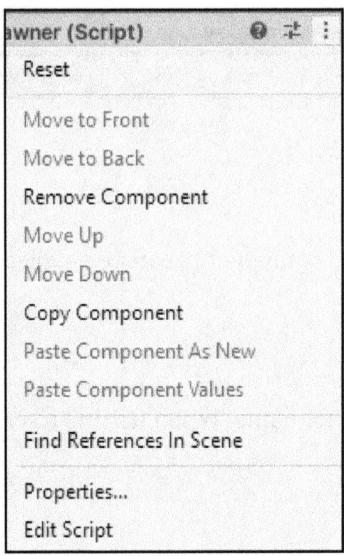

Here's an overview of what these commands do:

- **Reset**: Reset a component to its default values. For example, a **Tranform** component will reset its position, rotation and scale back to **(X:0, Y:0, Z:0)**.
- **Move to Front**: Move a UI element to the front. This can only be used on **Rect Transforms** on a **Canvas**. More on that in Chapter 7.
- **Move to Back**: Same as above, but this moves the UI element to the back.
- **Remove Component**: Remove the component from the GameObject.
- **Move Up**: Move the component one spot up in the component list.
- **Move Down**: Move the component down.
- **Copy Component**: Copy the component and all of its values to the clipboard.
- **Paste Component As New**: Add the copied component as a new component, with all the values added.
- **Paste Component Values**: Paste just the copied values onto a component. This can be useful for quickly applying the same settings across a range of components.
- **Find References In Scene**: This filters the Hierarchy and Scene view to a certain component type.
- **Properties…**: Open the properties of this component in a new window.
- **Edit Script**: This option only appears for custom components. Opens the script that created this component.

There may be even more options here depending on the type of component. A **Transform** component allows for copying and pasting only certain values — like its position, for example.

Component properties

Most components come with lists of properties. These can be numbers, vectors, sentences, colors, lists and references to GameObjects and other components.

If you take a look at a **Transform** component, it has a property for its position, rotation and scale. These are simply **Vector3** properties — meaning each property has an X, Y and Z value.

The Ammunition Spawner, on the other hand, has a lot of different properties going on!

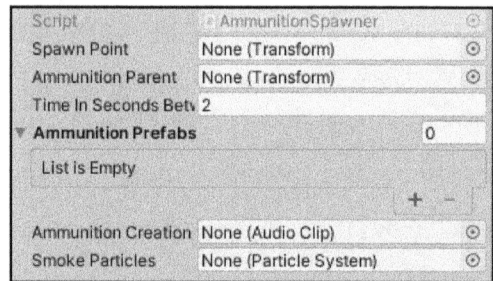

Any property with a button next to it with a circular icon is a reference to another GameObject, component or asset. To illustrate this, create a new empty GameObject, name it **Ammunition** and reset its **Transform** component (right-click on **Transform** from Inspector ▸ Reset). This GameObject will serve as the parent for all pieces of ammunition that will get spawned. Select **Ammunition Spawner** again and click the little button next to its **Ammunition Parent** property.

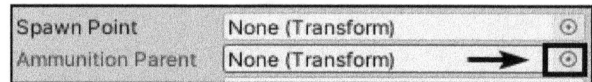

A new window will open up prompting you to select a **Transform**. Double-click **Ammunition** in this list to set it as the **Ammunition Parent**.

There's an even easier way to set up references like this! First, click the little button again next to **Ammunition Parent**, and this time, set it to **None**. This is simply to clear its value. Now drag the **Ammunition** GameObject to the **Ammunition Parent** property to quickly set it as the value.

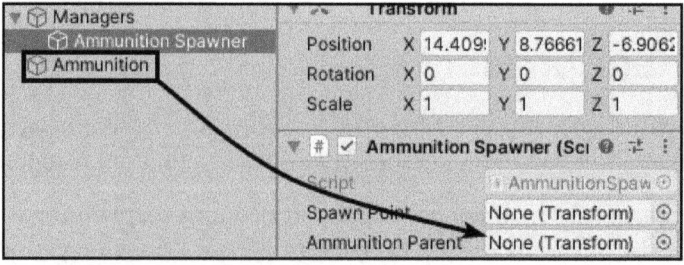

This is a lot faster (and more satisfying) than finding and clicking a value in a list.

Prefabs

Now that you know the basics of GameObjects and components, it's time to discover the power of **prefabs**! Prefabs are ready-made GameObjects, comparable to templates. A GameObject can be created once with all of its components and properties set up and stored as a prefab asset. This prefab can then be instantiated, which means an instance or copy of the prefab is spawned into the scene.

Instancing prefabs

Instancing a prefab can be done manually in the editor or at runtime with the use of scripting. The starter project comes with a lot of prefabs in the **RW / Prefabs** folder. To instance your first prefab, drag **Environment** from **RW / Prefabs** to the root of the Hierarchy.

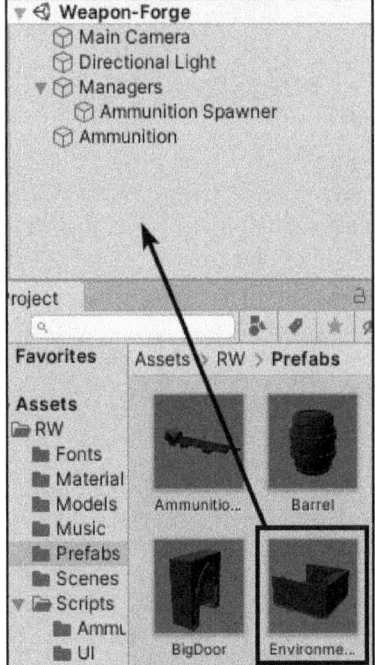

Just like that, you've now added a full 3D environment to your scene!

With the way the camera is positioned, the **Game** view shows a corner of the room.

If you take a look at **Environment** in the Hierarchy, its little cube icon is colored blue to indicate that the GameObject is linked to a prefab. If you expand it, you'll notice it acts like a folder for the walls, pillars, floor tiles and the different props scattered around.

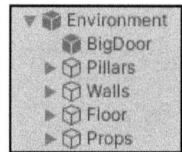

Creating a prefab

Creating a prefab is just as easy as instancing one. Just drag a GameObject to a folder in the Project view and a prefab will be created. Drag the **Directional Light** from the Hierarchy to the **RW / Prefabs** folder to turn it into a prefab.

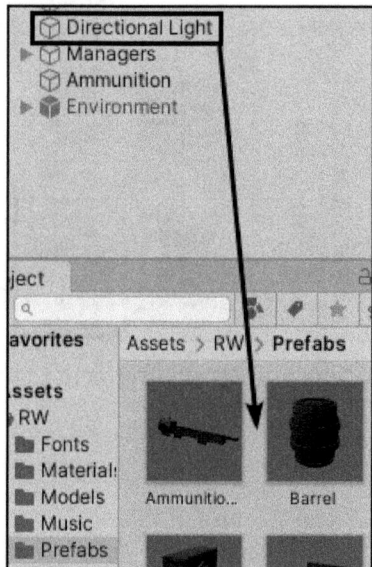

To test out the new light prefab, delete **Directional Light** from the Hierarchy and drag an instance of **Directional Light** from **RW / Prefabs** back to the Hierarchy.

Editing prefabs

You can edit prefabs directly, allowing any changes to flow to all of its instances. This is where prefabs really start to shine and can save a tremendous amount of time.

For example, you might have a power-up prefab in your game that looks like a floating orb and you have a bunch of these in your scene. If you ever decide that these power-ups should look like cubes with some fancy particles, you can simply edit the prefab and all instances will be replaced with the new graphics. If you weren't using prefabs in this case, you'd have to painstakingly replace the graphics for every power-up in the scene one by one.

There are two ways of editing prefabs, depending on the complexity of the prefab:

- Edit the prefab directly from the folder it resides in.
- Open the prefab in **Prefab Mode**.

First, try editing a prefab from its folder. Select **Directional Light** in **RW / Prefabs** and take a look at the Inspector. All of the properties of **Directional Light** are showing up, ready to be edited. Change the **Intensity** of its **Light** component to **2** and select any other property to apply the change. You'll see that the light in scene gets a lot brighter as the **Directional Light** instance in the Hierarchy changed as well. Be sure to change **Intensity** back to **1**, as everything will look kind of washed out otherwise.

Editing prefabs in this way is quick. It's fine for simple GameObjects without any children. However, what if you wanted to move one of those barrels in the **Environment** prefab? If you select **Environment** in **RW / Prefabs**, there's not much to edit here except for its **Transform** component — and even then, only the **Scale** will affect the scene. This is where Prefab Mode comes in!

To enter Prefab Mode, either double-click **Environment** in the **RW / Prefabs** folder or press the **Open** button at the top of the Inspector.

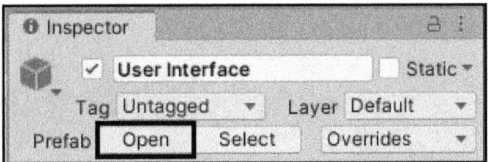

You'll now see just the **Environment** GameObject in the Hierarchy. When you take a look at the **Scene** view, it has a different look. The background is transformed into a blueprint-like grid.

Anything you change in this mode is saved to the prefab, and as a result the changes flow to any existing instances. The **Game** view is still showing the actual scene instead of the Prefab Mode view, so that's a good indicator of your changes being applied. Select one of the barrels in the **Scene** view standing near the door and move it to the other side of the arch.

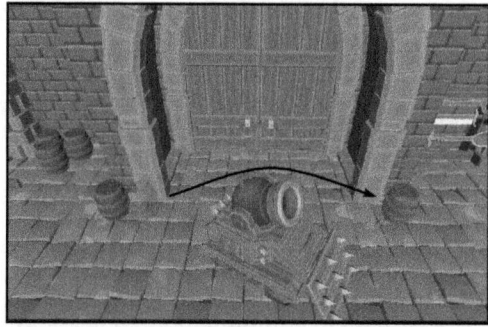

Now save the scene by pressing **Control-S** or **Command-S**, or by choosing **File ▶ Save** in the top menu. After doing this, you'll notice the same movement happened in the **Game** view. Prefab Mode allows you to edit prefabs isolated in full detail. This is another great tool to use when developing your own games!

To exit Prefab Mode, click the left-arrow at the top left of the Hierarchy.

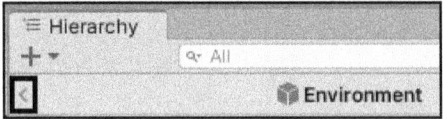

At this point, you might want to save again. It's good practice to do this sporadically so you won't lose any progress if disaster strikes.

Making it all come together

Now you know how GameObjects, components and prefabs work together to create a game, but the actual gameplay isn't working just yet. For that, you'll need to get the heart of the game — the **Ammunition Spawner** — working and introduce some way of providing input to your player so there's some interaction going on. Before all that though, you'll need to add the machine that will create the ammunition — or will appear to do so, at least.

Filling in the blanks

Drag the **AmmunitionMachine** prefab from **RW / Prefabs** to the root of the Hierarchy. This will add the machine to the middle of the room.

While you're at it, drag the **Smoke** prefab to the root of the Hierarchy as well. It has a **Particle System** component attached that can generate a small puff of smoke on command.

Now to fill in some of the missing properties of the **Ammunition Spawner**! Select **Ammunition Spawner** in the Hierarchy and start off by dragging **AmmunitionMachine**'s child, **SpawnPoint**, to the **Spawn Point** property.

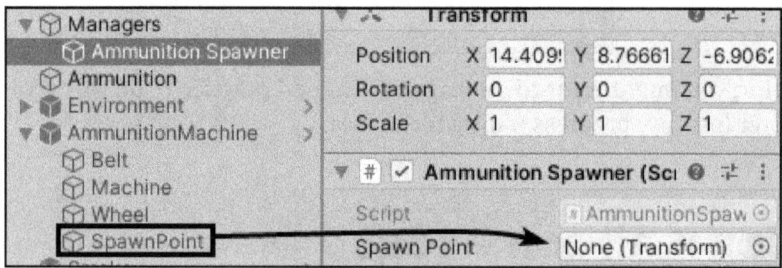

The **SpawnPoint**'s position will be used as the location for the ammunition to spawn from. Next up is the **Ammunition Parent**. All ammunition will be parented to this GameObject to keep the **Hierarchy** clean. Drag **Ammunition** from the Hierarchy to the **Ammunition Parent** property to assign it.

The **Ammunition Prefabs** is a list. These can be filled up by simply dragging objects of the correct kind to them (GameObject or prefabs in this case). You can also click the **Plus** icon at the bottom right to add a new element to the list and then assign a prefab to it.

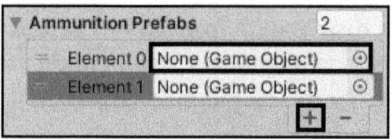

In this case, it's simpler to just drag the prefabs. Drag **LargeFork** and **LargeSkewer** from the **RW / Prefabs** folder to **Ammunition Prefabs**. You'll need to drag them onto the name of the property — left from where it says **0**.

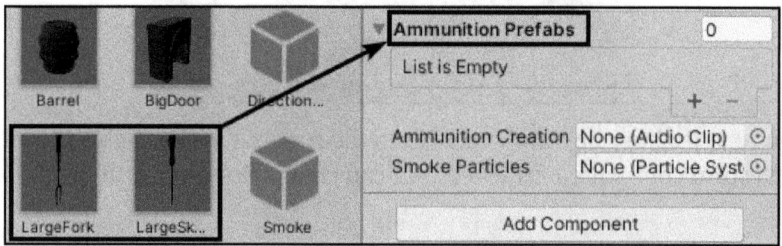

You might be able to tell at this point that this isn't ordinary ammunition — the tank will shoot sharp and pointy cutlery!

The last property to fill in for now is **Smoke Particles**. This refers to the **Smoke** GameObject you added earlier. Drag **Smoke** from the Hierarchy to the **Smoke Particles** property to assign it.

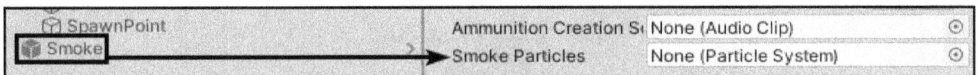

After all this, there are still three things missing to make this into a playable game: some tunes, sound effects and most importantly, a user interface.

Music and sound effects

Besides visuals and the feeling of keys and buttons, we humans love music and sounds to immerse ourselves in. Surely there are soundtracks you fondly remember from some of your favorite games — there are some iconic sound effects just about everyone knows about, like the discovery of treasure in *The Legend of Zelda* or the alert sound from *Metal Gear Solid*.

The starter project comes with a soundtrack called **Pippin The Hunchback** by the legendary **Kevin MacLeod** in the **RW / Music** folder. To add the soundtrack to the scene, drag the single music asset from **RW / Music** to the root of the Hierarchy and rename the newly created GameObject to **BGM**.

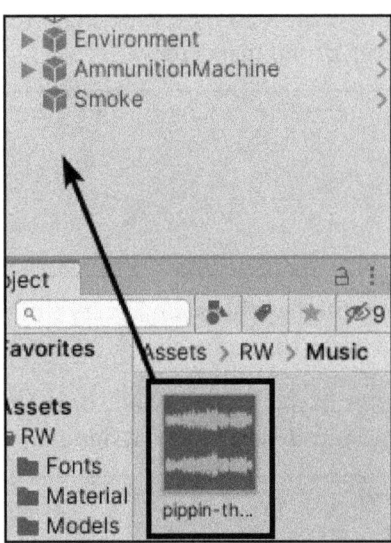

Now, select **BGM** and you'll see in the Inspector that there's an **Audio Source** component attached to it. This is what will communicate with Unity's audio system to play audio through your device, whether it's music or sound effects.

By default, the **Audio Source** will play the music a single time and then stop. As you can imagine, dead silence after a few minutes of playing can be a bit awkward, so you want the music to loop. To achieve this, check the **Loop** checkbox and you'll be golden.

Run the game by pressing the **Play** button at the top, and a nice tune will greet you. You can stop running the game by pressing that same button again.

Next up is the **Drill** sound effect. This is a WAV audio file that lives in the **RW / Sounds** folder. You can preview the sound by selecting it in the folder and clicking the **Play** button at the bottom of the Inspector.

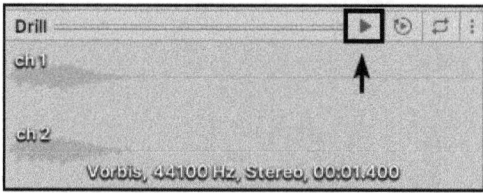

The **Ammunition Spawner** will play this sound every time a piece of ammunition is created, so it needs a reference to the audio clip.

Select **Ammunition Spawner** in the Hierarchy and drag **Drill** from **RW / Sounds** to the **Ammunition Creation Sound** property to assign it.

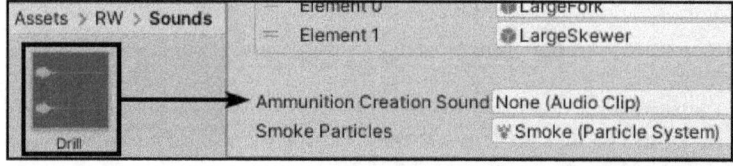

The final piece of the puzzle is the minimalistic UI for this game.

Adding a user interface

A user interface allows the player to interact with the game via buttons, toggles, sliders and text. For some genres of games, this is all you'll need. This is the case for this little project, too, because the player only needs to press a single button for the game to advance.

The user interface for this first project is provided in a prefab so as to not wander too far from the essence of this chapter. No worries though — Chapter 7 will delve deeper into user interfaces!

Drag the **User Interface** prefab from **RW / Prefabs** to the root of the Hierarchy to add it to the scene. You'll see a huge white border appear in the **Scene** view and a black bar with several UI elements in the **Game** view.

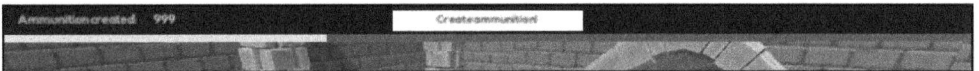

If you hold **ALT/Option** while clicking on the arrow next to **User Interface** in the Hierarchy, the GameObject will expand all of its children, their children and so on.

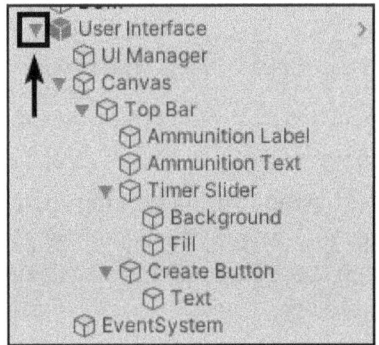

Take a look at how the UI built up, but for this chapter you'll want to focus on the **Create Button**, as that needs to trigger the **Ammunition Spawner** to create a new piece of ammunition if it can. Select **Create Button** and take a look at the **Button** component in the Inspector. Below the list of visual properties, there's an **On Click ()** property.

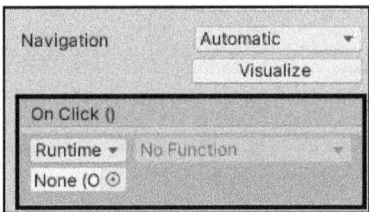

This is a **Unity Event**, and it expects one or more functions to perform. This can range from enabling a GameObject to triggering a piece of code in a script. The button needs to call a method called `AttemptAmmunitionSpawn` on the **Ammunition Spawner**. In order to set this up, start by dragging **Ammunition Spawner** onto the **Object** property of the first entry in the **On Click ()** list.

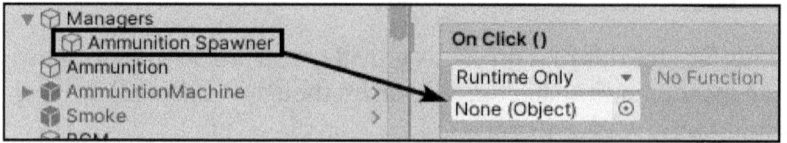

The function selection drop-down on the right is now filled with all the possible functions. Click on the dropdown and select **AmmunitionSpawner ▸ AttemptAmmunitionSpawn ()**.

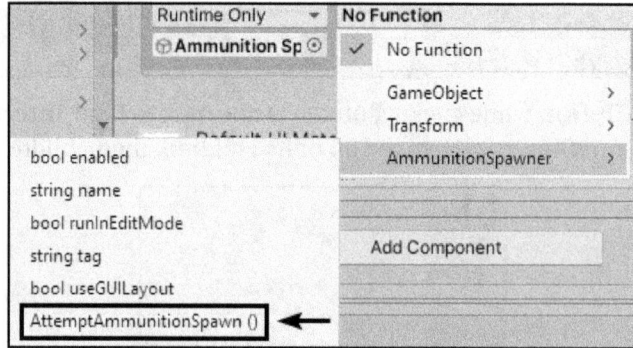

That's it! Now every time the button is pressed, a new piece of ammunition is created with a puff of smoke. You can only spawn a new piece of ammunition every two seconds though, although there's no way to tell this just yet. Give it a try by pressing the **Play** button at the top.

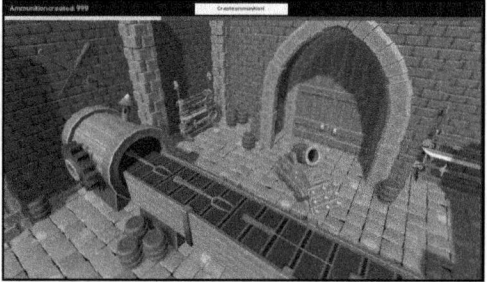

Congratulations on getting to the end of this chapter! With a good grasp of GameObjects, components and prefabs, you're now ready for the next chapter — which is an introduction to scripting in Unity.

Key points

- **GameObjects** are the basic building blocks and act as containers for components.

- Use a GameObject to give structure in the Hierarchy by using it as a folder or divider.

- **Components** are the brains of GameObjects. They give GameObjects features.

- **Prefabs** are assets that hold the state of a GameObject and all of its components. They are comparable to templates or blueprints.

- **Instancing** a prefab means creating a copy of the original and spawning it into the world.

- You can instance prefabs in the editor or at runtime with scripting.

- Creating a prefab can be done by dragging a GameObject to the **Project** view.

- Prefabs can be edited in **Prefab Mode** by double-clicking them in the **Project** view, or by simply selecting them and using the Inspector to change their properties.

- Import music and audio files into Unity as audio clips that can be played back with an **Audio Source** component.

Chapter 4: Creating & Using Scripts With C#

By Eric Van de Kerckhove

In the last chapter, you learned about GameObjects, components and prefabs. You learned that components are the brains of GameObjects and can be created via scripting. In this chapter, you'll learn how to create your own scripts using C# and how they can affect components in the scene.

At the end of the previous chapter, you made the humble beginnings of a small game. In this chapter, you're going to expand on that game and get things moving to make the experience more engaging.

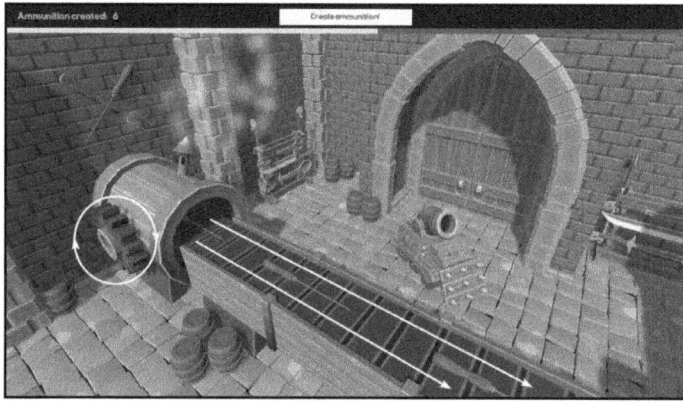

A key tool you'll wield for this is **Scripting**, an essential skill for any developer — Unity or otherwise. Even the smallest games need some logic to drive them, after all.

Scripting with C#

Unity uses **C#**, an extremely powerful and versatile object-oriented programming language developed by Microsoft around the year 2000. This was an excellent choice by the Unity developers, as C# is a widely used, mature language for client, server and even mobile software development. This means there's a ton of information out there on how to use the language to do just about anything — including making games!

Where to learn C#

There's way too much to cover in a single chapter about scripting in Unity with C#, so this chapter will focus on the basics to get you started. Don't fret though — it won't leave you hanging! There's a lot of information on C# out there, but where should you start your journey?

Well, it just so happens that there is a full video course on programming with C# on **raywenderlich.com**: Beginning Programming with C# (https://www.raywenderlich.com/603984-beginning-programming-with-c)

If you're more interested in a written C# tutorial with an emphasis on Unity, look no further than the Introduction to Unity Scripting (https://www.raywenderlich.com/4180726-introduction-to-unity-scripting-part-1) tutorial.

Where to find documentation

There are several ways to get more information about scripting for Unity. For starters, Unity comes with a scripting reference that covers the scripting API and the Unity manual that covers all things Unity in good detail.

Both of these can be found in the **Help** menu in the top bar of the Unity Editor. They're also just a click away at Unity's Scripting API Reference (https://docs.unity3d.com/ScriptReference/index.html) or the Unity User Manual (https://docs.unity3d.com/Manual/index.html), should inspiration strike elsewhere.

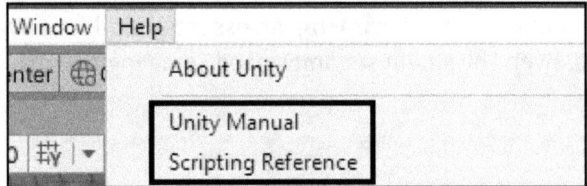

There's also Unity Answers (https://answers.unity.com), a platform that makes it easy to search for questions and answers. You can ask your own questions there, and the community is quite active, so you'll probably get an answer quickly.

And, there's the Unity Forum (https://forum.unity.com), which is similar to **Unity Answers**, but the topics are split up per category. A lot of the Unity developers are active there, so you can get answers straight from them.

Finally, there's the official Unity Discord (https://discord.com/invite/unity), a place to discuss game development with others and ask questions. The Discord server is extremely popular, so there's a good chance there will be someone online to help you.

Choosing an IDE

In theory, you could write all of your C# scripts using applications like *Notepad* or *Textedit* — but only if you're feeling particularly adventurous. A better solution is to use an IDE — an Integrated Development Environment. That's a fancy way of saying a code editor. :]

There are a lot of editors that are compatible with C# in some way, but there are two applications that rule when it comes to C# because of their features and price tag (or their lack thereof, rather).

If you're a Windows user, all you need is Visual Studio Community (https://visualstudio.microsoft.com/vs/community), the free tier of **Visual Studio**. When you install Unity, the installer even provides an option to install **VS Community** by default and will set it up for Unity game development. How considerate! VS Community is an absolute beast of an IDE that you can expand on with extensions and fully customize to your liking.

If you're a macOS or Linux user (or you simply want to try a lighter IDE), try Visual Studio Code (https://code.visualstudio.com), the little brother of **Visual Studio**. Make no mistake though — VS Code is a fully-fledged IDE with a ton of features, just like its older sibling. The setup required for VS Code to work nicely with Unity is a bit longer, but Microsoft has written a good guide (https://code.visualstudio.com/docs/other/unity) to get you started quickly.

Or, if you want to try something else entirely, here are some free alternatives (that might involve a bit more work setting up):

- VSCodium (https://vscodium.com)
- Atom (https://atom.io)
- Consulo (https://consulo.io)
- Emacs (https://www.gnu.org/software/emacs)
- Vim (https://www.vim.org)

After installing and configuring the IDE of your choice, you're ready to enter the wonderful world of C# scripting.

Scripting fundamentals

Why write scripts, anyway? Unity comes with a lot of built-in components, after all. While it's true that you *could* make a game solely with the built-in components — to an extent — you'd be extremely limited. The built-in components are like building blocks for you to work with or extend to get the logic you need working.

For example, you might attach a **Box Collider** and a **Rigidbody** to a wooden crate so it can fall to the floor with simulated gravity. You might want the crate to break and spill its contents when it drops from a great height, but there's no way to do this with the built-in components. This is where scripting comes in! You can write a script that hooks onto the event that triggers whenever a collision happens, replaces the crate with a broken one when the collision is a hard one, and your problem is solved.

Before diving right into creating your own scripts, though, it's a good idea to take a look at what makes a script tick.

Inspecting a script

Let's begin by opening the starter project. Navigate to the **Chapter 4 Starter** folder, and open it in the Unity Editor. Take a quick look, and you'll see that the structure is quite similar to the previous chapter.

This starter project comes with a few scripts that you can find in the **RW / Scripts** folder. For example, double-click on the **Ammunition** script in **RW / Scripts / Ammunition** to open it in your IDE of choice. This script moves (or "translates") a GameObject it's attached to the right by manipulating its **Transform** component.

When the GameObject moves past 20 units on the x-axis, the GameObject gets destroyed.

Here are the different parts, broken down:

```
using UnityEngine;
```

The using directive allows you to use the types defined in the UnityEngine namespace. This includes classes like MonoBehaviour, Transform and GameObject.

```
public class Ammunition : MonoBehaviour
```

Ammunition is the class name and should match with the file name (**Ammunition.cs** in this case) for it to work as a component. The : MonoBehaviour part means that this script derives from Unity's MonoBehaviour, which is the base class from which all Unity components are derived. It provides hooks into useful events such as Awake, Start, Update, OnCollisionEnter and OnDestroy. Every script you want to become usable in the Unity editor as a component should derive from MonoBehaviour. The Order of Execution (https://docs.unity3d.com/Manual/ExecutionOrder.html) page from Unity is an excellent resource to understand the lifecycle of these key event functions.

You may be confused at this point in differentiating between a script, a MonoBehaviour and a component. To clarify:

- A **script** is a C# code file that lives in your assets, just like prefabs, sound effects and 3D models.
- **MonoBehaviour** is the class you derive your script from to hook into built-in Unity events like Awake and Update.
- All scripts derived from MonoBehaviour are compiled and turned into **components** that can be attached to GameObjects in the editor to give extra functionality to said GameObjects.

Next up is this line:

```
public float movementSpeed = 5f;
```

This is a public float variable that saves the speed at which the GameObject should move. A float is a real number — meaning it can represent any negative or positive numerical value to the order of a **hundred undecillion**. That's **38 zeroes** after a number!

Below that, there's the `Update` method:

```
private void Update()
```

Anything inside the `Update` method will be executed every single frame. This is one of the events built into `MonoBehaviour`.

Next is this line of code:

```
transform.Translate(Vector3.right * movementSpeed *
Time.deltaTime,
    Space.World);
```

This piece of code moves the GameObject this component is attached to smoothly to the right. There are a few things to note here:

- `transform` is shorthand for `GetComponent<Transform>()`, which gets a reference to the **Transform** component attached to the same GameObject the **Ammunition** component is attached to.

- The `Translate` method moves a GameObject by providing it with a `Vector3` that has an X, Y and Z value.

- `Vector3.right` is a pre-defined value that's shorthand for the `Vector3` value of **(X:1, Y:0, Z:0)**. This is multiplied by `movementspeed` and `Time.deltaTime`.

- `Time.deltaTime` is the time in seconds between the previous frame and the current one. Remember that `Update` is called every single frame, so multiplying any values that change gradually by `Time.deltaTime` smooths the changes out as the game's frame rate is not guaranteed to be a steady 60 frames per second, for example. You might have tried playing some ancient games that play way too fast on modern machines, but played perfectly back in the day. That's because the developers tied the game speed directly to how fast a new frame can be generated instead of using delta time.

- `Space.World` is an argument provided to `transform.Translate` so the movement happens in **World** space instead of **Local** space.

The last part to consider is this if-statement:

```
if (transform.position.x > 20f)
{
    Destroy(gameObject);
}
```

The if-statement simply checks if the GameObject has moved 20 units to the right of the center of the scene, and if so, it will **destroy** the GameObject the **Ammunition** component is attached to. As you can see, these few lines of code make for an interesting behavior.

Return to the Unity editor and click the **Play** button at the top center. Then click the **Create ammunition!** button to see a weapon spawn. You can repeat this to make as many weapons as you like, but with some delay. You'll address this soon.

Now, in Play mode, take a good look at the **Game** view, and you'll notice the weapon moves along the x-axis of the scene until it's out of the view of the game camera and then simply disappears. That's what making games is about — smoke and mirrors to create the illusion that there's something more to it!

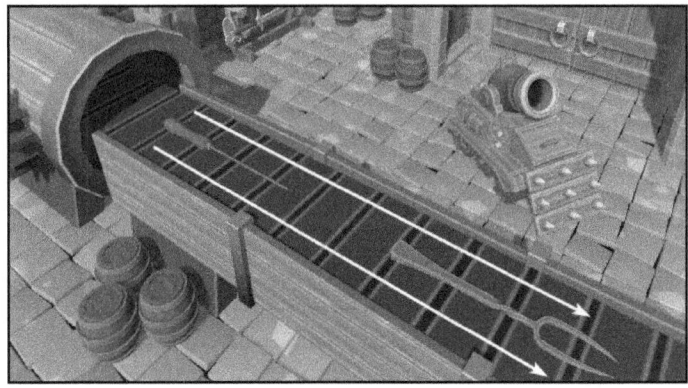

Fixing the UI

Before creating a script of your own, open the **AmmunitionSpawner** script in **RW / Scripts / Ammunition**. Don't worry — you don't have to understand all of this script. In broad terms, this script has a timer running in the background, and it can react to a button press by checking if the timer has been running for long enough. If this cool-down time has elapsed, a random piece of ammunition (picked from a list of prefabs) is instantiated into the scene and the timer is reset. That's it!

At the moment, the user interface is kind of passive — as in, it doesn't do anything except react to button presses. You're here to fix that while learning about comments along the way. Take a look around the script to get your bearings first. Did you notice anything strange?

There are a bunch of double slashes (//) spread around the file. These are comments, and anything after them is excluded from the compiler. This means you can add useful remarks ("comments") or remove ("comment out") certain pieces of code so they won't be used. In the case of the **AmmunitionSpawner** script, everything that references the **UIManager** component has been commented out. No wonder the user interface was so lifeless!

Simply remove all of the double slashes and save the script (you can use **Control-S** or **Command-S** for this). Next, return to the Unity editor and you might see a small window pop up that says "Compiling C# Scripts." This means Unity detected changes to one or more scripts and is (re)compiling so they can be used as components.

When this small window disappears, select **Managers / Ammunition Spawner** in the Hierarchy and take a look at the Inspector. A new property named **Ui Manager** has appeared.

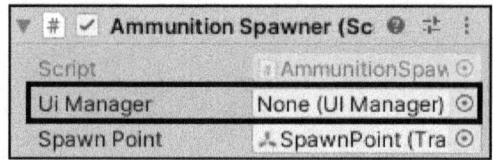

The **Ui Manager** property needs a reference to a **UI Manager** component, so go ahead and drag **User Interface / UI Manager** to the property.

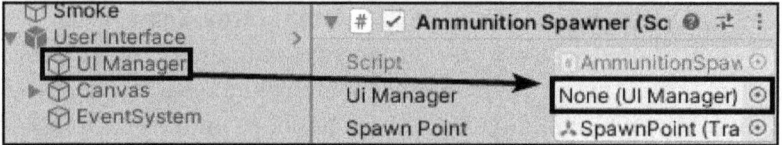

Next, play the game again in the editor and you'll notice the UI actually works now. The yellow bar now fills to indicate when the machine is ready to create another piece of ammunition and the text on the left shows the amount created.

This improves the feel of the game quite a bit!

Your first script

Now that you know the basic structure of scripts, it's time to make your own. This first script will rotate the giant gear of the machine to make it more lively. Create a new folder named **Transforms** inside **RW / Scripts** by right-clicking the folder in the **Project** view and selecting **Create ▸ Folder**.

Right-click this new **Transforms** folder and select **Create ▸ C# Script**.

Name this new script **RotateAround** and double-click the asset to open it in your script editor.

You'll be greeted by Unity's default C# script template. At the top are using directives that include UnityEngine, and the class itself is derived from MonoBehaviour so the script can be compiled into a component. There are already two Unity events added: Start and Update. You only need the Update method for this script, so go ahead and delete the Start method.

```
// Start is called before the first frame update
void Start()
{

}
```

Next, add the following variables right above the Update method:

```
public Vector3 rotationSpeed;
public Space rotationSpace;
```

rotationSpeed is a Vector3 used to set the direction and speed of the rotation. rotationSpace sets the coordinate space — either **Self** (local) or **World**. Since both of these variables are public, they can be changed in the Unity Editor once this script is compiled into a component.

Finally, add the following inside of the `Update` method:

```
transform.Rotate(rotationSpeed * Time.deltaTime, rotationSpace);
```

Just like `Transform.Translate` moves a GameObject, **Transform.Rotate** rotates it around the provided axes in a certain coordination space. Notice there are no actual values provided except for the variables and `Time.deltaTime` to smooth the rotation out over time. Now save this script and return to the Unity Editor.

Select **AmmunitionMachine / Wheel** in the Hierarchy. Add your newly created **Rotate Around** component by clicking the **Add Component** button at the bottom of the Inspector, searching for "Rotate" and selecting **Rotate Around**.

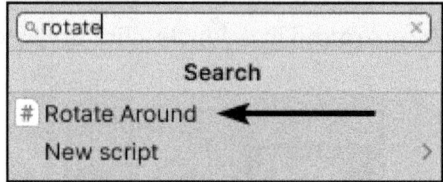

As-is, this won't do anything because the **Rotation Speed** is set to **0** on all axes. Go ahead and set the **Rotation Speed** to **(X:60, Y:0, Z:0)** to give it some speed. Next, set the **Rotation Space** to **Self** so the gear will spin around its own x-axis instead of the world's x-axis.

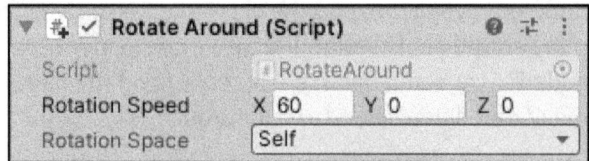

Start the game again, and you'll notice the gear on the machine is continuously spinning. Pretty nice!

Congrats on making your very own script!

Using scripts with other components

Scripts can reference other components, just like how the **Ammunition Spawner** triggers the **UI Manager** to change certain parts of the user interface. Any script can read the values of other components and change them or call methods on other components.

You might have noticed it's a bit strange how the weapons are sliding along the belt even though it's not moving! One way to solve this would be to actually move the belt itself, but this is just a small **plane** — a flat piece of geometry that lays on the machine. Moving that would result in something like this:

The belt would move for a bit and then reveal the wood below. This isn't any good of course. The belt needs to infinitely appear to move. To achieve this, you'll need to manipulate the material's texture of the belt to make it visually slide without affecting the GameObject's position. You can manually scroll this texture to see what happens by selecting **M_Belt** in **RW / Materials** and dragging its **Y Offset** property to the left.

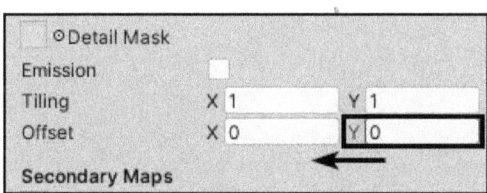

While dragging the offset, look at the **Game** view and you'll see the belt moving toward the screen. This is called scrolling the texture offset. It's a cool trick that's used all over for faking movement or rotation. To implement this effect yourself via scripting, create another folder inside of **RW / Scripts** and name it **Rendering**. Create a C# script in this folder via the right-click menu, name it **ScrollTexture** and double-click it to open it in your script editor.

The script you're about to create is generic, so it can be used for all of your scrolling texture needs — not just for the belt! To get started, add the following three variables right above the `Start` method:

```
public Vector2 scrollSpeed; // 1

private Vector2 offset; // 2
private Renderer rend; // 3
```

Here's what these will be used for:

1. `scrollSpeed` is a **Vector2**. That means it has an X and a Y value, but not a Z value like a **Vector3**. This variable is used to set axes and speeds at which the texture needs to scroll. Note that this is a `public` variable, so it can be changed in the Unity Editor.

2. The `offset` is used to keep track of how far the texture has been scrolled. For example, this value starts out at **(X:0, Y:0)** and after running the script for 10 seconds with a `scrollSpeed` of **(X:0, Y:10)**, the offset will be **(X:0, Y:100)**.

3. This is a reference to a **Renderer** component, which in itself holds a reference to the material.

Now, add this line inside of the `Start` method:

```
rend = GetComponent<Renderer>();
```

This line gets the **Mesh Renderer** component on the same GameObject the **Scroll Texture** component is attached to and saves it in `rend`.

Next, add the final piece of code inside of the `Update` method:

```
offset += Time.deltaTime * scrollSpeed; // 1
rend.material.SetTextureOffset("_MainTex", offset); // 2
```

Going through the comments, this code:

1. Cumulatively adds the delta time multiplied by the `scrollSpeed` to `offset` every frame.
2. Sets the texture offset on **_MainTex**, which is the regular color texture (the **Albedo** when you look at the material).

That concludes this script! Save the script and return to the Unity Editor to take it for a spin.

Select **AmmunitionMachine / Belt** in the Hierarchy and add a **Scroll Texture** component to it.

Set the **Scroll Speed** to **(X:0, Y:-0.4)** and start the game again. You'll see the belt steadily moving towards the screen. Pretty cool!

Now you know how to create your own scripts, and you know that these get turned into components in Unity. In the next chapter, you'll learn about Unity's camera and lights to make a scene look good.

Key points

- Unity uses **C#** as its scripting language.
- A script provides **functionality** to a GameObject as it's compiled into a **component**.
- **Visual Studio** and **Visual Studio Code** are recommended IDEs.
- You can open scripts by double-clicking their assets in the **Project** view.
- New C# scripts can be created by right-clicking in any folder in the **Project** view and selecting **Create ▸ C# Script**.
- Scripts expose variables that you can modify from the Unity Editor.
- Unity automatically calls event methods in the script to perform operations on the associated component.

Section II: Now You're Building With Components

Cameras, lights, sound, action! This section introduces you to a new game, where you'll learn how to build cameras, lights, sound and interactivity! These are essential elements for any game because they make games compelling and fun to play.

You'll also learn how to add a user interface and build a dialogue system to allow players to talk to your game's avatars. The project in this section is set in a dining hall, so head on down there right away and you'll meet some very strange characters indeed!

Chapter 5: Setting Up a Scene

By Eric Van de Kerckhove

In the previous section, you discovered the basics of GameObjects and prefabs. You also took the first steps toward creating your own components by using scripting in Unity. That will come in handy in the following chapters as you explore how to use scriptable objects to create a dialogue system.

In this chapter, you're going to take a closer look at how to set up a scene to make it look appealing.

Just like in a movie set, a scene in Unity needs a camera and lights, so that's what you'll focus on. You're also going to learn more about shadows and the different types of lighting modes. This will mark the start of a game that takes the player to a dining hall populated with vegetable gladiators preparing for the next battle.

Getting started

First, open the starter project for this chapter in Unity and take a look at the **Project** view. Just like in the previous two chapters, the assets are neatly grouped by their uses in the RW folder.

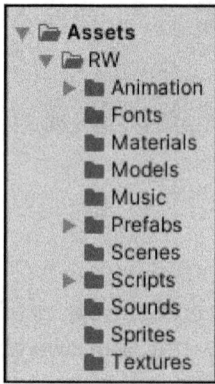

This time around, there are a few more folders to cover. Here's a brief overview:

- **Animation**: This folder contains the animations and controllers for the vegetable warriors and a treasure chest.

- **Fonts**: The main font used for all user interfaces is in here.

- **Materials**: The folder containing all the material files that hold the data for what a 3D model should look like.

- **Models**: All 3D models live in here.

- **Music**: This contains two sweet soundtracks by *Kevin MacLeod*.

- **Prefabs**: This folder holds all the prefabs, organized per category.

- **Scenes**: There's only one scene asset in here for now — **DiningHall**.

- **Scripts**: A few scripts that include a simple interaction system for later use and a script that makes an image blink on and off.

- **Sounds**: There are two sound effects in here that will be used for the treasure chest.

- **Sprites**: This folder has a single image in it that will act as a cursor in menus.

- **Textures**: A folder containing image files that are used as the textures for the 3D models.

Open the **DiningHall** scene if it isn't opened yet, and take a look around in the **Scene** view. It might be hard to tell because it's quite dark, but there's a single medieval-looking room with stone walls and wooden tables and benches.

You'll turn this into a lively dining hall throughout this chapter, even though it might look more like scenery out of *Dark Souls* at the moment.

Finally, take a look at the Hierarchy to see what GameObjects are present.

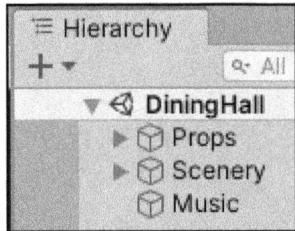

There are three GameObjects at the root of the Hierarchy:

- **Props**: The term *props* comes from the film industry and means movable items like hats, knives, carpets, barrels, crates and so on. In the **DiningHall** scene, these are objects like the food on the dishes and the torches. This GameObject acts like a folder, so expand it fully to see all of its children.

- **Scenery**: This is another folder GameObject with a lot of children and grandchildren. These are GameObjects that won't move like walls, pillars and stairs.

- **Music**: This GameObject has an **Audio Source** attached that loops a soundtrack.

With the project tour out of the way, it's time to get cracking. Lights, camera, action!

Camera

Every new scene you create starts with a single camera and a directional light — but what do these GameObjects do, exactly? To illustrate why you need these objects, the **DiningHall** scene doesn't start with either of these. If you take a look at the Game view, you'll notice there's just a black background and a text saying "Display 1 No cameras rendering".

Try playing the scene by clicking the **Play** button at the top of the editor. The game actually runs fine in the background as you can see in the Scene view. The fire particles are emerging from the torches and fire pits.

Adding a camera

Do you hear that? Listen carefully... the sound of total silence. There should be a merry soundtrack playing in the background as the **Music** GameObject has a looping **Audio Source** attached to it. What gives?Well, you can't hear anything if you don't have ears, and it's the same in a Unity scene. There might not be an ears component, but there sure is an **Audio Listener** available to listen to audio sources. This can be found on a camera.

Go ahead and add a camera to the root of the Hierarchy by clicking the + button at the top left of the Hierarchy and selecting **Camera**.

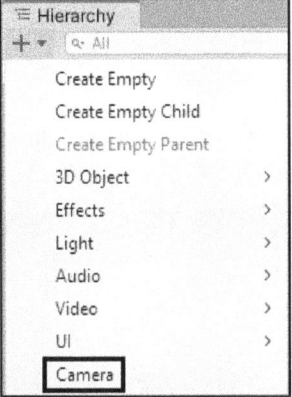

Rename this camera to **Main Camera** and set its tag to **MainCamera** via the **Tag** drop-down in the Inspector.

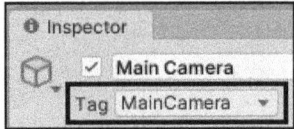

This tag tells Unity this is your primary camera, and it allows you to easily find it again via scripting. Unity caches all cameras tagged with **MainCamera** when the game starts, allowing you to call `Camera.main` to get access to the camera. Pretty nifty!

Now, take a look at the Inspector with **Main Camera** still selected and reset the **Transform** component by right-clicking it and selecting **Reset**. This will position the camera at **(X:0, Y:0, Z:0)**. The camera is now lodged into the floor.

Next, look at the bottom of the component list. You'll see the **Audio Listener** component is sitting there, ready to hear some sweet tunes. Play the scene again and you'll hear nice music playing with some medieval feast vibes!

Setting up the camera

To give **Main Camera** a better view of the scene, adjust its **Transform**'s position and rotation to **(X:26, Y:5, Z:4)** and **(X:25, Y:-90, Z:0)** respectively.

Time to dive a bit deeper into what makes a camera tick!

In the context of Unity, a camera is a complex component that generates a list of models visible to it and then iterates that list from far to near models. Every model is drawn to a buffer, a canvas of sorts, which is then displayed as a 2D image since your display can only show two dimensions in the physical world.

Each one of these images is a **frame** — a snapshot of what everything looks like at a certain moment in time. In that regard, cameras in game engines are similar to those used on movie sets and the one that's attached to your smartphone — making pictures in quick succession to create a video. While the movie industry has settled on 24 **frames per second** (FPS) for movies, video games demand 30 FPS at a bare minimum for smooth motion, and 60-120 FPS is currently the gold standard, depending on the game.

As you can imagine, having only 1/60th of a second (that's only **16 milliseconds**!) to render isn't a lot of time to render all the models and do the complex calculations you'd expect from a modern game. For this reason, you want to strike a balance between attractive visuals and good performance so you don't drop any frames.

Now take a closer look at the **Camera** component, which has an impressive list of properties.

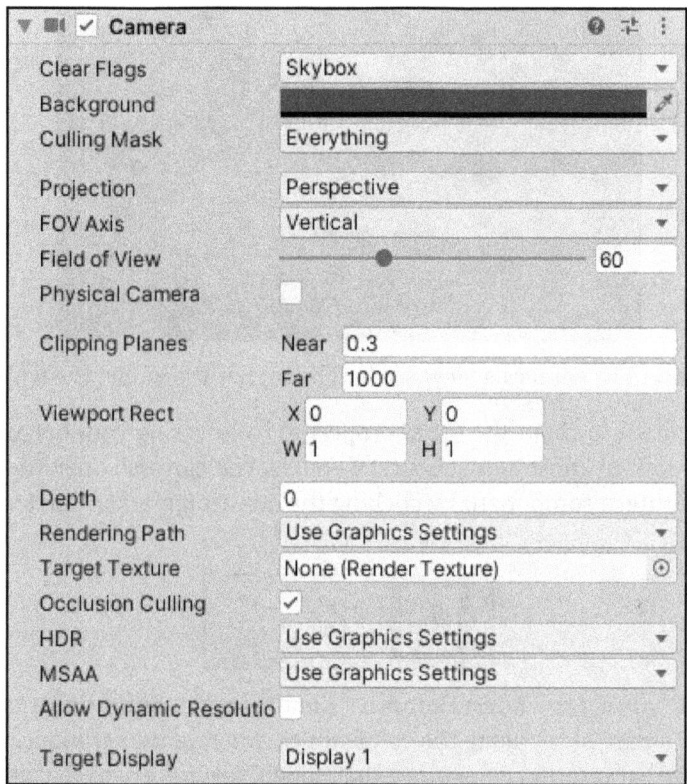

Most of these can be left at their default values for this game, but here's an overview of the most commonly used properties:

- **Background**: The color of the background. Use this when the **Clear Flags** property is set to **Solid Color**.

- **Culling Mask**: This is a **Layer** filter. Anything that isn't selected in the culling mask won't be drawn by this camera.

- **Projection**: The projection can be set to either **Perspective** or **Orthographic**. The former is how we perceive reality around us, with objects closer to us appearing bigger and objects that are farther away looking smaller. This is the default setting, and that's why the cups and plates closer to the camera look bigger than the ones on the tables near the banners. The orthographic projection displays objects as if they were all at the same distance. This is the same projection of classic isometric games like *Diablo*, *Fallout 2* and *Age of Empires* used for their sprites.

To illustrate, here's how the dining hall looks with orthographic projection set up to be isometric:

- **Field of View**: The camera's view angle. The higher the value, the wider the view.

You can get more info about the other properties by hovering your cursor over the property you want to know more about. Of course, you can also open the reference page for the **Camera** component by clicking the question mark at the top right of the component.

For the dining hall, set the **Main Camera**'s **Clear Flags** to **Solid Color** and set the **Background** to pure black using the color wheel. You might be wondering why to bother with the background color since the models seem to cover the whole view. There are actually small gaps between some of the floor tiles that can show the background through them. You can see this clearly by temporarily changing the background color to something bright like white or magenta.

Be sure to change the background color back to black afterwards.

Lighting a scene

Until now, the scene has been quite dark except for the light coming from the fire pits. To fix that, you'll add some lights to make the room more appropriate to use as a dining hall instead of a moody dungeon.

Types of lights

Unity comes with four types of light for you to use. Here's a quick primer:

- **Point light**: A point light shines its light evenly in all directions from a single point. You can think of this type of light as a light bulb or a sphere of light, with objects closer to it appearing brighter while objects further away appearing darker.

- **Spot light**: This behaves exactly like the real life spotlight you can find in a flashlight or a street lamp. Light emits from a single point in a direction in the shape of a cone.

- **Directional light**: A directional light is arguably the most important one, as it acts like the sun and lights up the whole scene. It's a point that's infinitely far away and shines its light in a certain direction. Since the position of the light isn't used for calculations, the brightness of this light is constant, meaning it doesn't matter whether objects are close to it or farther away.

- **Area light**: An area light casts light rays from within a rectangle towards a position. This could be compared to a window or a softbox studio light (a light with a screen in front of it to diffuse the light). This type of light cannot be used in real time, but has to be baked by the game developer. More on that later.

The illustration below shows the difference between the behavior of a point light, a spotlight, a directional light and an area light:

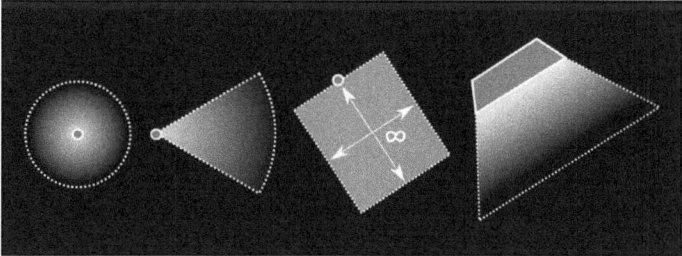

Note how the light for the directional light is constant and infinite, while the intensity of the others depends on the distance from the light source.

Point lights are often used for lighting up a small area of a scene or for showing magical auras and for adding light to particle effects. Spot lights are used for putting focus on a single object or small part of a scene and are ideal for use as flashlights in horror games. Below is a direct comparison of a point light and a spot light in Unity.

In this case, the point light is hovering right above the floor. The spot light is at a similar height and is pointed at the wall.Now that you know all about the different types of light, it's time to work on the dining hall!

Adding lights

To start, add a new empty GameObject named **Lights** to the root of the Hierarchy and reset its **Transform** component. Next, add a **Directional Light** GameObject by clicking the + button at the top left and selecting **Light ▸ Directional Light**.

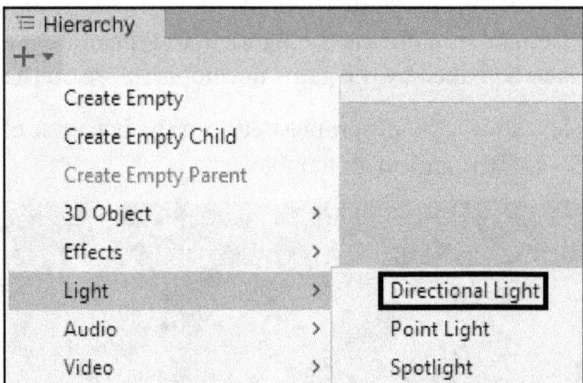

Drag the **Directional Light** on top of **Lights** to set it as its child. **Lights** will act as a folder for the different lights you'll add to the scene.

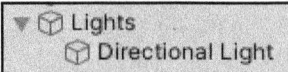

With some light added, the scene looks very different already! Now, take a look in the Inspector of the **Directional Light** you added. As you can see, it's a GameObject with a single **Light** component added to it.

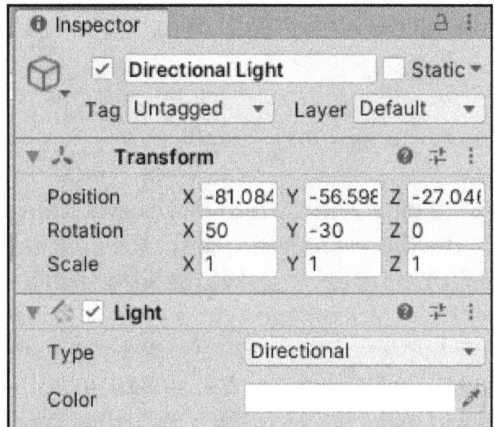

Directional lights

This **Light** component is shared between all types of light. The only difference is the **Type** property. This is how you can change a light to be of the type you need — in this case **Directional**.

A directional light behaves as if it's infinitely far away, so its position doesn't actually matter. You can try this out by moving **Directional Light** around in the scene view. It won't change the way the light behaves. Now try rotating the light and watch what happens. You'll notice this does have a big impact on how the scene looks as the light changes the mood.

Before moving on to other types of light, it's time to set up the directional light to set the mood for the scene. For starters, move **Directional Light** to **(X:0, Y:3, Z:0)** to have it in a convenient location right above the stairs. Now, set its rotation to **(X:75, Y:-85, Z:0)**.

It will make the light shine from above with a slight angle toward the big door at the far back.

The light is currently set to pure white, which makes everything look a little boring. To change that, click on the **Color** property and set the light color to **(R:206, G:239, B:255)**. This is a nice light blue color. It makes the scene feel a bit colder, but it will improve the contrast with the nice orange lighting you'll add later. The **Color** property can have a huge impact on the general mood of a scene. For example, making it a green color will make the scene feel as if there's poison hanging in the air. Making it dark blue will make it feel as if it's nighttime. You should always play around with the lighting to get a feel for what moods fit your game best.

Light modes

Next up is the light **Mode**, which can be set to **Realtime**, **Mixed** or **Baked**. In this scene, all lights will be realtime — which means the lighting and shadows will be recalculated every frame by the game engine. While this may be more heavy on the CPU, it allows objects to move and animate freely while their shadows and lighting look correct at all times.

While realtime lighting shouldn't be a problem for this scene as it's not too heavy graphics-wise, for more complicated scenes you might need the **Baked** or **Mixed** mode. The **Baked** lighting mode "bakes" the lighting and shadows from the light into textures that get applied to the models. This is a process that happens at design time. It's up to the game developer to bake out all the lighting ahead of time so the textures are included with the final game. This saves a ton of CPU cycles and moves the performance hit to a single load on the RAM and storage as the texture gets loaded in. Another benefit is that the baked shadows and lighting can include high-quality shadows and even light bounces for beautiful effects. So why not use baked lighting for everything?

There's a huge caveat to baked lighting, and that's that it only works correctly for non-moving objects like scenery and static props. Because the lighting and shadows are baked in, they can't be altered at run time. Take the little scene below for example:

Looks pretty good, right? Light in the scene is even disabled, but that doesn't matter because all light and shadow data are preserved in the textures. Move the barrels a bit to the right because that will make things look nicer, and notice what happens.

The shadows stay put even when the object was moved! To fix this, you'd have to re-bake the whole scene again. In this case, that will only take about 10 seconds when using GPU baking, but the bigger the scene and the more lights you add, the longer this will take. Baking can easily take a few hours for complex scenes, and even the dining hall scene will take a few minutes of baking on a beefy GPU. For this reason, it's best to use the realtime lighting mode until you're sure what objects will never move.

Finally, there's the **Mixed** mode, which combines realtime and baked lighting. The way the lighting modes are mixed can be set up with different modes of their own, like the **Subtractive** mode always uses the baked data except for dynamic objects.

Below is an example of a baked scene with mixed lighting.

The shadows cast by the barrels are baked in, while the potato warrior casts its own realtime shadows. The performance of the mixed mode lies somewhere in between baked and realtime lighting, depending on how many dynamic GameObjects are visible in the scene.

Light intensity and shadows

Next up in the list of **Light** component properties is the **Intensity** and **Indirect Multiplier**. The intensity of the light can be set with the **Intensity** property. The higher the value, the brighter the light will be. The default value of **1** is fine for this scene, but you might want to tone it down for night scenes or up the value a bit for extremely bright scenes. Increasing this value too much will make the scene look washed out, so be careful not to overdo it.

The indirect (light) multiplier is used when baking lightmaps. As light rays bounce around the scene, it takes the color of the objects it collides with along with it. This effect can also be observed in real life. If you take a bright red object, put it near a white wall and shine a bright light on it. You'll see the color red will bleed onto the wall. You may even see this effect happening around you right now if you have any colored objects standing or hanging near a white wall or a desk. The **Indirect Multiplier** strengthens that effect in Unity.

Now for the big one — shadows! The **Shadow Type** property has three options: **No Shadows**, **Hard Shadows** and **Soft Shadows**. By default, a light casts no shadows because the calculations of shadows are one of the most expensive operations when it comes to lighting. For directional lights, the performance hit is minimal, as Unity only has to calculate the shadows for one direction.

However, point lights like those used for the fire pits are six times more expensive as they cast shadows in every direction. It's for this reason the fire pits have their shadows disabled.

Both hard and soft shadows cast shadows in the scene. All models will cast shadows onto other objects and themselves, resulting in realistic results. Shadows are processed and written to a **shadow map** that's applied over the existing textures. Soft shadows add an extra step to average the shadow map pixels with a shader, resulting in a smooth result at the cost of some extra GPU processing.

Select **Soft Shadows** in the **Shadow Type** drop-down, and you'll immediately see the results in both the **Scene** and **Game** view.

The shadows are especially prominent below the benches and in the stone door frames. Some shadows add a lot to the scene in terms of contrast and mood.

If you look back at the Inspector, you'll notice more properties appeared for the shadow settings labeled **Realtime Shadows**.

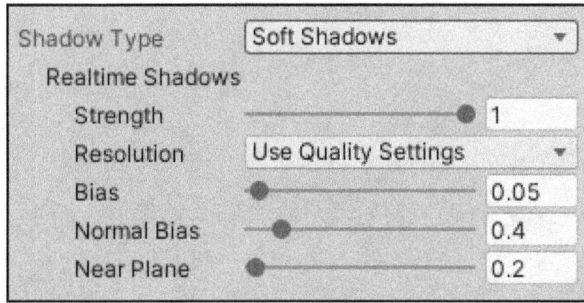

These properties let you specify the details of the shadows.

For starters, tone down the **Strength** to **0.5** to make the shadows less harsh, as it decreases the opacity that results in a softer look.

The **Resolution** sets the size of the shadow map, with bigger values resulting in crisp shadows and lower values making the shadows fuzzy. Of course, higher resolutions will require more processing power by the GPU and will eat up more memory. The default value is **Use Quality Settings**, which uses the values found in the **Quality** tab of the **Project Settings**, with the default set to **High Resolution**.

> **Note**: A whole book could easily be dedicated just to setting up a project for maximum fidelity or performance, but for the sake of simplicity, this book skips the setup of the project settings as the defaults are a good compromise between performance and visuals. If you're curious, you can take a look at the **Quality** tab in the **Project Settings** by selecting **Edit ▸ Project Settings...** in the top menu and clicking on **Quality** on the left side.

You can play around with this setting to get a feel for the difference. Below is a comparison between **Low Resolution** and **Very High Resolution** to show the huge impact of this single setting.

Next up are **Bias** and **Normal Bias**. These properties are here to solve two common shadow problems: **shadow acne** and **light bleeding**. Shadow acne occurs when an object is incorrectly shadowed by itself because the calculation of the distance between the light and the shadow caster on the shadow map is off by a pixel or two. You don't have to remember the cause, but it's important to recognize when it's happening and how to fix it by using the bias.

There's a little bit of shadow bias by default to prevent shadow acne. If you set **Bias** to **0**, shadow acne will appear on some objects in the scene. You can tell by the subtle dark wavy pattern on some of the objects and by some objects becoming just a bit darker overall. It's especially clear on the plates at the lower right corner and on some of the floor tiles in the middle. Below is a zoomed-in view to make the acne more visible, with the bias turned all the way down on the right side.

It might be hard to tell, but there's a wavy pattern on the tile that shouldn't be there. If you ever see this with your own shadows, slightly increase the bias in increments of 0.01 until the issue disappears. Increasing the bias too much will make the shadows move too far away from the objects, so it's a subtle balance that requires a bit of tweaking.

The **Normal Bias** fixes light bleeding, an effect where light bleeds through objects that should be solid. The default value of **0.4** slightly shrinks the normals of each model used for shadow casting. In other words, the higher you set the normal bias, the thinner the shadow will be in most cases. For some models, this default shrinkage can cause light to spread between the "cracks" and seep out — causing holes in the shadow.

For example, take a look at this barrel scene again with the normal bias set to **0.4**:

Notice how the shadows have holes in them while you'd expect these barrels to be solid without any gaps. The fix in this case is dropping the normal bias down to 0 as no other artifacts appear when doing so:

The takeaway from all of this is to look closely at your shadows and play with the bias values until you're satisfied with the results.

Finally, the **Near Plane** is the minimal distance from the light source from where shadows will start to be drawn. For directional lights, this setting won't do anything because the light's distance is infinite. The directional light is ready, and you know a lot more about lights now! Next up are the point lights for the torches.

Point lights

If you play the scene, you'll notice there are a bunch of torches hanging against the walls of the dining room. These have fiery particles, but they don't emit any light yet.

Each of these torches will need to have a point light near them to give the illusion that they're providing light to the scene. To start off, add a Point Light to the root of the scene by clicking the + icon at the top left of the Hierarchy and selecting **Light ▸ Point Light**.

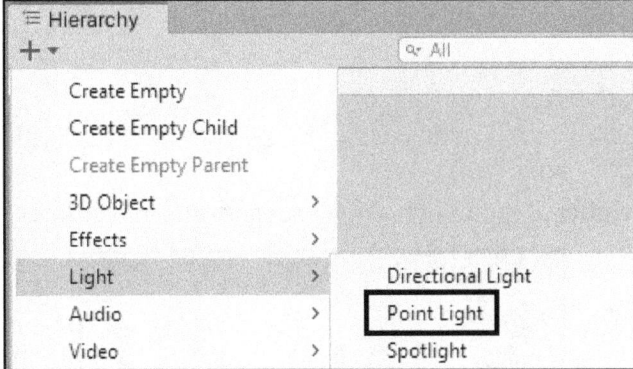

Now, drag this new **Point Light** GameObject onto **Lights** to make it a child of **Lights**.

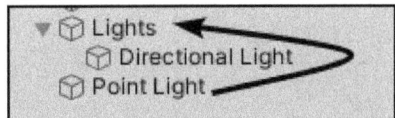

Next, position the light to the torch left of the big door at the back of the scene by setting its position to **(X:-9.2, Y:4, Z:-2.2)**. This will move the point light right in front of the torch.

At the moment, the light emitted by the point light is a weak white glow. This might be suitable for a small white LED, but this is a flame! The light needs to be powerful and somewhere on the orange spectrum of color. To achieve this, edit the following properties of **Point Light** in the Inspector:

- **Range**: 20

- **Color**: (R:255, G:188, B:129)

- **Intensity**: 1.5

- **Indirect Multiplier**: 0 (point lights don't support this in realtime)

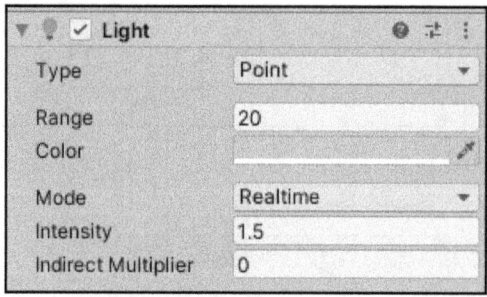

That's a lot better! The light now glows brightly and illuminates the door and the platform on the left.

Now, duplicate the point light by selecting it in the Hierarchy and pressing **Control-D** or **Command-D**. This will add a copy named **Point Light (1)** below the existing point light. Select the new copy and move it to the other torch next to the door by using the **Move** tool in the **Scene** view.

Keep duplicating and moving the point lights until there's a point light next to each torch. Don't worry about the exact position. As long as every light is near a torch, it'll look good!

The end result should look similar to the image below when running the scene.

With that, all of the lights are in place — making the dining hall feel a lot more cozy! All that's missing are some people to dine on the delicious food.

Adding characters

The characters in this scene will be veggie gladiators — fierce warriors that fight daily in the arena. They are getting themselves ready by munching on the fine food and drinks provided. The character the player will control is known as an **avatar**, a graphical representation of the player in the virtual world. The avatar in this game is a veggie gladiator himself that will be able to interact with the world around him in later chapters. For now, he will be a character that's just standing around.

The player avatar and the others have been prepared beforehand and saved as prefabs.

To add the avatar, drag **Player Avatar** from the **RW / Prefabs / Avatar** folder to the root of the Hierarchy.

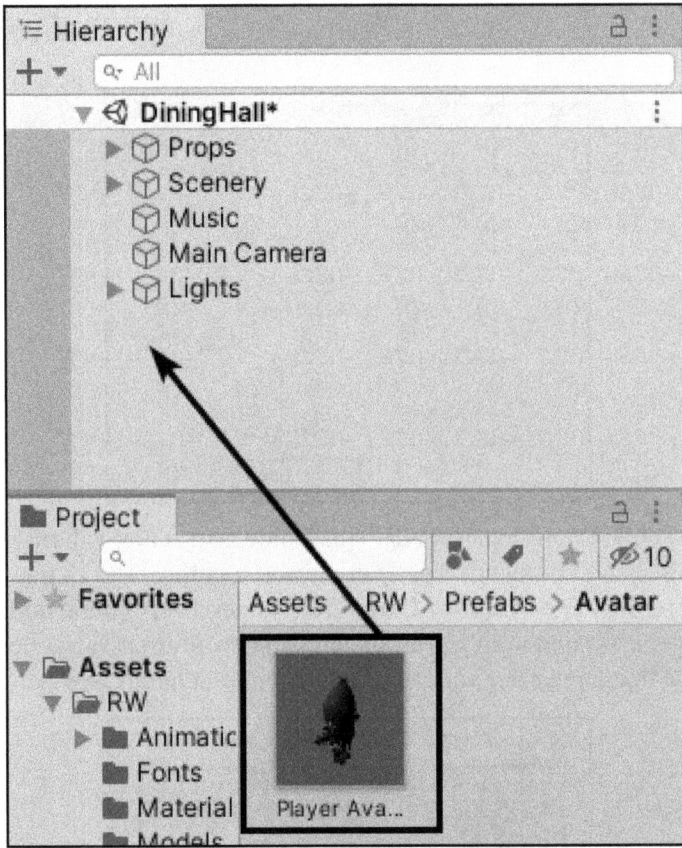

The player avatar is a potato warrior that has an animation controller attached to it on its child **Model**. By default, he's in a **T-pose**, which means he's standing upright, with his "arms" spread out. If you play the scene, you can see that he starts doing his idle animation. Now for the other characters. Create a new empty GameObject named **Interactable** in the root of the Hierarchy. Next, reset its **Transform**.

Finally, add an empty GameObject as a child of **Interactable** by right-clicking **Interactable** and selecting **Create Empty**.

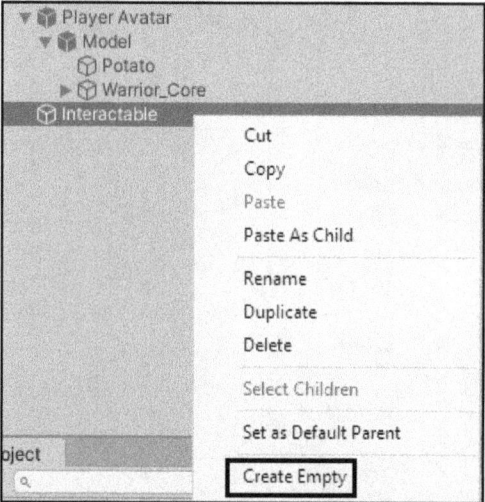

Name this new child GameObject **NPCs**. This "folder" structure will make it easier to keep the non-playable characters neatly organized together. The characters are prefabs living in the **RW / Prefabs / Characters** folder. Every character has three versions: a regular version wielding a weapon and two alternative versions named **Alt 1** and **Alt 2** that have color variations and have their hands empty.

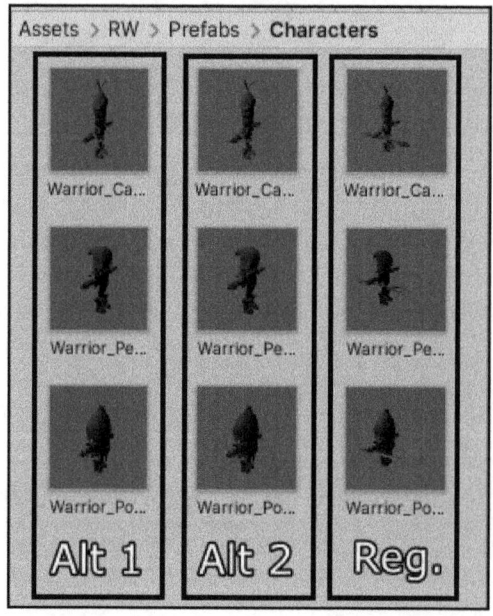

For the sake of adding the characters, it may be easier to scale the icons down in the Project view until you can see their full names without any thumbnails. You can do this by sliding the slider at the bottom right all the way to the left.

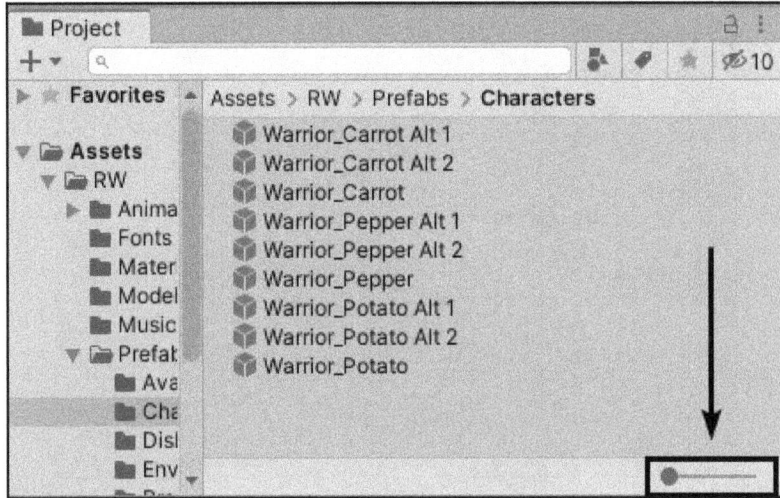

To add the characters to the scene, drag each character to the **NPCs** GameObject in the Hierarchy and set their position and rotation. The first one will be a guard standing in front of the left stairway. Drag **Warrior_Potato** from the **Prefabs** folder onto **NPCs** and name it **Guard 1**. Set its position and rotation to **(X:3, Y:0.2, Z:-9.4)** and **(X:0, Y:0, Z:0)**, respectively.

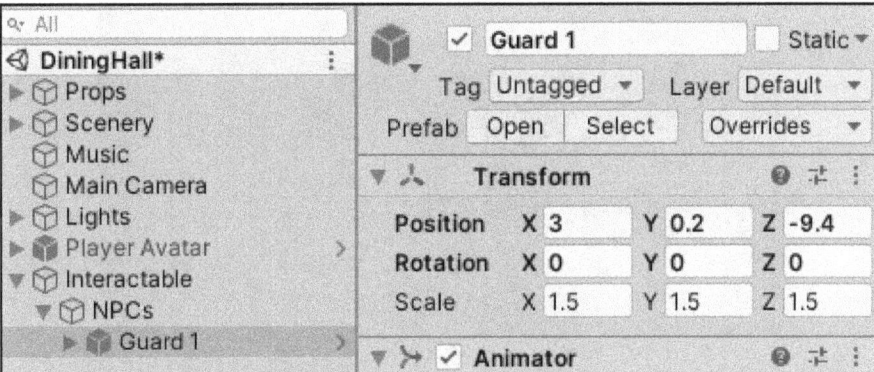

The guard should now be standing near the stairway on the left.

Repeat the same steps, but this time use the **Warrior_Carrot** prefab. Name this NPC **Guard 2** and set its position and rotation to **(X:2.5, Y:0.2, Z:12.7)** and **(X:0, Y:180, Z:0)**, respectively. This will position the carrot warrior at the other stairway on the right, facing the first guard.

For the next warriors, place them like so:

> **Note**: You can skip this step if you want, because the starter project of the next chapter has these NPCs already placed for you.

- A **Warrior_Pepper** named **Boss** at position **(X:-12.65, Y:1, Z:2.12)** and rotation **(X:0, Y:90, Z:0)**.

- A **Warrior_Pepper Alt 1** named **Pepper Warrior** at position **(X:11.15, Y:0, Z:-5.5)** and rotation **(X:0, Y:0, Z:0)**.

- A **Warrior_Carrot** named **Carrot Warrior** at position **(X:10, Y:0, Z:-3.2)** and rotation **(X:0, Y:185, Z:0)**.

- A **Warrior_Potato** named **Potato Warrior** at position **(X:15.5, Y:0, Z:0)** and rotation **(X:0, Y:180, Z:0)**.

- A **Warrior_Carrot** named **Carrot Warrior** at position **(X:11, Y:0, Z:6.4)** and rotation **(X:0, Y:0, Z:0)**.

- A **Warrior_Pepper** named **Pepper Warrior** at position **(X:20, Y:0, Z:9)** and rotation **(X:0, Y:180, Z:0)**.

With all these characters added, run the scene and you'll notice all of them will be in their idle animations. The dining hall is a lot more lively now. :]

That concludes this chapter! In the next chapter, you'll learn all about Unity's input system and how to set up collisions. This will allow you to make the player avatar walk around in the dining hall.

Key points

- You need a **Camera** component to render the scene to the **Game** view. To hear sounds, you need an **Audio Listener** component.
- A camera generates frames. These are like pictures that are taken at a swift rate. The **framerate** is the amount of these frames that can be generated per second.
- The target framerate is often 60 to 120 frames per second (FPS). This is only 16 to 8 milliseconds per frame!
- Lights allow you to see models in the scene, and they can create shadows to improve the contrast and realism.
- **Point lights** shine light evenly like a sphere of light.
- **Spot lights** emit light from a single point in a cone shape.
- **Directional lights** are like the sun — they shine from infinitely far away in a direction.
- The **Realtime lighting mode** allows you to move objects in real time and the shadows will move with them. This is heavier on the CPU.
- **Baked lighting mode** bakes the shadows and lights in the scene, which takes a long time. After moving objects, you need to bake again. Baked lighting is easy on the CPU.
- The **Mixed lighting mode** combines realtime and baked lighting. The performance lies between realtime and baked.
- Shadows add a lot to a scene and can be either hard or soft. The latter is a bit more expensive on the GPU.
- Play around with the shadow **Strength** and **Resolution** properties to fit your game and target device.
- Use the shadow **Bias** and **Normal Bias** to fix common rendering issues.
- An **avatar** is a graphical representation of a player in a game.

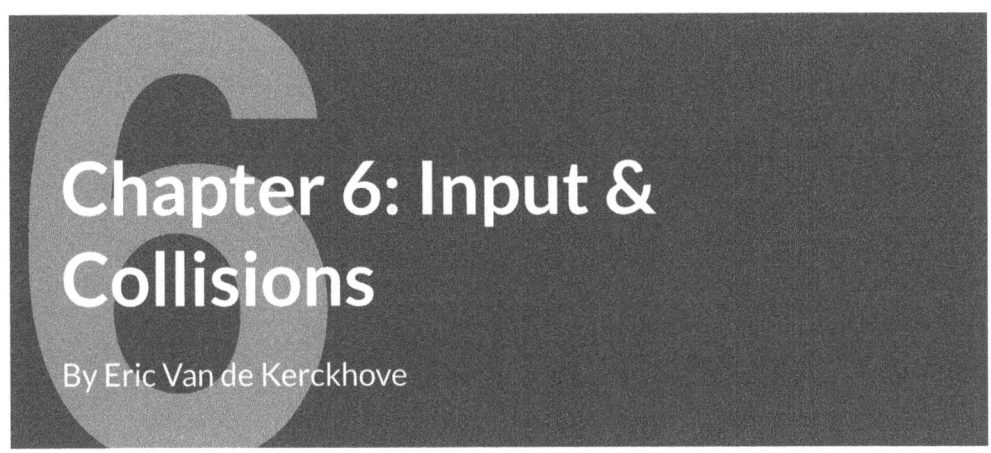

Chapter 6: Input & Collisions

By Eric Van de Kerckhove

In the last chapter, you learned how to add a camera to the scene and set it up. You also mastered the art of using lighting and shadows to make the scene look great. In this chapter, you'll learn about Unity's input systems and how to use them to make the player avatar walk around.

Besides reading and using the player's input, you'll also discover how to use Unity's physics system to make sure objects can't fall through the floor. The combination of an input system and a physics system is the foundation for a lot of games out there. For example, it allows an avatar to run around on platforms, jump and bonk enemies on their heads.

Even real-world games like *Jenga* use a combination of the player's dexterity and gravity to create fun gameplay! Once you've mastered the concepts in this chapter, you'll be ready to create quite a few fun projects of your own.

Input systems

To get started, open the starter project for this chapter in Unity. If it wasn't opened automatically, open the **DiningHall** scene located in **RW / Scenes**. You'll see the familiar scene from the last chapter: a dining hall full of gladiators spreading their arms wide.

Before diving into setting up the input system, you need to understand what an input system is and what choices Unity offers.

The old code way

This might be glaringly obvious, but every game needs **input** from the player. Whether it's a button press, the movement of a mouse or the swipe of a finger on a touchscreen, input is essential for games. In Unity, there are a few ways to go about capturing a player's input — one of which is simply calling the Input class in a script like this:

```
void Update()
{
    if (Input.GetKeyDown(KeyCode.Space))
    {
        Jump();
    }
}
```

This will check if the Space key was pressed this frame when it wasn't before with Input.GetKeyDown(KeycCode.Space). If so, a Jump method will be called. This will work perfectly, and you can use the Input class for both keyboard key presses and mouse clicks. Great! However, there are some huge limitations, as you can't poll for gamepad button presses or joystick movement. On top of that, the key to jump in this example is hard-coded to **Space** with no easy way of changing that except for editing the script. Since players won't be able to remap the key themselves, this way of implementing input won't score you any accessibility points — as some disabled players won't even be able to play.

Old input system

Of course, that's only one way of going about polling for the player's input. Unity comes with two input systems — the old one and the new one. The old input system is still the default and has been since the first release of Unity way back in 2005. Time for a small history lesson!

Instead of simply using KeyCode.Space in your script, you would define a **virtual axis** in the **Input Manager**, which can be found in **Edit ▸ Project Settings ▸ Input Manager**. The setup for mapping jumping to the **Space** key would look like this:

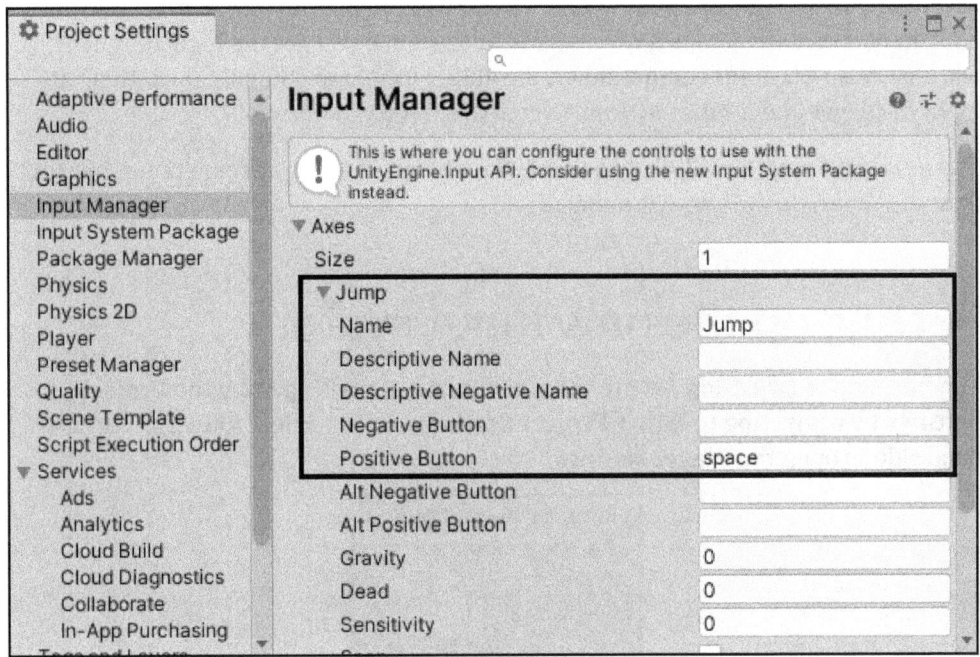

Every "virtual axis" has to have a name and at least one button, key or joystick axis. In this case, **Jump** is the name of the axis and **space** is the key. You would then be able to check if the key was pressed in a script like this:

```
void Update()
{
    if (Input.GetButtonDown("Jump"))
    {
        Jump();
    }
}
```

This allows you to remap the key or button in the Input Manager, and even allows you to map multiple keys to the same axis name. This system even allowed for remapping keys by players *before* starting up the game in a configuration screen, but the developers have removed this feature in recent versions. This system was usable, but it's clunky, hard to set up and about as fun as filling in tax forms. You need to know the names of the keys, buttons and joystick axes to use them because there's no drop-down or system where you simply press the key or button you want to map. Not ideal!

New input system

This is where the new input system comes into play! This system has been in development since 2018 and has been officially out of preview since 2021. It's now a built-in part of Unity and is much more intuitive once you get the hang of it. It features cross-platform compatibility, the ability to remap controls at runtime, an input debugger and it binds actions to controls. Pretty sweet!

The new input system will likely become the default in Unity at some point, but for now you'll have to switch to it manually.

Setting up the new input system

The first step to switching over to the new input system is opening the **Project Settings** by navigating to **Edit ▸ Project Settings…**. Now select **Player** at the left-hand side to open the **Player** settings.

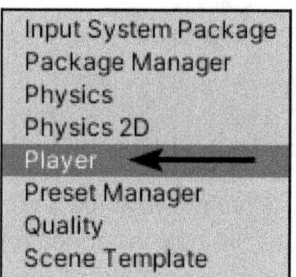

Next, scroll down in the **Other Settings** section of the **Player** settings until you see **Configuration**. The last option here is **Active Input Handling** with a drop-down next to it. Make sure that **Input System Package (New)** is set here.

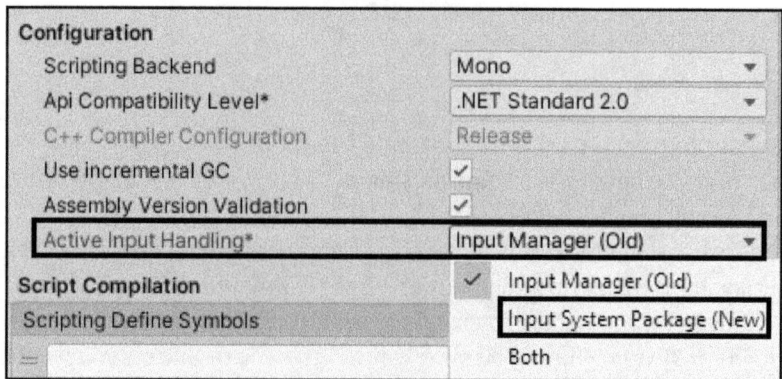

If you changed the setting, a dialog window will now pop up asking if you would like to apply the change. Click **Apply** to let the Unity editor restart itself.

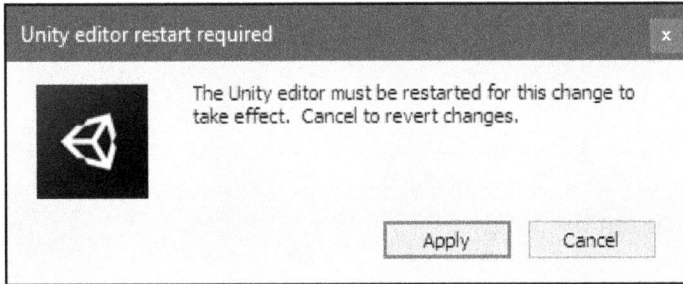

Next, wait for the editor to reload and then close the **Project Settings** window.

Input actions

Now the new input system is activated, you'll need to create an **Input Actions** file to map the player input to actions. To do this, first create a new folder in the **RW** folder named **Input**.

In this new folder, create a new **Input Actions** file by pressing the + button at the top left of the **Project** window and selecting **Input Actions** (the last option in the list).

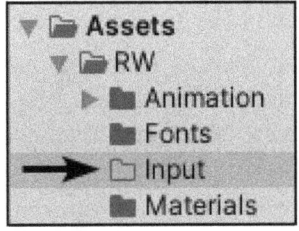

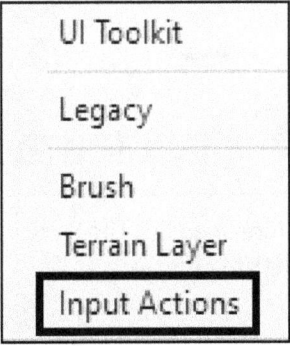

Name this file **Input**, then double-click it to open the **Input** window.

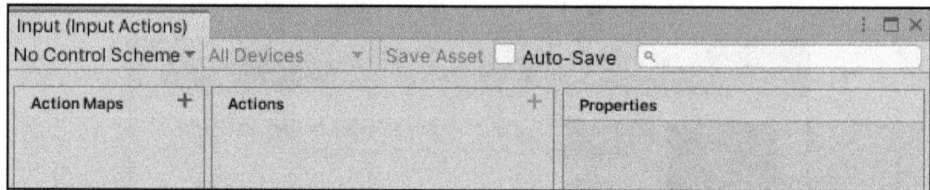

This is where you define your **control schemes**, **action maps**, **actions** and the accompanying **input bindings**.

Control schemes

First, you'll need to add control schemes. These are the **physical devices** you want to support, like keyboards, gamepads, touchscreens and even accelerometers.

Click on the control scheme drop-down at the top left that says "No Control Scheme" and select **Add Control Scheme…**

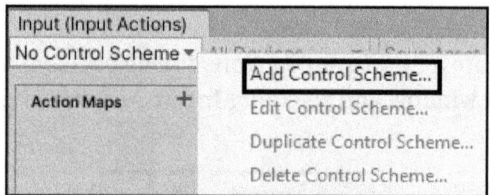

A popup window will open to let you add a control scheme. Change **Scheme Name** to **Gamepad** and click the **+** button at the bottom left of the control list that says "List is Empty." A selection screen will pop up to allow you to select a control scheme.

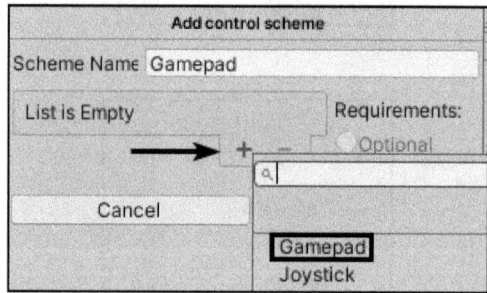

Select **Gamepad ▸ Gamepad** here and click the **Save** button to add the **Gamepad** control scheme to the **Input Actions** file.

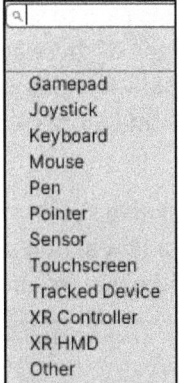

You can now link gamepad button presses and analog stick inputs to actions, but you'll surely want to be able to use your keyboard as well. So, add another control scheme via the drop-down at the top left. This time, name the new control scheme **KeyboardMouse** and add two entries to the empty control list: **Keyboard** and **Mouse ▸ Mouse**.

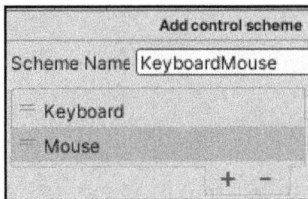

Like before, click the **Save** button to add the control scheme. Next, select **All Control Schemes** in the drop-down at the top left. This makes it so you can now poll input from game controllers, keyboards and mice when creating input bindings. Nice!

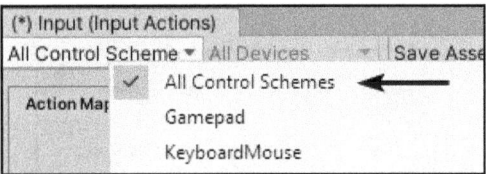

Action maps

Now that you've decided on the input methods, the next step is to create an **action map**. This is a **set of actions that are related** to each other in some way. For example, take a game that has the player avatar walking on foot, but also occasionally riding on horseback.

You can create two action maps in this case to separate the controls — one called "On foot" and one "Riding horse." Each of these action maps can have unique actions for the player to do. This separation also allows you to let the player rebind the controls per action map easily — and more customization options are always better!

For the sake of simplicity, you'll stick to a single action map that handles all of the player input for this project. Create a new action map by clicking the + button at the top right of the **Action Maps** list and name this new action map **Player**.

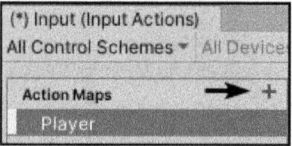

You'll notice Unity has automatically added an action named **New action** to the **Actions** list.

Actions

An **action** is something that can be done in-game that needs to be linked to the player's input. This can be a jumping, shooting, moving, whistling, etc. You need an action for just about anything an avatar can do so the player can perform it.

First, rename the default action to **Interact** by right-clicking **New action** and selecting **Rename**. Or, press the **F2** key (for Windows) or the **Enter** key (for Mac) to start renaming.

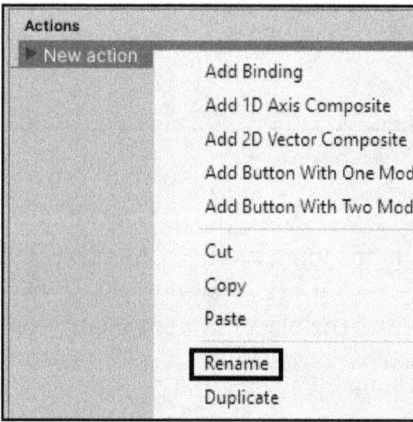

With the action named properly, take a look at the **Properties** list on the right.

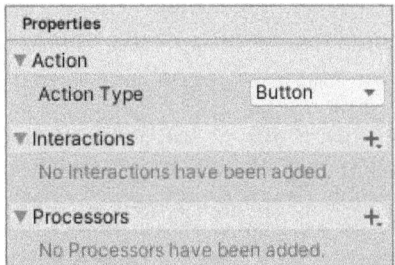

This panel changes depending on the selected item in the **Actions** panel, but **Interactions** and **Processors** are always present. The **Interact** action you've selected has an **Action Type** property. This is a drop-down with the following options:

- **Button**: This is the default action type. It's used for actions that are triggered every single time by a single button or key press. This can be used for a jump or interacting with an NPC, for example.

- **Value**: This action type is used for actions with continuous changes in value where a joystick or button is held down — like for movement or looking around. When multiple buttons or directions tied to the action are input at once, the most dominant one is chosen.

- **Pass Through** : The **Pass Through** action type works exactly like **Value**, except that there's no dominant input chosen, meaning all inputs will be used at once.

In most cases, you'll use either use the **Button** or **Value** action type.

Interactions and **Processors** are modifiers of an action. These can enforce that a button needs to be held down for a certain amount of time before triggering an action by using the **Hold** interaction, for example. An **Invert** processor simply inverts the input. These are used for more advanced inputs so this book won't cover them in detail.

Now, click on the little arrow to the left of the **Interact** action. This will reveal the list of **bindings** tied to the **Interact** action. The list only holds a single empty binding for now.

Bindings

A **binding** is the player's input, like button presses, the state of a joystick or even the movement of a VR controller. This is what connects an action to the physical world.

The player avatar should be able to interact with its surroundings when the player either presses the **Space** key or presses the bottom face button on their gamepad (A on Xbox controllers, X on PlayStation controllers).

Select the **<No Binding>** entry. If you now take a look at the **Properties** panel, you'll see some **Binding** options.

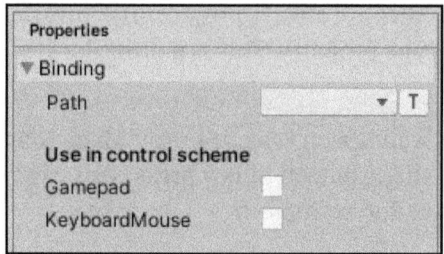

Here's a brief overview:

- **Path**: This is where you set the input path — like a specific button, key or other input, for example. The **T** button next to it allows you to set the path string manually instead of choosing it from the list.

- **Use in control scheme**: These checkboxes allow you to restrict this binding to a certain control scheme. When no checkboxes are checked, the binding is active for all control schemes.

Time to bind some input to the **Interact** action! The first input you'll bind is the **Space** key, so click on the **Path** drop-down to open the selection screen.

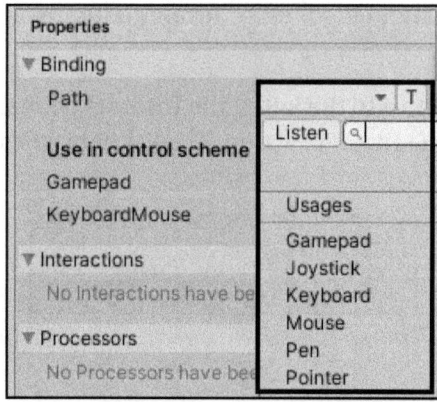

You can select the **Space** key by selecting **Keyboard ▸ By Location of Key (Using US Layout) ▸ Space** or by simply clicking the **Listen** button at the top left, pressing the **Space** key on your keyboard and selecting **Space [Keyboard]**.

Your first binding should now be named **Space [Keyboard]**. To add another binding to the same action, click the **+** button next to the **Interact** action and select **Add Binding**. Another empty binding will now appear in the list.

This time, the binding should be linked to the bottom face button of any supported gamepad. In traditional input polling, this would be a nightmare, since just about every brand of controller binds their buttons differently. Luckily, Unity's new input system allows you to bind gamepad buttons to their physical position based on the cardinal directions (north, east, south and west).

To add a gamepad south button binding, select the empty binding, click on the **Path** drop-down and select **Gamepad ▸ Button South**.

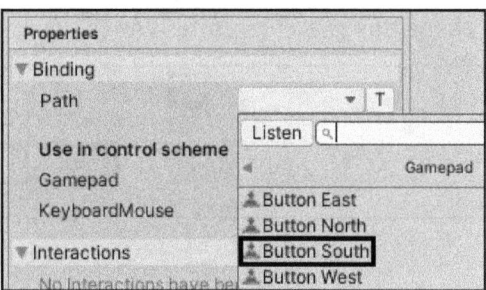

The **Interact** action is now complete! When the player presses the **Space** key or the bottom button, the action will be triggered.

Next up is the movement, for which you'll want to poll the following player inputs:

- **Left analog stick** on gamepads
- **WASD** keys
- **arrow** keys

As you can imagine, the setup for this action will be quite different from the **Interact** action. Create a new action by clicking the + button next to the **Actions** label and name the new action **Move** .

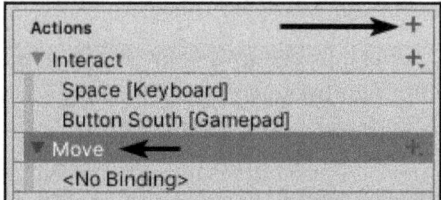

Change its **Action Type** to **Value** and its **Control Type** to **Vector 2** in the **Properties** panel on the right. The **Value** type allows for continuous input needed for movement while the **Vector 2** control type means the movement input will have an x- and a y-axis value between -1 and 1. For example, **(X:1, Y:0)** is the same as pointing an analog stick to the right.

Adding the left analog stick as a binding is straightforward. Click on the empty binding of **Move** and select **Gamepad ▸ Left Stick** in the **Path** list. The Left Stick input outputs a **Vector 2** out of the box, so there's no extra setup needed.

The next binding is the **WASD** keys. For this you'll need to add a **2D Vector Composite**, so click the + button right from the **Move** action and select **2D Vector Composite** in the list. Name this new composite **WASD**.

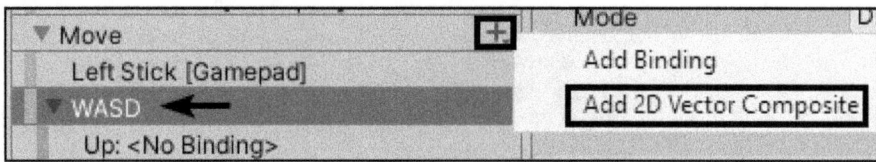

If you take a closer look at the **WASD** composite, you'll see it's composed of four bindings named **Up**, **Down**, **Left** and **Right**.

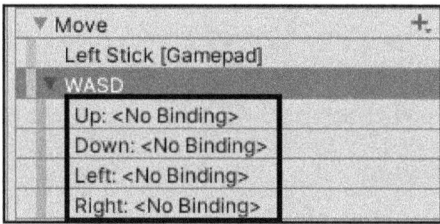

A binding is a simple one-input, one-value system, while a **composite** allows for multiple inputs that result in one final value. The illustration below shows how the **WASD** keys can be mapped onto the x-axis and y-axis to generate a **Vector 2**, with an X and a Y value:

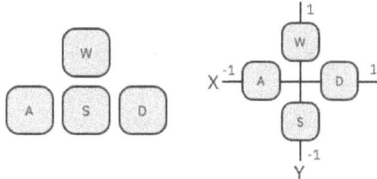

To apply this to the **WASD** composite, set the following paths for the four bindings. Do this by clicking the **Path** drop-down, clicking on the **Listen** key and pressing the appropriate key on your keyboard. This is exactly like you did it for the **Space** key in the **Interact** action.

- **Up**: W [Keyboard]
- **Down**: S [Keyboard]
- **Left**: A [Keyboard]
- **Right**: D [Keyboard]

The end result should look like this:

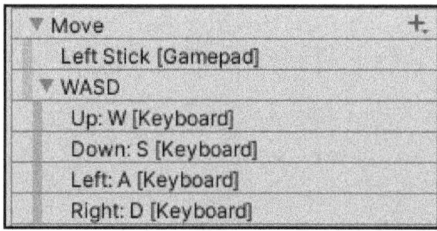

For the arrow keys, add another **2D Vector Composite** to the **Move** action and name it **Arrow Keys**. The concept here is exactly the same as with the **WASD** keys, but this time set up the following bindings for the four directions:

- **Up**: Up Arrow [Keyboard]
- **Down**: Down Arrow [Keyboard]
- **Left**: Left Arrow [Keyboard]
- **Right**: Right Arrow [Keyboard]

Here's what that should look like:

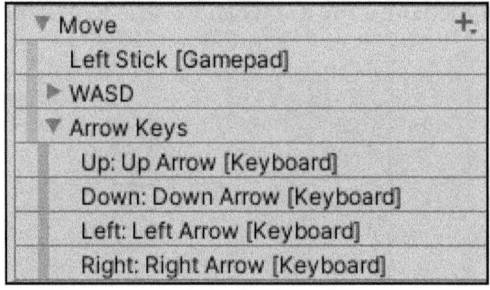

That's it for the input! You now have a full input scheme set up to make the player avatar move and interact with the world. Don't forget to click the **Save Asset** button at the top to save the **Input Actions** file.

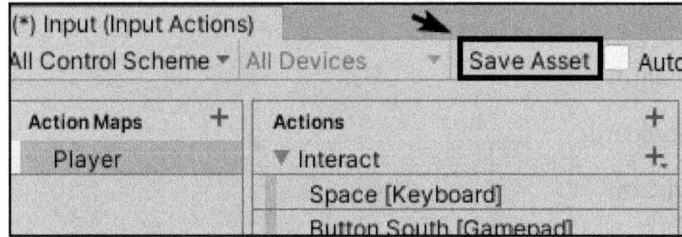

Now close the **Input** window and get ready to get the player avatar moving!

Linking input to movement

An Input Actions asset by itself isn't enough to poll for the player's input. For that, you'll need to add a **Player Input** component.

Select **Player Avatar** in the Hierarchy and add a **Player Input** component to it by clicking on the **Add Component** button at the bottom of the Inspector.

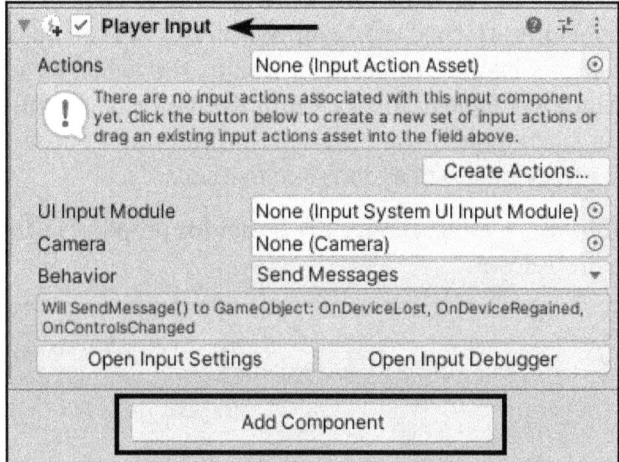

Player Input component

This component uses an Input Actions file as its input, checks for any triggered actions and can pass the results along to a script. Click on the circular selection button next to the **Actions** property and select the **Input** Input Actions file you created earlier. Doing so adds some extra properties below Actions. Here's what these are for:

- **Default Scheme**: The default control scheme (device) to use. You can set this to a particular scheme if you only want to poll input from a certain device. The default value of <Any> goes through the list of control schemes and uses the first one that's connected.

- **Auto-Switch**: When this property is enabled, the control scheme will automatically switch when input is detected on a supported device. For example, if the player is using a keyboard to play the game and then decides to connect a gamepad and use that instead, the control scheme will switch from **KeyboardMouse** to **Gamepad** automatically. In games with multiple players (and multiple **Player Input** components) this won't work. In that case, you'll have to dedicate a controller or the keyboard to each player via the **PlayerInput API**.

- **Default Map**: The action map to start with. In a game with multiple action maps, this could be set to "UI" or "Menu," for example, as the player starts at the title screen and needs some way to traverse that. In the case of the game you're working on for this chapter, there's only a single action map named **Player**.

By default, a **Player Input** component uses **Unity Messages** to call methods on a component on the same GameObject. For example, if the **Interact** action was triggered, an attempt to call an **OnInteract** method would be performed by **Player Input** on all components attached to **Player Avatar**. As you can imagine, this isn't effective performance-wise and the behavior would break when an action gets renamed. A good idea would be to invoke **Unity Events** instead - this can also call methods, but it's a much more flexible system that you can set up in the editor instead of relying on the names of actions and methods.

To get started with Unity Events, change the **Behavior** property to **Invoke Unity Events** using the drop-down.

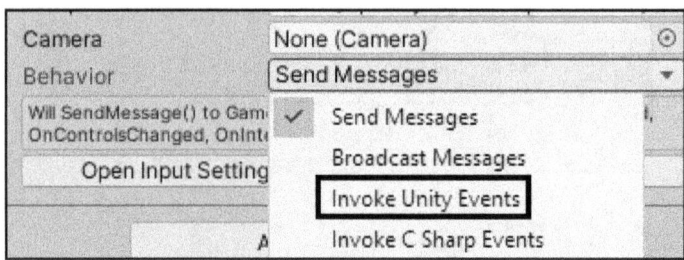

A new property called **Events** has now appeared below **Behavior**. If you expand **Events**, another property named after the **Player** action map and a set of Unity Events show up.

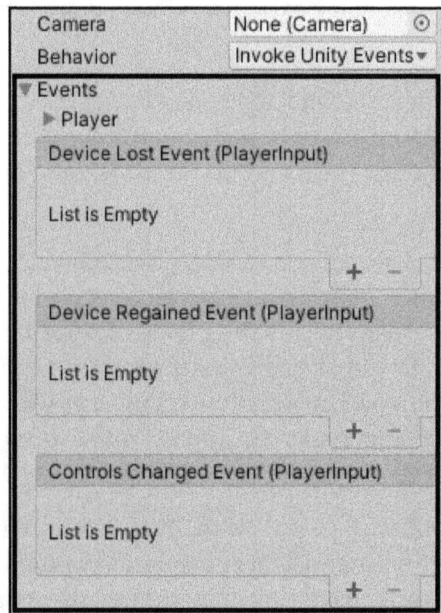

The first two of the events, **Device Lost** and **Device Regained** can be used when a device has been disconnected and reconnected, respectively. This can be used to detect when a gamepad has been unplugged or ran out of battery, for example, and you could pause the game as a reaction. The **Controls Changed** event triggers whenever the player switches their active device, like from a keyboard to a gamepad.

That's all good and well, but how do you react to the **Interact** and **Move** actions? That's where the **Player** property comes in! It's linked to the **Player** action map, so if you expand it, you'll see that events appear for both the **Interact** and the **Move** actions.

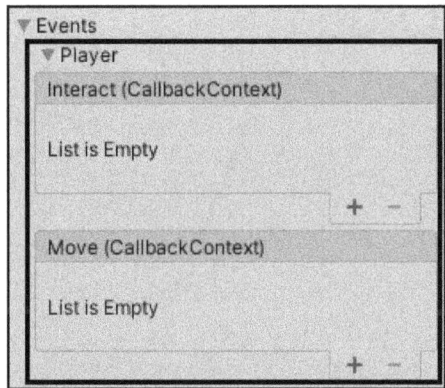

To test out if this works, you can turn off the lights in the scene when you trigger the **Interact** action by pressing **Space** or the bottom button on your gamepad. Click on the + button at the bottom right of the Interact event to add a new empty **function call**.

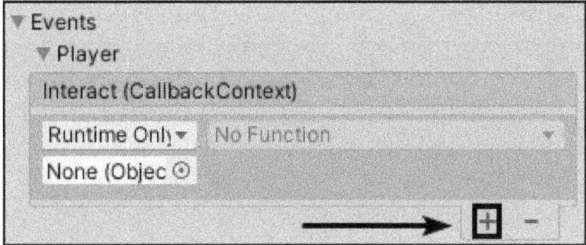

A **function call** can access the properties and methods of components that should be called or changed.

In this case, the **Lights** GameObject in the Hierarchy should be disabled. Drag **Lights** to the **Object** field of the **Interact** event to fill the function list on the right.

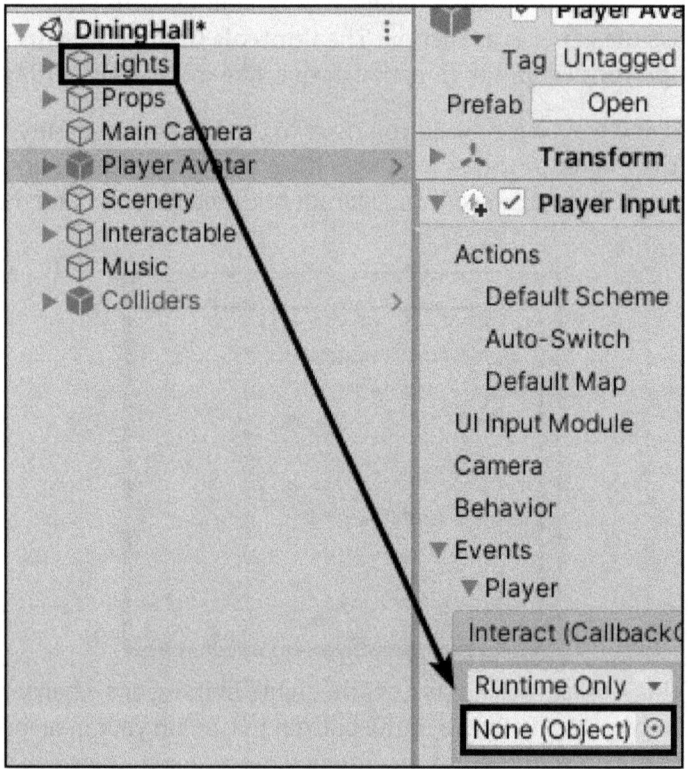

Now select **GameObject ▸ SetActive (bool)** in the function drop-down (it says "No Function" at the moment).

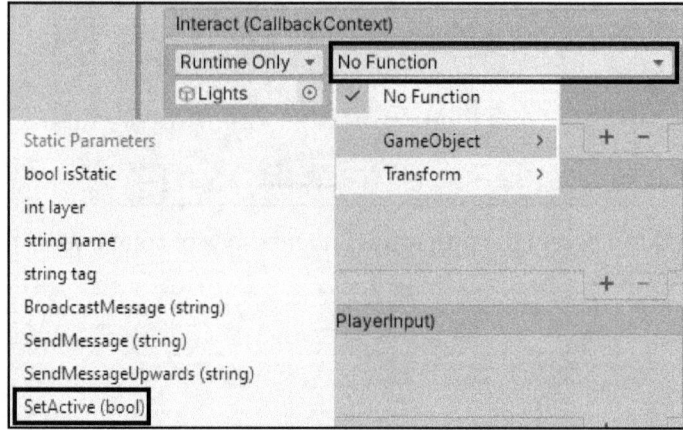

A property will appear that fits the type of property of the selected function. In the case of `SetActive`, this is a **Boolean**, so a checkbox appears. The lights should be disabled when the event is triggered, so the default off state is perfect. Now run the scene by clicking the **Play** button at the top of the editor. Try pressing **Space** on your keyboard — the lights should go off!

This is one reason why Unity Events are so powerful — it's easy to wire things together like this.

Before moving on, remove the function call to the **Lights** by selecting **Player Avatar**, expanding **Events ▸ Player** and clicking the - button at the bottom right of the **Interact** event.

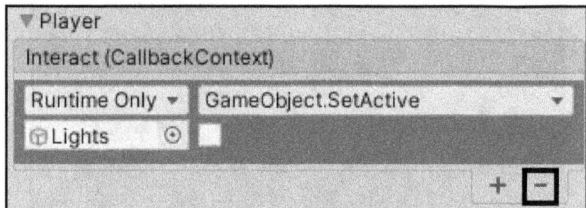

Character Controller component

At this point, you can take the player's input and use it in any way you want. To get the avatar moving through the scene, you'll need a component that handles the avatar's movement without moving through the floor or walls. You could script this yourself, but Unity comes with a handy component built-in: a **Character Controller**. Add one to the **Player Avatar** by clicking the **Add Component** button at the bottom of the Inspector, searching for "Character" and selecting **Character Controller** in the list.

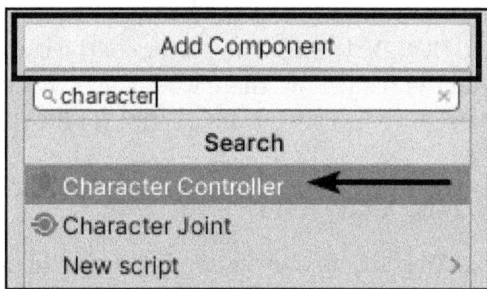

The **Character Controller** component adds a capsule-shaped collider to **Player Avatar** that can be moved in any direction via scripting. The component will automatically walk up stairs and slopes and will be stopped by walls if they have colliders.

The default values for the **Character Controller** component's properties are just right for the potato warrior model, except for **Center**, which is used to set the center of the capsule. The default value of **(X:0, Y:0, Z:0)** lodges the capsule in the ground as you can see in the **Scene** view.

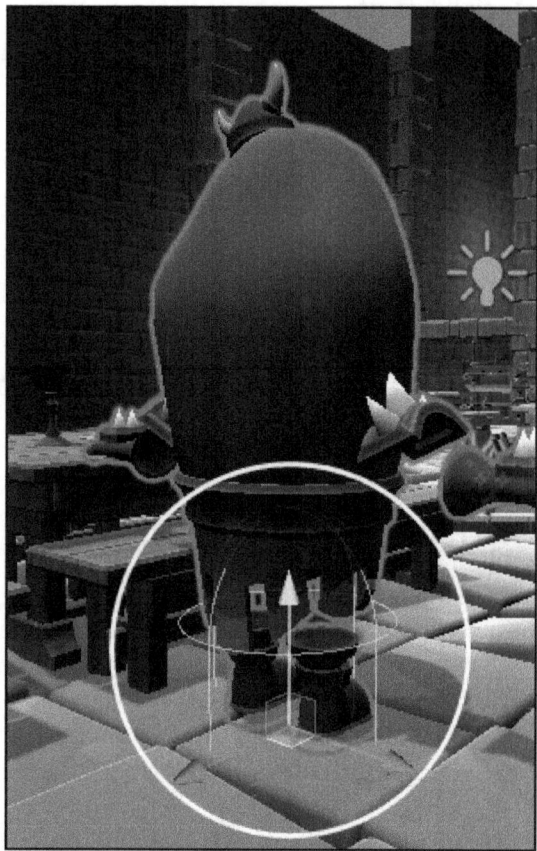

To fix this, set **Center** to **(X:0, Y:1, Z:0)**. The bottom of the capsule will now touch the ground. If you played the scene now, there would be no difference just yet, as the **Character Controller** needs to be called from a script for it to work.

Scripting the movement

Time for some scripting! To start, the movement input should be processed and passed to the **Character Controller**. Create a new folder in **RW / Scripts** and name it **Player**. Right-click inside this folder, select **Create ▸ C#** Script and name the script **PlayerAvatar**.

Double-click the script to open it in your code editor.

To start, add this **using** directive just below using UnityEngine; at the top:

```
using UnityEngine.InputSystem;
```

This adds a reference to the InputSystem namespace, which is needed to access methods and variables of the new input system. Now, add these variable declarations right above the `Start` method:

```
public float movementSpeed = 5f; // 1
public float rotationSpeed = 10f; // 2
public float gravity = 20f; // 3
public Animator animator; // 4

private CharacterController characterController; // 5
private Vector2 movementInput = Vector2.zero; // 6
private bool allowInput = true; // 7
```

Here's what these are for:

1. The speed of the movement in meters per second.

2. When the character changes direction, it will turn to face the direction it's moving in. This is the speed of that turning in degrees per second.

3. The force of the gravity that will be applied to the avatar every second.

4. A reference to the 3D model's **Animator** component, which can change the currently playing animation. This will be used to switch between the idle and the walking animation.

5. A reference to the **Character Controller** component to be able to make it move.

6. This keeps track of movement input provided by the **Player Input** component.

7. A **Boolean** to easily allow or disallow input to be passed through. The dialogue system will use this later to disable movement input when the avatar is talking to an NPC.

Next, rename the `Start` method to `Awake` and add this line to its body:

```
characterController = GetComponent<CharacterController>();
```

This line gets a reference to the **Character Controller** component and saves it to `characterController`. Now, add the `Move` method below `Update`:

```
public void Move(InputAction.CallbackContext context) // 1
{
    if (!allowInput) // 2
    {
        return;
    }

    movementInput = context.ReadValue<Vector2>(); // 3
}
```

This `Move` method will be called from the **Move** event in the **Player Input** component every time the player presses the **WASD** keys, the **arrow keys** or move the **left joystick** on their gamepad. Here's a breakdown of the code:

1. `Move` accepts a single parameter `context` of the type `InputAction.CallbackContext`. The `CallbackContext` contains all information about the input action — like when exactly it was started and what the current phase and value is.

2. If no input is allowed, don't do anything and simply return.

3. Read the `Vector2` value from the `CallbackContext` and store it in `movementInput`.

Next, add this method below `Move`:

```
private void UpdateMovementAndRotation()
{
    // 1
    Vector3 movementVector = new Vector3(-movementInput.y, 0, movementInput.x);
    // 2
    characterController.Move(movementVector * movementSpeed * Time.deltaTime);
    // 3
    transform.rotation =
        Quaternion.Slerp(transform.rotation,
            Quaternion.LookRotation(movementVector),
                    Time.deltaTime * rotationSpeed);
}
```

This code will read the movement input and send it to the character controller. It will also rotate the avatar towards the direction of the movement. Here's what's happening line by line:

1. Convert the 2D X and Y input to 3D movement and store it in `movementVector`. The illustration below shows a top-down view of the dining hall scene. Moving toward the door at the back means moving along the x-axis while moving side to side is along the z-axis. The movement input however maps left and right to the x-axis and up and down to the y-axis.

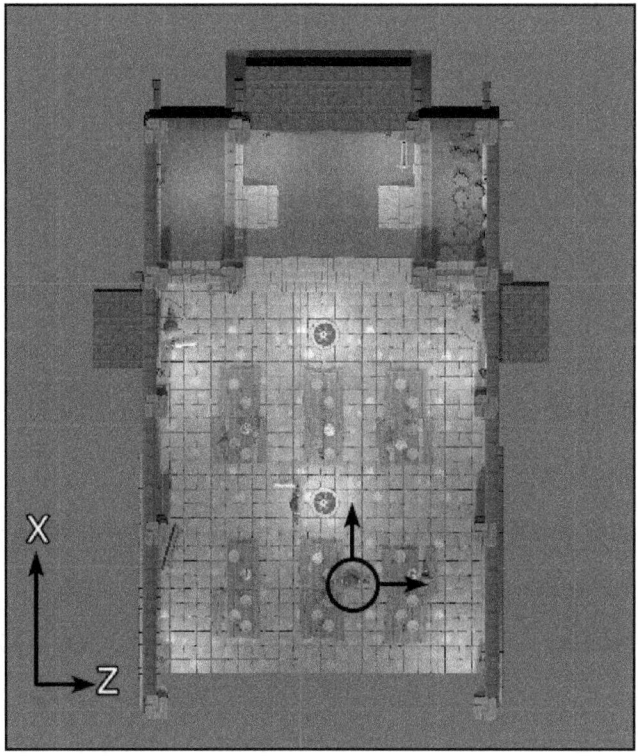

2. Call the `Move` method on the character controller. `movementVector` is the direction, `movementSpeed` is the speed and `Time.deltaTime` is used to ensure the movement is steady and frame-rate independent.

3. Smoothly modify the rotation of the avatar over time by using a **spherical linear interpolation** (slerp). The slerp takes the current rotation and will change it each frame until the avatar is facing in the direction of `movementVector` at the speed set in `rotationSpeed`. This is a way to animate GameObjects with scripting. More on that in Chapter 12!

Next, you'll apply the gravity — so add this code below the
UpdateMovementAndRotation method:

```
private void UpdateGravity()
{
    characterController.Move(Vector3.down * gravity * 
Time.deltaTime);
}
```

All this does is use the character controller to move the avatar down toward the floor with a force set in the `gravity` variable.

To bring it all together, add this to `Update`:

```
if (movementInput != Vector2.zero && allowInput) // 1
{
    UpdateMovementAndRotation(); // 2
    animator.SetFloat("Speed", 1f); // 3
}
else // 4
{
    movementInput = Vector2.zero;
    animator.SetFloat("Speed", 0f);
}

UpdateGravity(); // 5
```

Here's what's happening:

1. If the movement input isn't **(X:0, Y:0)** and input is allowed, proceed.

2. Update the movement and rotation based on the input.

3. Call the **Animator** component's `SetFloat` method to start the walking animation.

4. If there's no movement input or input isn't allowed, reset the movement input and stop the walking animation.

5. Update the gravity so the avatar can't float.

That finishes up the script! Save it and return to the Unity editor. Select **Player Avatar** in the Hierarchy and add the newly created **Player Avatar** component. Change **Movement Speed** to **3** and **Gravity** to **15**.

Next, expand **Player Avatar** in the Hierarchy and drag **Model** to the **Animator** property to add it as a reference.

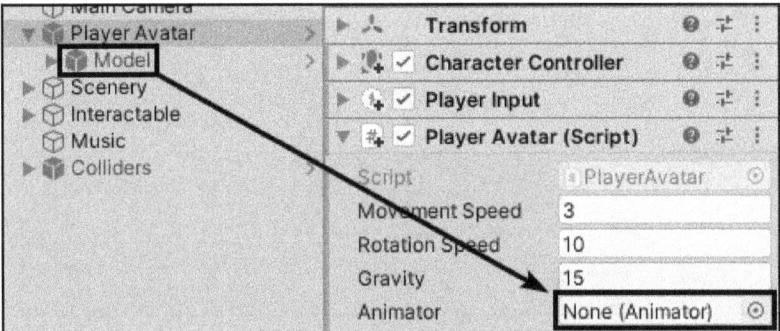

The final step is to link the **Move** action to the Move method you just added in the script. In the **Player Input** component, expand **Events ▸ Player** and create a new empty function to the **Move** event by clicking the + button at the bottom right.

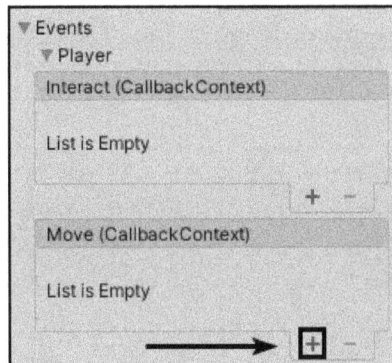

Finally, drag **Player Avatar** to the **Object** property and select **PlayerAvatar ▸ Move** in the **Function** dropdown.

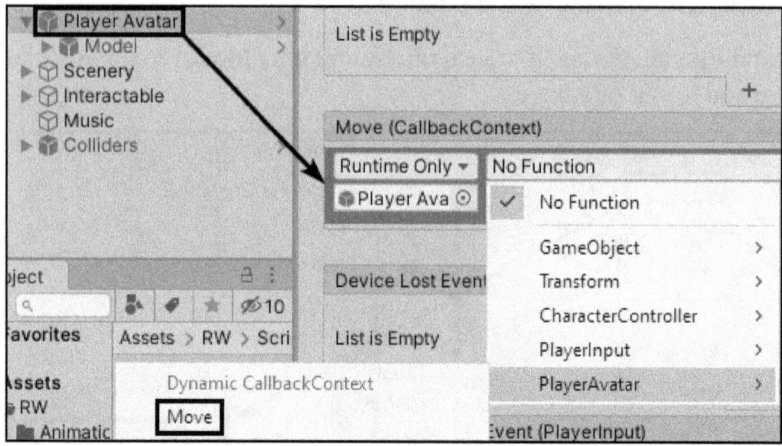

Now, play the scene and enjoy the magic of locomotion! Use either the WASD keys, the arrow keys or the left analog stick on a gamepad to move the player avatar around. Can you find all the moved player avatars in the image below? :]

It can get a bit awkward to walk around while the camera remains stationary because it can be hard to see the avatar when it's at the back of the scene.

Use the included simple component called **Third Person Camera** to make the camera follow a GameObject around. Add this component to **Main Camera** and drag **Player Avatar** to its **Transform To Follow** property. As a final step, set the value of **Position Offset** to (**X:6, Y:5, Z:0**).

Play the scene again and move the avatar around. The camera will now follow along!

Physics

Now that you can move the character around, you might have noticed you can move through the tables and the NPCs. While the scene comes with the colliders needed for the geometry, no colliders have been added for most props. Select **Colliders** in the Hierarchy and take a look at the scene view. All of the green boxes you see around the scene are **box colliders** that have been set up for the geometry.

To get a better look, you can change the **Shading Mode** to **Wireframe** from **Shaded**, as shown below. Remember to change it back!

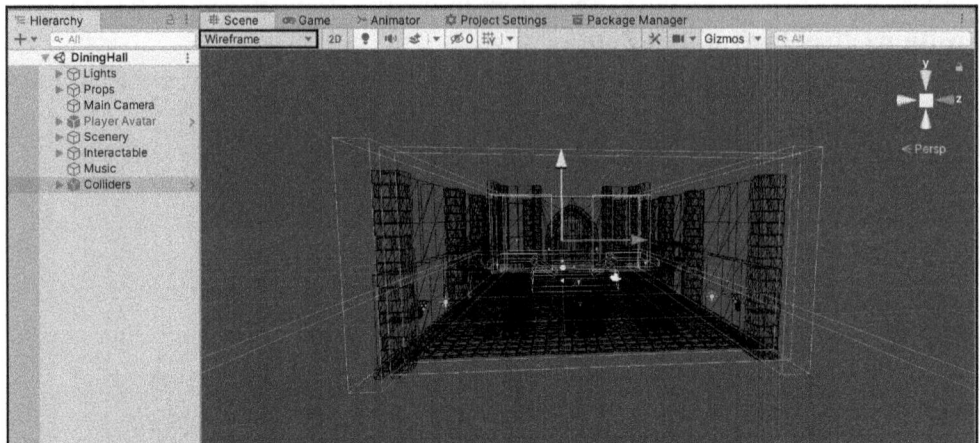

Unity uses a physics engine called **PhysX** that calculates collisions between **colliders**. Colliders are simple 3D shapes that represent their high resolution counterparts. Some examples include boxes, spheres and capsules. Each of these colliders has a dedicated component.

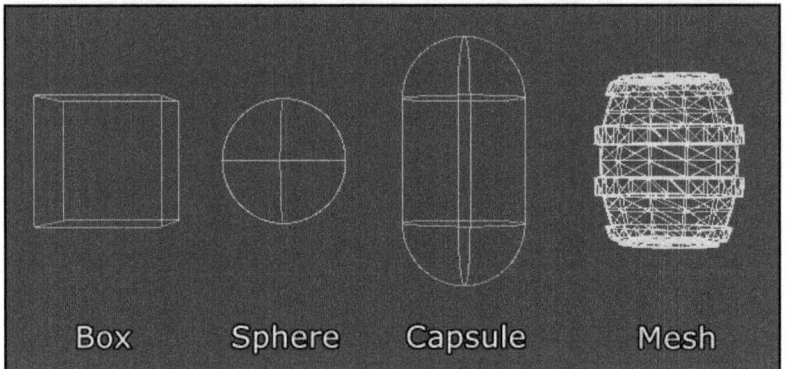

The **Character Controller** component Unity provides only does a small subset of the physics calculations — so while it may not be realistic, it's optimal for avatars that simply need to be able to move around without falling through floors while being able to climb stairs and slopes.

Adding colliders is a matter of adding a collider component with the most appropriate shape and setting up its size.

To start off with the tables, expand **Props ▸ Tables & Benches ▸ Tables** in the Hierarchy. This will unveil all of the tables. Next, select all of the **Table** GameObjects and add a **Box Collider** component to all of them via the Inspector.

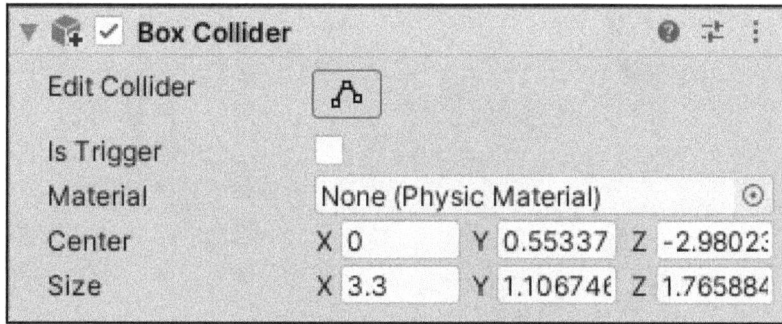

Here's a quick overview of a collider component's properties:

- **Edit Collider**: This button enables the collider editing mode and allows you to drag around handles in the Scene view to adjust the shape of the collider.

- **Is Trigger**: By default, a collider is used to make a GameObject solid when it comes to physics — allowing for collisions that call the OnCollisionEnter function. By checking the **Is Trigger** checkbox, the collider becomes a **trigger** and will let colliders pass through. When a collider enters the trigger, the OnTriggerEnter function gets called.

- **Material**: You can choose a **physics material** here if you made one. A physics material provides custom properties to a collider to make it more grippy or bouncy for example.

- **Center**: The local position of the collider in the scene.

- **Size**: The size of the cube.

If you now look at the **Scene** view, all of the tables have a green colored collider around them.

The great thing about adding collider components to GameObjects that have a **Mesh Renderer** attached to them is the collider auto sizes itself as best it can. In the case of the tables, it's a perfect fit! Next up are the benches. Expand **Props ▸ Tables & Benches ▸ Benches**, select all of the **Bench** GameObjects and add a **Box Collider** component to them. This will make for perfect fits again.

Now, play the scene again and try bumping into the benches and tables. You might step onto them in some cases, but you won't be able to phase through them like a ghost anymore. :]

The last geometry colliders to add are for the fire pits in the middle of the room and the barrels at the back. You'll use capsule colliders for these, since they have a round shape. Expand **Props ▸ Fire Pits** and select both of the **FirePit** GameObjects. Now add a **Capsule Collider** component to both of them. This will add a sphere-shaped collider to both of the fire pits. Next, do the same thing for the barrels found in **Props ▸ Barrels**.

If you play the scene now, you'll see the colliders around the fire pits will prevent the avatar from walking through the fire, but you can still stand atop the flames. Yikes!

Fix this by changing the height of the Capsule Collider to **3**.

Now, play the scene and see if you can make the avatar move through objects. It shouldn't work anymore — except for the poor NPCs who keep getting ghosted, of course.

Can you guess what collider shape you'll need to use for the NPCs? That's right — even more capsule colliders!

Expand **Interactable ▸ NPCs**, select all of the NPCs inside and add a **Capsule Collider** component to all of them. This time, the collider didn't even make an attempt to get the position and the size right because there's no **Mesh Renderer** attached to the root GameObject of the NPCs. Not a problem though — just set **Center** to **(X:0, Y:1, Z:0)**, **Radius** to **0.5** and **Height** to **2** just like you did for the player avatar.

Play the scene once again and bump into the NPCs. Their vegetable bodies are now solid like they should be.

Congratulations on finishing this chapter! You've learned all about implementing input in a game and the basics of the **Unity Physics** system. In the next chapter, you'll take a look at how to add a user interface to the game.

Key points

- Unity comes with two input systems: the old one and the new one. The former is enabled by default.
- You can enable the new input system via **Edit ▸ Project Settings… ▸ Player**.
- To start mapping controls to actions, you need to create an Input Actions file.
- A **control scheme** is a collection of physical devices like keyboards and gamepads.
- An **action map** is a **set of actions that are related** to each other in some way.
- An **action** is something that can be done in-game that needs to be linked to the player's input.
- A **binding** is the player's input. It connects an action to the physical world.
- A **composite** allows for multiple input bindings that result in one final output value.
- To use the **Input Actions** file and poll for input, you need a **Player Input** component.
- Events get called when input actions are triggered. These events can call functions, which can change properties of components and/or call methods.
- A **Character Controller** is a simple component for moving an avatar around a scene. Its `Move` method needs to be called from a script.
- **Colliders** are simple 3D shapes that represent their high-resolution counterparts. Some examples include boxes, spheres and capsules.
- A collider component automatically adjusts its size when a **Mesh Renderer** component is also attached to the same GameObject.

Chapter 7: User Interfaces

By Eric Van de Kerckhove

In the last chapter, you explored the wonderful world of Unity's input systems, and you learned the basics of the physics system. Now that you can move the player avatar around in the world, it's time to add a title screen and make a user interface for the dialogue system. Along the way, you'll learn all about the most common UI elements and how to create windows that can automatically resize to fit their contents. You can use this to let the NPCs tell the player avatar anything you want — like silly dad jokes, for example!

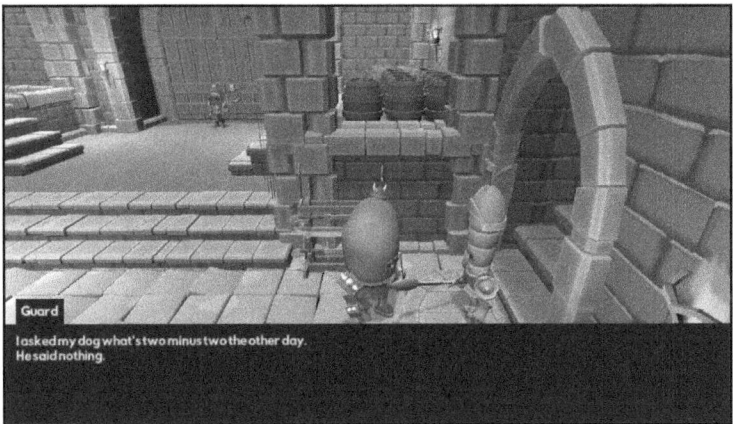

Whether it's bouncy hearts that show your remaining lives, a green stamina meter that lets you know how many more dodge rolls you can perform or a simple piece of text that explains the stats of your equipped weapon, user interfaces are everywhere.

A user interface — commonly referred to as the UI — can consist of text, images, sliders, buttons and more. The combination of these elements is crucial to delivering information to the player.

Title screen overview

As a minimum, a title screen should show a game's name and a way to start playing. More elaborate title screens can include an options screen and a way to show the credits. They might even have dynamic backgrounds. In the case of the Veggie Gladiators game you've been tinkering with for the last two chapters, the title screen is simple, but it does use several types of UI elements, like text, an image and a button.

First, open the starter project for this chapter in Unity. Create a new empty scene by right-clicking the **RW / Scenes** folder in the **Project** view and selecting **Create ▸ Scene**. Name this new scene **Title** and double-click the scene asset to open it in the editor.

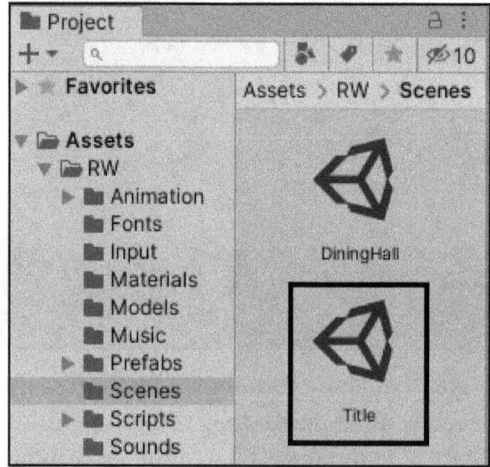

When adding a new scene to your game, it's good practice to add it to the **Scenes** list in the **Build Settings** because that includes the scene in the final game. Not doing this will result in errors when you try to load the scene.

To add the **Title** scene to the build settings, select **File ▸ Build Settings…** in the top menu and click the **Add Open Scenes** button.

Next, close the **Build Settings** window; it's time to get the scene ready.

Take a look around the editor. You'll see a beautiful blue sky in both the **Scene** and **Game** views. Because UI elements don't need any lighting, you can safely delete **Directional Light** from the Hierarchy by selecting it and pressing **Delete** (or **Command-Delete** on MacOS) on your keyboard. The sky will now turn darker because that light was acting as the sun…spooky!

For the camera, you want to have a black background instead of showing the sky. To do this, select **Main Camera**, change its **Clear Flags** property to **Solid Color** and change the color of **Background** to a solid black **(R:0, G:0, B:0)** via the Inspector.

Perfect! Now you have an empty void that's begging to be filled with UI elements.

Canvas

Unlike the GameObjects you've seen until now, UI elements can't be placed just anywhere in the Hierarchy — they need to be children of a **canvas**. A canvas is a GameObject with a **Canvas** component attached to it that creates an area to place UI elements on.

Create a new canvas by clicking the **+** button at the top left of the Hierarchy and selecting **UI ▸ Canvas**. This will create two GameObjects at the root of the Hierarchy: **Canvas** and **EventSystem**. The latter is used to pass input to the canvas, like button presses and mouse clicks.

Unfortunately, Unity adds a **Standalone Input Module** component to the **EventSystem** by default — which is used by the old input system, not the new one you're using. To fix this, select **EventSystem** and click the **Replace with InputSystemUIInputModule** button in the Inspector.

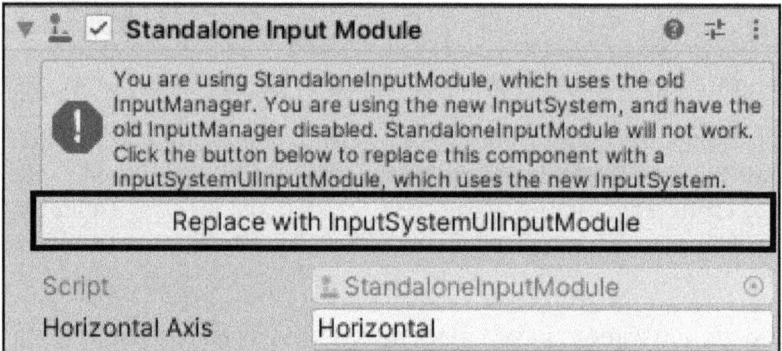

This will remove the **Standalone Input Module** component and replace it with an **Input System UI Input Module** component. Now, select **Canvas** in the Hierarchy and take a look at the Inspector. By default, a canvas comes with four components: **Rect Transform**, **Canvas**, **Canvas Scaler** and **Graphic Raycaster**.

Each of these components plays an important role in how the canvas behaves.

Rect Transform component

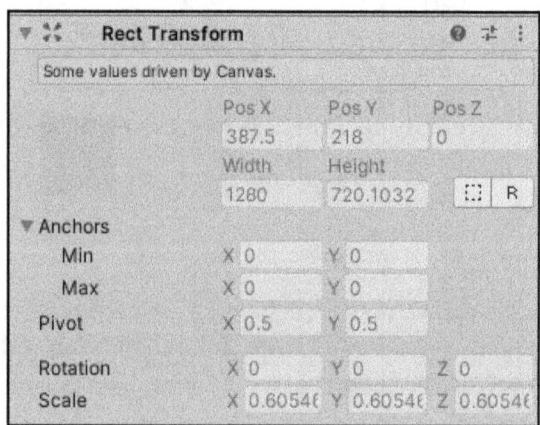

A **Rect Transform** component is the 2D counterpart to the familiar **Transform** component. You'll use it for all UI elements. Instead of just having X, Y and Z values for its position, rotation and scale, it also has a width and a height, along with anchor points and pivot points. It's essential to know what these terms mean, so here's a quick overview:

- **Position**: The **Pos X**, **Pos Y** and **Pos Z** properties are used to set the position of a **Rect Transform**. These are used to move the UI element on the canvas. These values are relative to the anchor points and the pivot point. By default, the anchors and pivot are centered, so that's why a value of **(X:0, Y:0, Z:0)** centers the UI element on the canvas.

- **Dimensions**: This is the width and height of the UI element.

- **Anchor points**: Anchor points are the points at which a UI element is attached to its parent. They're represented by the white "flower" and its four petals. These values are **normalized** — in other words, they range from 0 to 1, with 0 being the utmost left or top and 1 being the utmost right or bottom. There are two anchor points — **Min** and **Max** — which make a rectangle. **Min** is the position of the **lower-left corner** of the rectangle, while **Max** is the position for the **upper-right corner**.
The zero position for these points is at the lower-left corner of the parent. For example, with the anchor points set to **(X:0.5, Y:0.5)** and **(X:0.5, Y:0.5)**, the UI element is anchored to the center of their parent — in this case, the canvas. With a value of **(X:0, Y:0)** and **(X:1, Y:0)**, the anchor is stretched at the bottom.

- **Pivot point**: The pivot point is the **normalized** position of the point on the UI element that's used for rotations and scaling. Imagine pricking a needle through a picture and then trying to rotate the picture. It will rotate around the needle. That's the pivot point!

As you may have noticed, in the case of the canvas, you can't edit the **Rect Transform** values. They are automatically set by the **Canvas** component.

All of this may seem daunting at first, but how these values are used together will become a lot more clear once you start using them. And, Unity comes with some handy shortcuts to help you along.

Canvas component

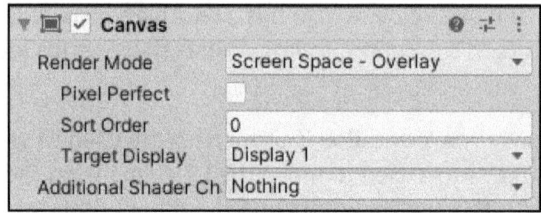

The **Canvas** is what's doing the heavy lifting. It adjusts its size based on the **Render Mode** and draws all of its children to the screen in order. Here's an overview of its properties:

- **Pixel Perfect**: Enabling this property forces all UI elements to snap to rounded pixel values, resulting in an image that is potentially more crisp.

- **Sort Order**: When using multiple canvases, you can decide the order in which they should be drawn using this property.

- **Target Display:** Use this to draw this canvas on another display if you're creating a game that spans over multiple monitors.

- **Additional Shader Channels**: Additional channels can be added to the canvas as data feeds for custom UI shaders.

For the title screen — and for most use cases — the default canvas values will be fine.

Canvas Scaler component

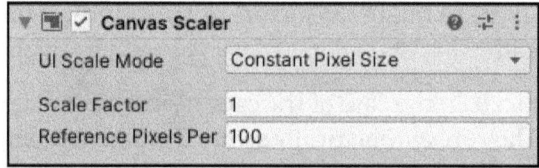

This component automatically changes the size of UI elements in the canvas based on its scale mode. In a nutshell:

- **Scale Factor**: Multiplies the size of all UI elements by this value.

- **Reference Pixels Per Unit**: Every image — called a sprite — used on a canvas has a **Pixels Per Unit** property, which can be used to decide how many pixels can fit in a single world unit. Unlike 3D models, 2D assets don't have real-world size, only pixels. These need to be mapped to units that Unity can use. By default, one world unit can hold 100 pixels, but you can change that via this value

Now, to make things easy, change the **UI Scale Mode** to **Scale With Screen Size** and set the **Reference Resolution** to **(X:1280, Y:720)**. This will make the canvas layout act as if the screen resolution was **1280x720** at all times, and it will scale the user interface up or down when the actual resolution is higher or lower, respectively. This makes creating the UI a lot more straightforward because you don't have to worry about dynamically resizing or moving certain elements to cater for every player's display. This will become a lot more clear once you start adding some UI elements to the canvas.

Graphic Raycaster component

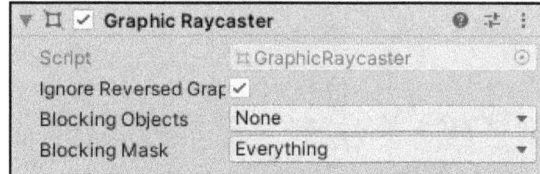

This component passes mouse clicks and finger taps to the event system. It has three properties:

- **Ignore Reversed Graphics**: Enabling this prevents interacting with UI elements that are turned away from the canvas, which are invisible.

- **Blocking Objects**: A drop-down to decide whether 2D objects, 3D objects or both can block interaction with UI elements in this canvas.

- **Blocking Mask**: The layers that will block interactions.

The defaults for this component make sense for this project, so you can leave them alone.

Adding UI elements

Time to get down to business! The first UI element you'll need to add is the title itself at the top. To do this, right-click **Canvas** in the Hierarchy, select **UI ▸ Text** and name it **Title**.

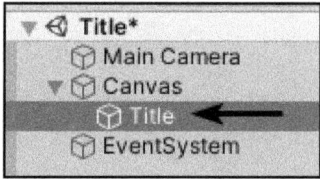

Now, click the **2D** button at the top left of the **Scene** view to switch to 2D mode, and zoom out until you can see the whole canvas.

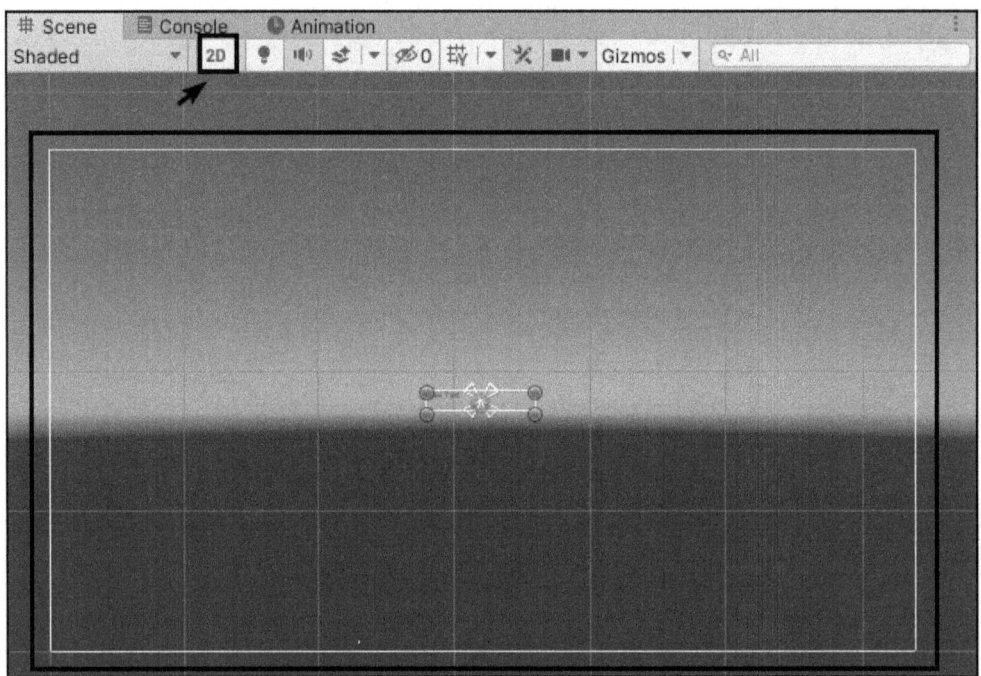

Look carefully, and you'll see tiny text that reads "New Text." Not really impressive, is it? Like all GameObjects, UI elements come with components, so take a look at the Inspector to see what makes this text tick.

Text

The very first component is a **Rect Transform**, which can be edited this time. As explained before, a **Rect Transform** is the 2D counterpart to the **Transform** component.

Before moving on, change the **Height** of **Title** to **200**. You'll need the extra space for the big font later on. Next, the text UI element should be stretched along the top of the canvas, with the text itself centered inside it both vertically and horizontally.

You *could* calculate the values for the anchor points yourself, but **Rect Transform** components come with a nifty **Anchor Presets** menu to make the process a lot more straightforward.

To anchor the **Title** along the top of the canvas, click the **Anchor Preset** button at the top left of the **Rect Transform** component.

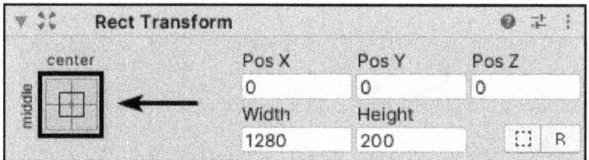

This opens up the **Anchor Preset** menu, which has the most common anchoring options right there for you to pick from.

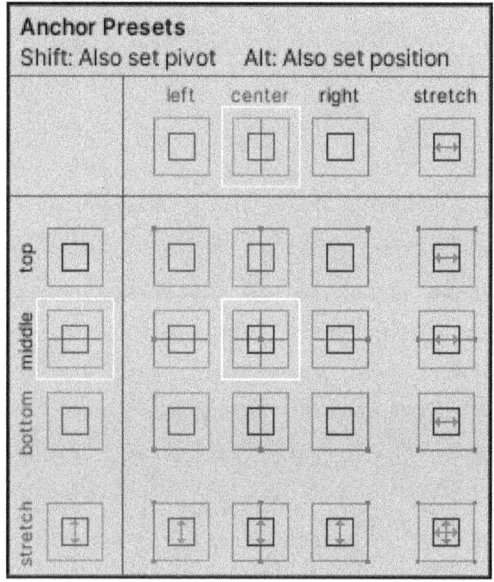

Simply clicking on any of these buttons will change the anchor points accordingly. Holding **Shift** and/or **Alt** while clicking will change the pivot point and/or the position, respectively.

To expand **Title** along the top of the canvas, hold **Alt** and click the button that has the rectangle at the top with blue lines from left to right indicating the stretch.

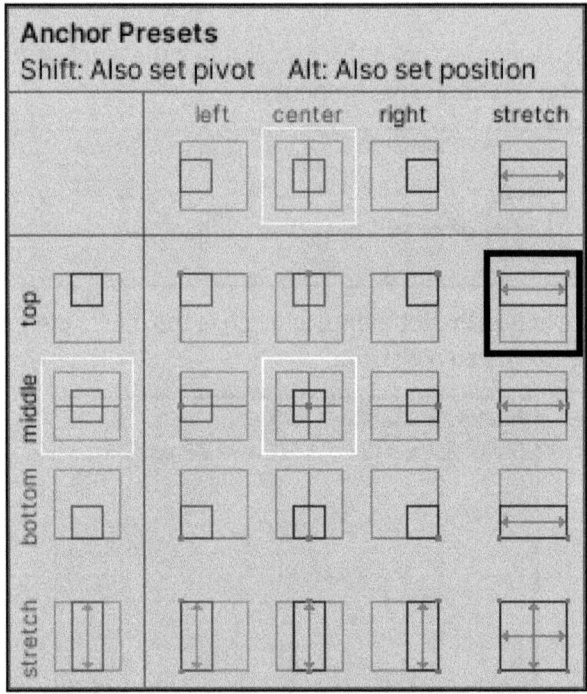

After doing this, you can see that the UI element is now stretched at the top of the canvas in the **Scene** view.

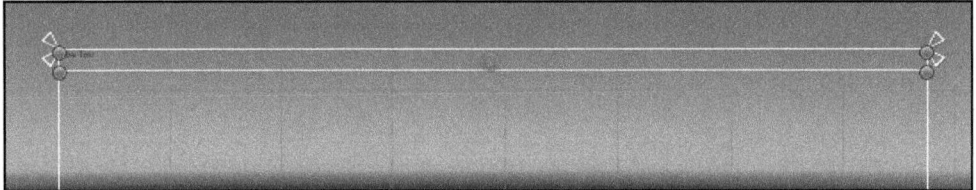

The text is still a bit small and not the right font or color, so divert your attention back to the Inspector again. Besides the **Rect Transform** component, there's a **Canvas Renderer** component which simply signals the canvas to draw the UI element. And, more importantly, there's a **Text** component that holds all the properties for the text. If you've ever used a rich text editor before, a lot of the properties will already be familiar to you.

First, change the value of the **Text** property to **Veggie Gladiators** instead of **New Text**. Then, click the **Picker** button next to the **Font** property and select the **RabbidHighwaySignII** font in the list. Next, change the **Font Size** to **80** and use the **Alignment** buttons to center the text both horizontally and vertically. Finally, change the **Color** to white **(R:255, G:255, B:255)**.

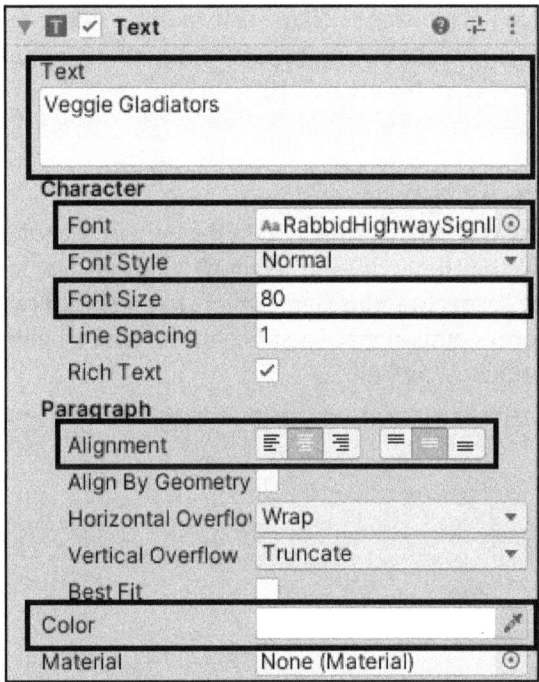

After doing all this, take a look at the **Game** view. You'll see the title prominently displayed at the top.

Other commonly used properties of the **Text** component include:

- **Font Style**: This changes the text style to **bold**, *italic* or ***both***.

- **Line Spacing**: This is a multiplier for the vertical distance between lines set in the **Text** property.

- **Horizontal Overflow**: When the text overflows its horizontal boundaries, there are two options to handle this: **Wrap** or **Overflow**. Wrapping the text will move any text that's outside the boundaries to the next line(s). The **Overflow** option simply lets the text go outside its set boundaries.

- **Vertical Overflow**: Similarly to the horizontal overflow, when text overflows its vertical boundaries, there are two options to handle this: **Truncate** or **Overflow**. Truncating — or shortening — the text will not draw any text that's outside the boundaries. The **Overflow** option lets the text go outside its set boundaries.
- **Best Fit**: By enabling this, the **Font Size** property will be ignored and the text will be enlarged as far as it's allowed until it fits its parent. While this may sound useful, it can make a UI look very cluttered when used with multiple text boxes, as the different font sizes can be jarring. Use with caution.

Image

Now that the title text is done, it's time to add the logo in the middle of the screen. Right-click **Canvas** in the Hierarchy and select **UI ▸ Image**. Name this new image **Logo**, and look to the Inspector. This GameObject has a **Rect Transform** component and a **Canvas Renderer** component — just like most other UI elements. There's an **Image** component attached, as well.

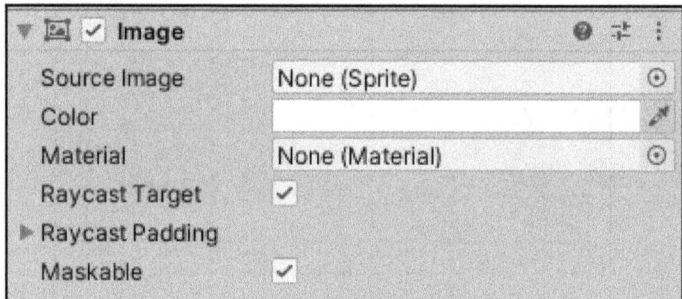

This is a simple component when compared to the dozen or so properties of the **Text** component. The **Source Image** property allows you to use a sprite as an image, and the **Color** property tints the image. Pretty straightforward!

Click the **Selector** button next to **Source Image** and select the **Logo** sprite from the list. These crossed weapons represent the power and unity of the veggie gladiators.

The image is a bit small though, don't you think?

Images, just like other UI elements, get their position and size from the **Rect Transform** component. To make the logo bigger, change its **Width** and **Height** to **400** units.

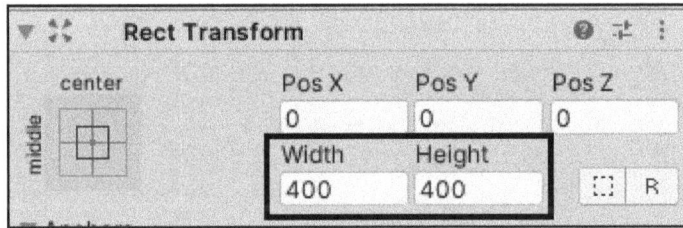

The final piece of the UI puzzle is the button that will start the game.

Button

Right-click **Canvas** again, select **UI ▸ Button** to add a button and name it **New Game Button**. Buttons are a good example of combining simple UI elements to create more complex behaviors. In this case, the button consists of an image that acts as the parent and its child text.

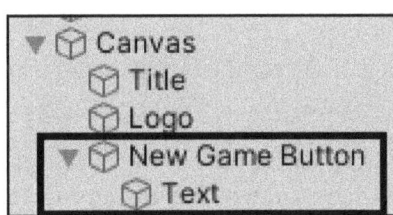

To make the button receive input and have optional animations, the parent GameObject comes with a **Button** component.

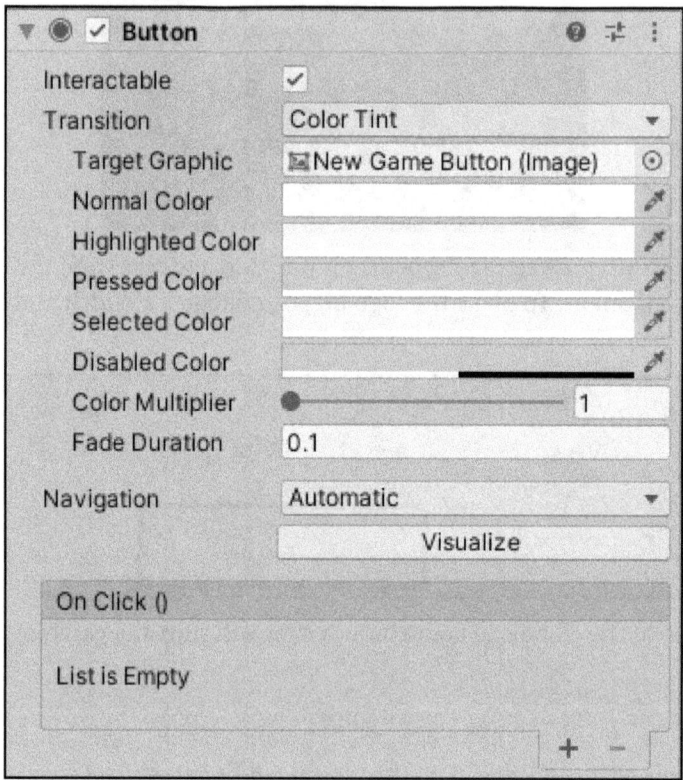

Most of the button's properties are actually used to animate its color when the button is hovered over, clicked and selected. Simply set a color for these, and the button will be tinted when the accompanying state change is triggered. Here's an overview of the other properties:

- **Interactable**: When this is checked, the button accepts input. When unchecked, the button is in a disabled state.

- **Transition**: The type of transition between the different states. **None** disables state changes, **Color Tint** fades between color tints and **Sprite Swap** changes the target graphic sprite depending on the state. **Animation** is the most advanced option, as it uses an animation controller to switch between the states — meaning just about anything can change depending on the state.

- **Target Graphic**: The **Image** that should be used for transitions.

- **Color Multiplier**: This multiplies the tint color with the target graphic's original color. The higher the value, the more of the tint color will get blended in.

- **Fade Duration**: The amount of time in seconds between color tint fades.

- **Navigation**: By default, Unity can automatically detect the order of the selection of interactable UI elements. When multiple buttons are in a horizontal row, for example, and you press the right arrow key, the button on the right side of the currently selected button will get selected. This property is useful when building forms.

- **On Click ()**: This event is triggered when a player presses the button.

Now that you know your way around the button, start by changing its **Width** and **Height** to **300** and **50** respectively. Next, change its anchor point to be at the middle point of the bottom of the canvas via the **Anchor Presets** menu. There's no need to hold **Alt** this time, though, because you'll set its position manually.

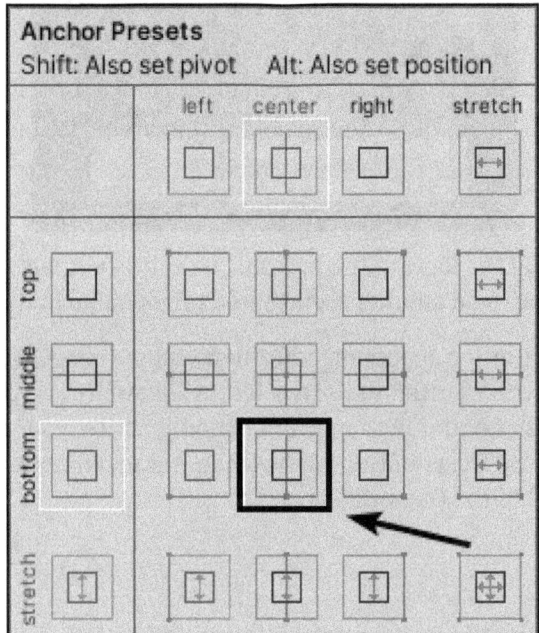

To set its position, move the button down a bit by setting **Pos Y** to **100**.

The final step is to tweak the button's text. Select the **Text** child of **New Game Button**, change its **Text** value to **New game** and change its **Font** to **RabbidHighwaySignII**. Now, change the **Font Size** to **20**, and you're done with the visuals.

All that's left is to add the logic to the button. You'll find a small script named **SceneLoader** that can load another scene based on its name in the project files.

To add it to the scene as a component, add a new empty GameObject to the root of the Hierarchy. Click the **+** button to the top left of Hierarchy and choose **Create Empty**. Name it **SceneLoader**. As a matter of good practice, you should reset the transforms through the **Reset** option in the three-dot menu of the **Transform** component attached to the GameObject.

Next, add the **Scene Loader** component to it. With the component in place, the **New Game Button** can now load a scene via its On Click event.

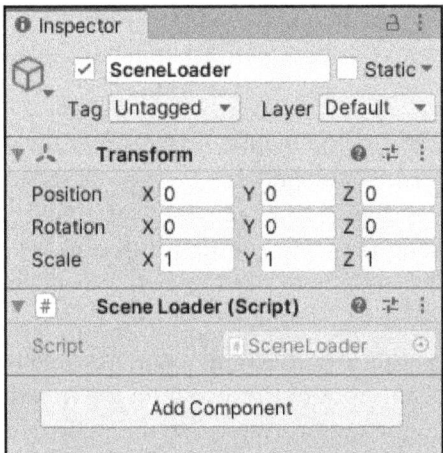

Select **Canvas ▸ New Game Button** in the Hierarchy and add a new empty function call to **On Click ()** by clicking the + button. Now, drag SceneLoader from the Hierarchy to the **Object** property of the function call and select **SceneLoader.LoadScene** in the function drop-down. The method LoadScene takes a string as an argument, so a text field will appear below the function drop-down. Enter **DiningHall** in this text field. That's the name of the dining hall scene asset found in **RW / Scenes**.

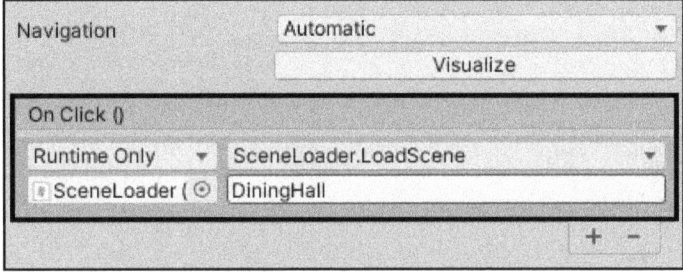

Now, play the scene and click the **New game** button. If everything is hooked up correctly, the dining hall scene will load.

With the title screen finished, it's time to use the skills you've learned and take another look at the dining hall scene!

Interaction system

Open the dining hall scene by double-clicking **DiningHall** in **RW / Scenes**. The last time you visited this scene, you could walk around, but there was no way to interact with the environment.

Compared to the project in the last chapter, this chapter's project has been given a simple interaction system. In a nutshell, the player avatar can now detect and interact with GameObjects that have a component attached to them derived from **Interactable Object** as long as they're on the **Interactable** layer.

Explaining this in more detail:

- There's now an **Interaction System** component attached to **Player Avatar**. It checks for GameObjects in front of the avatar on the **Interaction** layer with **Interactable Object** components attached to them. If it finds any, it keeps an eye on them. If the player triggers the **Interact** action by pressing **Space**, for example, an interaction is attempted with the nearest interactable GameObject. You can find the source script in **RW / Scripts / Interaction**.

- The **PlayerAvatar** script now implements the `Interact` method to call the **Interaction System**.

- There's a new abstract class named `InteractableObject`. It stores the name and the verb for the interaction and has an abstract method called `Interact` that needs to be implemented by any class that derives from it. The source code for this script is also located in **RW / Scripts / Interaction**.

- There's an example component named **Play Animation On Interaction**, which derives from the abstract `Interactable` class. This component can play an animation and a sound effect when interacted with. Again, find the source in the **RW / Scripts / Interaction** folder.

> **Note:** An abstract class or method indicates that the class or method is not completely implemented yet, so it can't be used on its own. It serves as a base to be built upon. In the case of the `InteractableObject` class, the `Interact` method won't do anything by itself — it's like a placeholder. That's why the **PlayAnimationOnInteraction** script derives from `InteractableObject` and fills in the blanks, starting an animation and playing a sound effect.

To show off what this does in practice, play the scene and walk the avatar towards the big door. Then, go left up the stairs. There's a treasure chest waiting there to be opened.

Now, stand facing the chest and press **Space** on your keyboard. The chest will animate and play a sound effect!

This chest can be found in the Hierarchy in **Interactable / Objects / TreasureChest**. It has an **Animator** component, a **Box Collider** and the **Play Animation On Interaction** component attached to it.

That last component is what holds the important information.

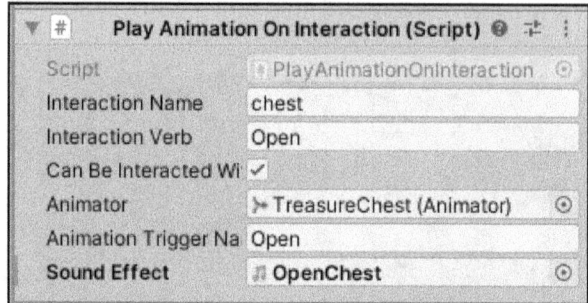

This component derives from `InteractableObject`, so its first three properties come from that script, while the others are specific to the **Play Animation On Interaction** component. At the moment, the name and verb can't be seen anywhere because the dining hall scene doesn't have UI elements yet. Ideally, a little window that says what action can be performed should pop up when the avatar can interact with an object. Time to add that!

Adding a user interface for interactions

Your goal is to add a window with some text — like the one pictured below — and extend the interaction system. The process is very similar to what you did with the title screen.

First, add a canvas to the root of the dining hall scene.

Click the **+** button at the top left of the Hierarchy and select **UI ▸ Canvas**. Now, change the **UI Scale Mode** of the **Canvas Scaler** component to **Scale With Screen Size**, and set its reference resolution to **(X:1280, Y:720)**. Next, select **EventSystem** in the Hierarchy and click the **Replace with InputSystemUIInputModule** button in the Inspector.

With the canvas set up, you can add a window as its first child. Right click **Canvas**, select **UI ▸ Image** and name it **Interaction Window**. You might wonder why there's no **UI ▸ Window** option. That's because the UI system doesn't actually know the concept of a window — so an image will have to do. :]

Change **Pos Y** of its **Rect Transform** to **80** to move it up a bit, and change its **Width** and **Height** to **250** and **45**, respectively. Next, go to the **Image** component attached to this GameObject and use the color picker to change its **Color** to a dark grey **(R:34, G:34, B:34)**. The window should now look like a wide, dark rectangle above the avatar's head.

Now, add some text inside of it by right-clicking **Interaction Window**, selecting **UI ▸ Text** and naming it **Interaction Text**. Change its **Text** value to **Interaction description goes here** and change its **Font** to **RabbidHighwaySignII**.

Finally, change its alignment to be centered both horizontally and vertically, and change its **Color** to a light grey **(R:221, G:221, B:221)**.

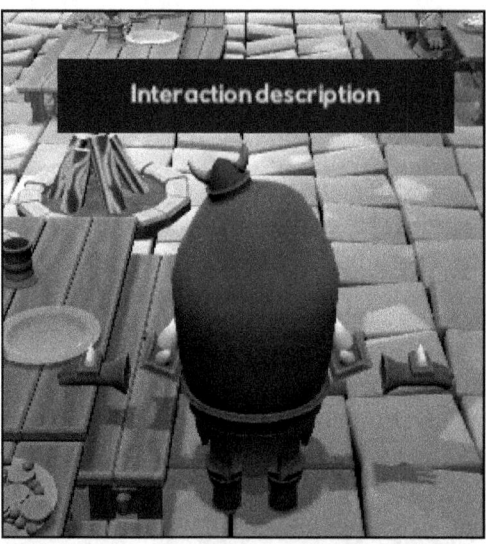

To connect the interaction window and its text to the interaction system, you'll need to make a few changes to the **InteractionSystem** script. Double-click the **InteractionSystem** script found in **RW / Scripts / Interaction** to open it in your code editor.

All of the checking for interactable objects happens in `FixedUpdate`, so that's where you'll want to hook up the logic for the interaction window. Before doing that though, the interaction system needs to be aware of the UI elements. First, add this using directive right below `using UnityEngine;`:

```
using UnityEngine.UI;
```

With this added, you can easily reference UI components. Now, add the following variable declarations above `private PlayerAvatar playerAvatar;`:

```
public GameObject interactionWindow;
public Text interactionText;
```

These will act as references to **Interaction Window** and **Interaction Text**. The final step is toggling the visibility of the window and setting its text to the right value. To do that, find the following code at the end of `FixedUpdate` (minus the comments):

```
if (closest != null)
{
    interactionTarget =
```

```
closest.GetComponent<InteractableObject>();
        // A
}
else
{
    interactionTarget = null;
    // B
}
```

This is the piece of code that checks if there's a valid interactable object, which then gets put in `interactionTarget` for later use. If the if statement rings true, that means an interactable object was found, so that's a good place to put the code to show the interaction window. Put the following code in the place marked by // A in the code snippet above:

```
if (!interactionWindow.activeSelf) // 1
{
    interactionWindow.SetActive(true); // 2
}
interactionText.text = interactionTarget.interactionVerb
    + " " + interactionTarget.interactionName; // 3
```

Here's what this does:

1. Checks if the interaction window isn't activated already.

2. Activates the interaction window, making it visible.

3. Sets the interaction text to "VERB NAME." This can be "Open chest" or "Pull lever," for example.

To hide the interaction window if there are no interactable objects nearby, add the following code below `interactionTarget = null`, in the place marked by // B:

```
if (interactionWindow.activeSelf)
{
    interactionWindow.SetActive(false);
}
```

In the case there's no interactable object in sight, this will deactivate the interaction window if it was activated before.

That's it for the scripting side of things! Save the script and return to the Unity editor to connect everything.

Select **Player Avatar** in the Hierarchy and take a look at its **Interaction System** component.

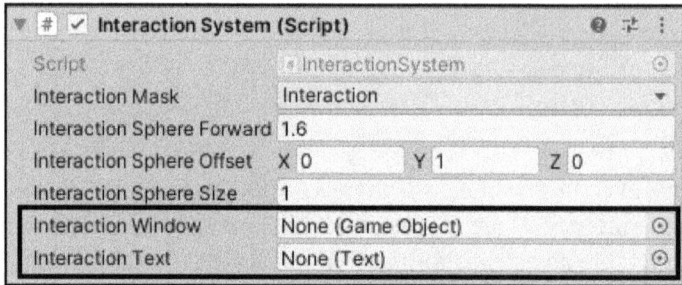

The two variables you've added to the script are now visible as properties. Drag **Interaction Window** and **Interaction Text** from the Hierarchy to the properties with the same name to link the references.

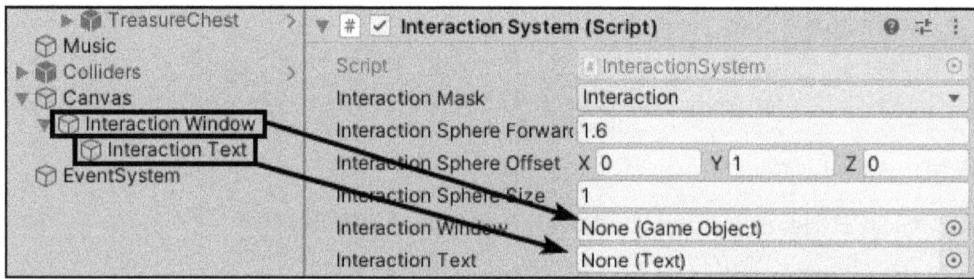

Now play the scene and walk up to the treasure chest again. The interaction window will pop up and show "Open chest" when you're looking at the chest. It will disappear when you move away.

Awesome! To make it even better, you can make the window automatically adjust its size depending on the text inside of it. This is where two useful UI components come into play: **Content Size Fitter** and **Vertical Layout Group**. Select **Interaction Window** and add both a **Content Size Fitter** and a **Vertical Layout Group** component to it.

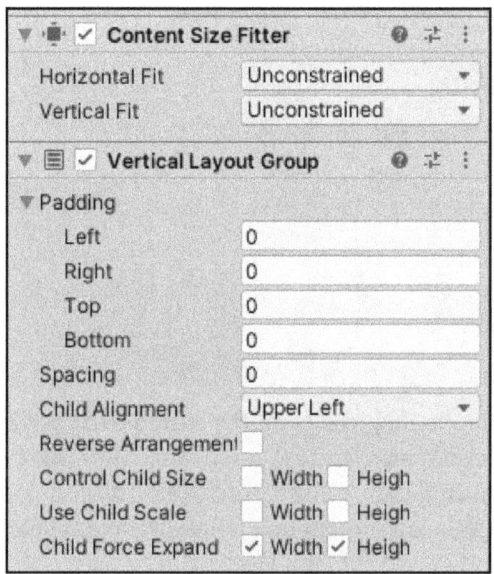

A **Content Size Fitter** is a layout controller that adjusts the size of the **Rect Transform** on the same UI element it's attached to. It can automatically resize the UI element based on the minimum size or the preferred size. By default, UI elements don't have either of these, though, which is where the **Vertical Layout Group** comes in.

Vertical Layout Group components can be added to a parent UI element and will automatically place and resize the children vertically. You can easily create lists with this component. To demonstrate this, select **Interaction Text** and press **Control-D** or **Command-D** a couple of times to duplicate it.

You'll notice that the text elements will nicely stack in a vertical line — although most will fall somewhere out of the window.

To prevent this from happening, you want the window to change its size depending on the text. Select **Interaction Window** and change the **Horizontal Fit** and **Vertical Fit** fields of **Content Size Fitter** to **Preferred Size**. This will enlarge the window to go around the text slightly, but not all text will be visible. The full sentence is "Interaction description goes here," but you can only see a part of it.

To fix that, let the **Vertical Layout Group** take care of text sizing by checking both the **Width** and **Height** checkboxes next to **Control Child Size**.

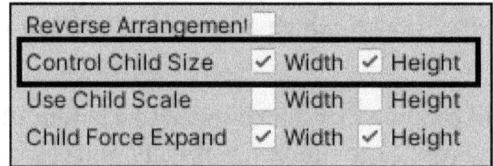

You'll see all of the text, but it's a bit cramped. You can add some padding to the borders of the window by setting all the **Padding** values in the **Vertical Layout Group** to **15**.

The text will now have some space around it.

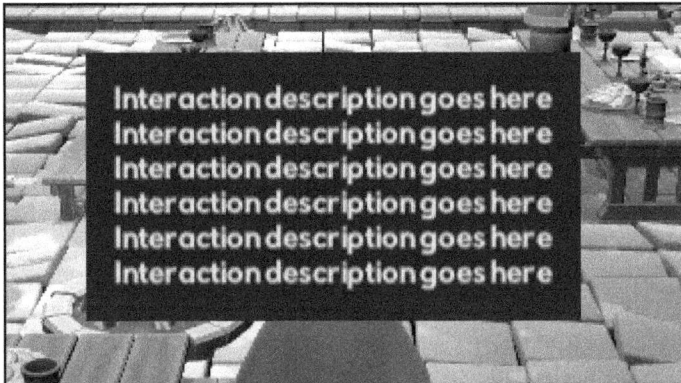

Now, delete the duplicate **Interaction Text** GameObjects. You'll only need one. Play the scene and walk up to the chest. The window fits perfectly around the text.

That concludes this chapter! Now you know about some of the most common UI elements and how to use them. In the next chapter, you'll complete the game by making the characters speak with a dialogue system that utilizes scriptable objects.

Key points

- UI elements need to be children of a **Canvas**.
- A **Canvas** component creates an area to place UI elements on.
- The **EventSystem** passes input to the canvas.
- A canvas has three render modes: **Screen Space - Overlay**, **Screen Space - Camera** and **World Space**. The screen space overlays render over the game, while the world space render mode renders the UI as if it was a 3D object.
- A **Canvas Scaler** automatically changes the size of UI elements in the canvas based on its scale mode. The easiest mode to work with is **Scale With Screen Size**.
- **Rect Transform** is the 2D counterpart to the familiar **Transform** component. It sets the position, size and anchor points of a UI element.
- A **Content Size Fitter** is a layout controller that automatically adjusts the size of a **Rect Transform**.
- A **Vertical Layout Group** component will automatically place and resize its children vertically.

Chapter 8: Scriptable Objects

By Eric Van de Kerckhove

In the previous chapter, you learned the basics of Unity's user interface system and used the most common UI elements to create a title screen and a window. This knowledge will come in handy when completing the game with a flexible dialogue system that you'll also be able to use in your own games with ease.

This chapter is all about giving the NPCs a way to talk to the player's avatar and letting the player choose how to respond. This lets you add some personality to the characters.

The dialogue system you'll create will teach you the basics of how to use scriptable objects to save conversations as files. This same concept will allow you to create items, weapons and settings presets as files for your own games. Scriptable objects are immensely powerful once you know how to use them, and they'll make your game development journey a lot easier.

Dialogue user interface

Before diving into the concept of the dialogue system, there's a new window you need to meet: the **Dialogue Window**. This GameObject is a child of **Canvas** in the Hierarchy and is disabled by default to hide it. Open the **Chapter 8 Starter** project in Unity and then open the **Dining Hall** scene in **RW / Scenes**. Then, expand the **Canvas** and select **Dialogue Window**. In the Inspector, click the checkbox in front of its name to make the window visible in both the **Scene** and **Game** views.

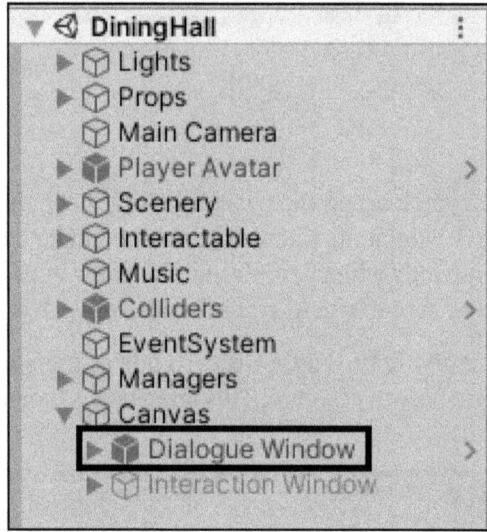

To get a good look at the different parts, fully expand and enable all of **Dialogue Window**'s children in the Hierarchy.

Take a look at the bottom of the **Game** view to see the **Dialogue Window**. The dialogue window might seem quite a bit more complex than what you've seen up until now, but it's actually just made up of some images and text.

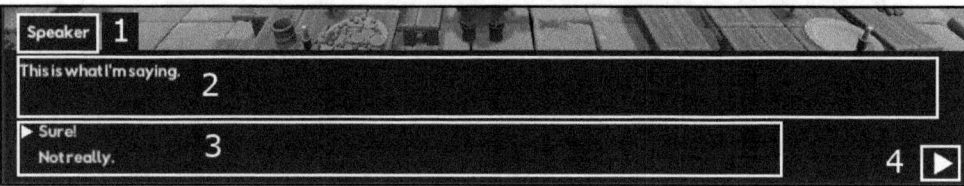

Here's an overview:

1. **Speaker Tag and Speaker Text**: The tag here is a dark image element that automatically resizes itself to the size of Speaker Text. Speaker Text is a text element that shows the name of the speaker — this can be "Guard" or "Potato guy," for example. You can test this out by changing the text value of Speaker Text.

2. **Line Text**: This is a text element that shows what the speaker is saying or asking.

3. **Option Selection Image and Answers**: The white triangle on the left is an image that acts like a selection cursor. It can be moved to highlight the selection option. The two text elements are the possible answers when a question is asked. All of these UI elements will only be visible when a question is asked.

4. **Continue Indicator Image**: This is an arrow image that blinks on and off via a small script. It's used to indicate that the interact button can be pressed to advance the conversation.

Now that you know the different parts of the dialogue window, disable **Option Selection Image** and **Answers** again, followed by the **Dialogue Window GameObject** itself so it won't be in the way. From now on, the different parts will be shown or hidden with scripting.

Dialogue manager overview

This brings you to the **Dialogue Manager** — it's a child of the GameObject called **Managers** in the Hierarchy.

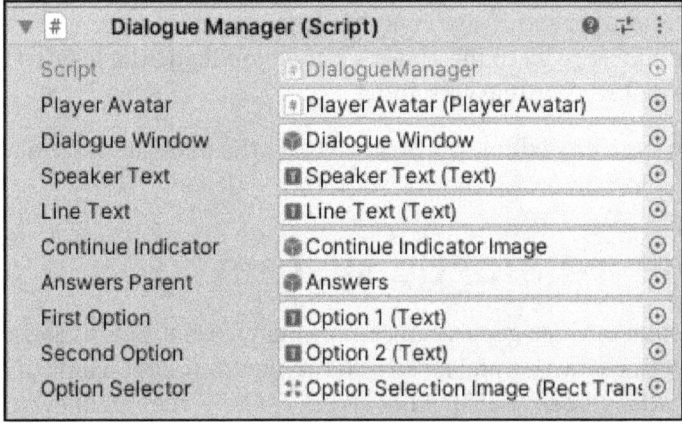

For now, this component only holds a bunch of references to the **Player Avatar** component, and all of the UI elements of the **Dialogue Window**. You'll build upon this component to create the dialogue system in this chapter. Open its source code file in a code editor by double-clicking **DialogueManager** in the **Script** property. All of the variable declarations are at the top of the class:

```
public static DialogueManager Instance;

// Player input

public PlayerAvatar playerAvatar;
private PlayerInput playerInput;

...

// Conversation
```

Most of these are references to components, but the first one is an exception. The `Instance` variable is `public static` and stores an instance of the `DialogueManager` class itself. It's paired with this code in the **Awake** method:

```
if (Instance == null)
{
    Instance = this;
}
```

This makes sure the value of `Instance` is set to an instance of the `DialogueManager` class as soon as the script starts. This is called the **Singleton pattern**, and it allows you to call methods and access public variables on the **DialogueManager** component from anywhere by using the `Instance` variable. It will prove very useful later on to let NPCs call on the **DialogueManager** when starting a conversation.

The **DialogueManager** script also contains some empty `Interact` and `Move` methods to be able to react to the player's input; you'll add the logic to these once the rest of the dialogue system gets going.

Now, return to the Unity editor. It's time to create the dialogue system itself!

Creating a dialogue system

A dialogue system in video games can assume many forms, but in essence it allows you to speak with characters and make a choice now and then. Think of old school RPGs like *EarthBound*, *Secret of Mana* or *Breath of Fire* — they all allow you to walk around and talk to the people (and creatures) around you.

Some games like visual novels and Choose Your Own Adventure games are entirely based upon having conversations and making meaningful choices.

In **Veggie Gladiators**, you can walk around the dining hall and talk to the other gladiators once you get near them — just like how you could open the treasure chest in the previous chapter.

The first step of the dialogue system will have NPCs with a Dialogue Starter component that holds a reference to a conversation file. A conversation has one or more lines of dialogue. Each line has a speaker name and the text the speaker is saying. When the player avatar tries to interact with a dialogue starter, this will trigger the Dialogue Manager to parse the conversation file and update the UI for it. These UI changes are done by modifying the UI elements of the Dialogue Window.

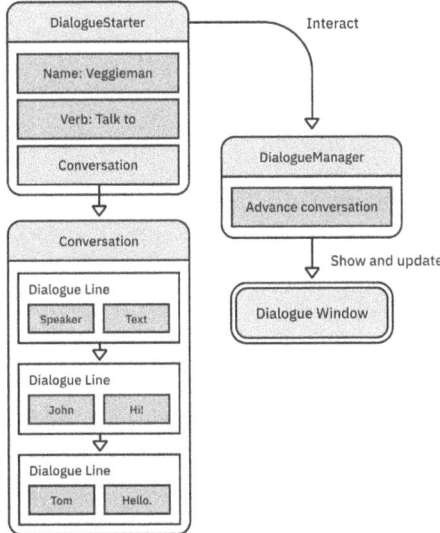

The logical order to create and edit the classes and components for this system is as follows:

1. The **DialogueLine**: A class that holds a single line of dialogue.

2. A **Conversation**: A scriptable object that will have a list of dialogue lines.

3. The **Dialogue Starter**: A component that has a reference to a conversation and can be talked to by the player avatar.

4. The **Dialogue Manager**: This needs to be aware of dialogue starters and conversations and needs to allow the conversation to progress.

Get ready for some scripting action!

Lines of dialogue

The first order of business is to create the **DialogueLine** class, which holds the data for a single line of dialogue. Create a new C# script named **DialogueLine** in **RW / Scripts / Dialogue** and open it in your code editor. Unity's default script template will make this yet another class that derives from MonoBehaviour to become a component. **DialogueLine** shouldn't be a component, though, but a simple class that holds some variables instead.

To stop deriving from MonoBehaviour, remove : MonoBehaviour from the class declaration line. While you're at it, strip away the Start and Update methods. You should now have a clean class to work with:

```
public class DialogueLine
{
}
```

Next, remove these lines from the top of the script:

```
using System.Collections;
using System.Collections.Generic;
```

Replace them with this:

```
using System;
```

The System namespace is necessary for the next part. Add this right above public class DialogueLine:

```
[Serializable]
```

A class in square brackets above a class or a variable is an **attribute**. In the case of Serializable, this attribute makes the DialogueLine class **serializable**, which means instances of the class can be saved to and loaded from a disk or memory. By making the class serializable, Unity can process the data and show it in the Inspector. The Serializable attribute is a part of the System namespace.

Now, add these lines inside the DialogueLine class:

```
public string speaker; // 1

[TextArea(2, 3)] // 2
public string text; // 3
```

Here's a quick overview:

1. This is the name of the speaker.
2. This **property attribute** will make the string defined below it editable in a big text area with a scrollbar in the Inspector. Unity comes with a bunch of property attributes that can make your life a lot easier, so be sure to check out the Unity Scripting Reference (https://docs.unity3d.com/ScriptReference). You can find all attributes in the **UnityEngine ▸ Attributes** section.
3. The line(s) of text the speaker will say.

Save this script and return to the Unity editor. The `DialogueLine` class won't do much by itself. Unlike a component, it can't be added to a GameObject; it needs to be part of a conversation.

Conversations

A basic conversation is a simple list of dialogue lines with one or more speakers that will play one line after the other like a movie script.

To create a list of dialogue lines, you could create a component with a list of `DialogueLine` variables, add that component to every NPC and call it a day. That would become unwieldy pretty fast though, because you'd have to hunt down the correct NPC in the Hierarchy for every little change you want to make.

To make the situation even worse, if you ever decide you want to let others translate the dialogues, you'd have to painstakingly copy and paste the text from every NPC and keep track of it somewhere.

Writing scriptable objects

There's a far better alternative for storing data in a central location, and it's built right into Unity: **scriptable objects**! You can use a scriptable object as a data container and store it as an asset, like an image or a sound effect. You can then reference the scriptable object in a component and read its contents. As a bonus, you can edit its properties right in the Inspector like components and the asset files are easily edited in a text editor. Yes, scriptable objects are truly marvelous, and you should use them when you can.

Here are some use cases for scriptable objects to spark your imagination:

- Store the inventory of an in-game store in a scriptable object, then have a shop component reference the inventory asset.
- Store the stats of enemies — like health, strength and defense — as separate assets in a central location.
- Use empty `Element` scriptable objects for storing elements like fire, ice and lightning. Now you can slot these in on objects in the world to set weaknesses and resistances.

Now that you know what a scriptable object is, it's time to create your own. Create a new C# script in the **RW / Scripts / Dialogue** folder, name it **Conversation** and open it in your favorite code editor.

This script isn't a component, so you'll need to remove everything `MonoBehaviour`-related. To do that, remove the `Start` and `Update` methods and replace `MonoBehaviour` with `ScriptableObject`. Next, add this line inside of the class:

```
public DialogueLine[] dialogueLines;
```

This is the array of dialogue lines you'll be able to populate via the Inspector. The complete class now looks like this:

```
public class Conversation : ScriptableObject
{
    public DialogueLine[] dialogueLines;
}
```

This is a complete scriptable object, but there's no way to create an asset out of it in the editor. To do that, add a special attribute right above `public class Conversation : ScriptableObject`:

```
[CreateAssetMenu(fileName = "Conversation", menuName = "Dialogue/Conversation", order = 1)]
```

This attribute will add a **Dialogue ▸ Conversation** entry to the **Create** menu of the Unity editor that will create a **Conversation** asset in a folder of your choice. Save this script and return to the editor to give that a shot.

Creating scriptable objects

Create a new folder in the **RW** folder named **Conversations**, and right-click on the new folder. Next, select **Create ▸ Dialogue ▸ Conversation** to create a new conversation, and name it **Weird Taste**.

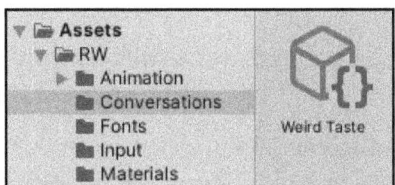

Now take a look at the Inspector, and you'll see an empty list of dialogue lines. Click the + button at the bottom right to create your first line of dialogue.

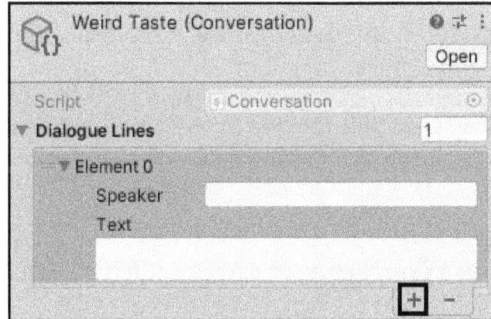

As you can see, you can easily create new lines of dialogue this way. Change the value of **Speaker** to **Pepper Warrior** and add the following text: "**Don't you think the food here has a weird taste to it?**" Next, add another line of dialogue by clicking the + button again. This will duplicate the line you added last. Change **Text** to "**It's familiar to me, but I can't put my finger on it…**"

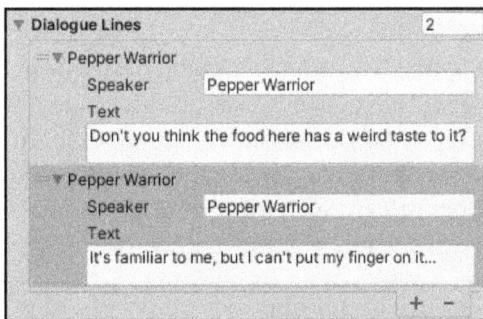

With the first conversation safely stored as an asset, it's time to give the NPCs a way to use this dialogue.

Dialogue starter component

To make the NPCs interactable, you'll use the interaction system. You learned about this in the previous chapter, but here's a quick refresher:

- There's an **Interaction System** component attached to the **Player Avatar**.
- This system checks for GameObjects on the **Interaction** layer with a component that derives from the abstract `InteractableObject` class in front of the avatar.
- If the player triggers the **Interact** input action by pressing **Space** for example, the interaction system will attempt to interact with the nearest interactable object.

This means you'll need to create a script that derives from `InteractableObject` and attach that to all NPCs you want to be able to talk with.

Create a new C# script named **DialogueStarter** in the **RW / Scripts / Dialogue** folder and open it in a code editor.

The basic version of this script will need to meet the following requirements:

- The class should derive from `InteractableObject` so it works with the interaction system.
- It needs a reference to a **Conversation** asset so the NPC will know what to say.
- It should have a way to start the conversation.

With this in mind, remove both the `Start` and `Update` methods and replace `MonoBehaviour` with `InteractableObject`. This will be the end result:

```
public class DialogueStarter : InteractableObject
{
}
```

You'll get an error saying that the Interact method hasn't been implemented yet. That's because the `InteractableObject` class is abstract and it has an abstract method called `Interact` — which means all classes that inherit from `InteractableObject` are required to provide their own implementation of this method. Most code editors will give you the option to automatically implement abstract classes, which will add any missing method overrides.

Of course, you can always choose to do so manually by adding the following method to `DialogueStarter`:

```
public override void Interact(PlayerAvatar playerAvatar)
{
}
```

This interaction system will call this method when the avatar interacts with the dialogue starter, so this method will start a conversation. To add a reference to the conversation, add this variable declaration right above the `Interact` method:

```
public Conversation conversation;
```

This allows you to add a reference to a **Conversation** asset via the Inspector once you're back in the editor.

Remember that to work with the interaction system, the GameObject needs to be on the **Interaction** layer. While you can set this up manually for every interactable object in the editor, it's easy to forget to do this — resulting in you frantically searching around for what's wrong. Luckily, there's a way to set a layer automatically via scripting. Add this Awake method above the `Interact` method:

```
private void Awake()
{
    gameObject.layer = LayerMask.NameToLayer("Interaction");
}
```

This piece of code changes the layer of the GameObject the component is attached to. `gameObject.layer` is the current layer, and `LayerMask.NameToLayer` gets the ID of the **Interaction** layer by its name. By adding this code, you'll never have to worry about setting the layer correctly again!

The `Interact` method won't be able to let the NPC talk yet, as it depends on the dialogue manager being able to start a conversation. That doesn't mean you can't test `DialogueStarter` out already, though. Add the following code to the `Interact` method:

```
foreach (var line in conversation.dialogueLines)
{
    print(line.speaker + " : " + line.text);
}
```

Whenever an NPC and the avatar interact, this will iterate over the dialogue lines in the conversation asset and print out the speaker and the line of text to the console for each line of dialogue. This isn't fancy, but it's more than good enough for now.

Save the script and return to the Unity editor.

Next, add a dialogue starter to the Pepper Warrior sitting at the table next to the avatar's starting location. To do this, start by selecting the last **Pepper Warrior** in the Hierarchy. It's in **Interactable / NPCs**.

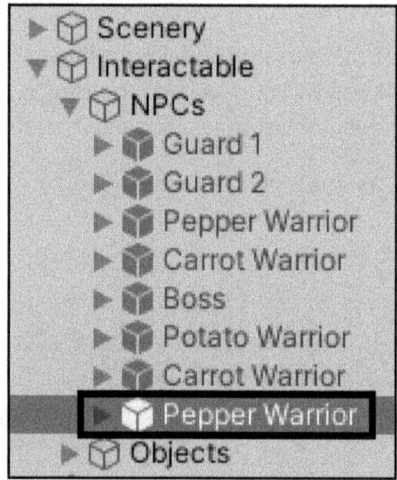

Then, add a **Dialogue Starter** component to it, set its **Interaction Name** to **Pepper Warrior** and set its **Interaction Verb** to **Talk to**. Finally, set the value of its **Conversation** property to **Weird Taste** by using the selection button.

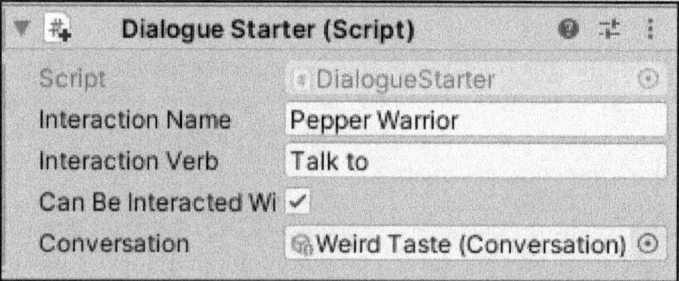

Play the scene and approach the Pepper Warrior on the right. The interaction window will pop up and show "Talk to Pepper Warrior."

Now, press **Space** to start a conversation. It will appear as if nothing happened, but if you take a look at the **Console** window (**Window ▸ General ▸ Console**), the dialogue lines of the conversation you set up earlier are visible — which means everything is working fine!

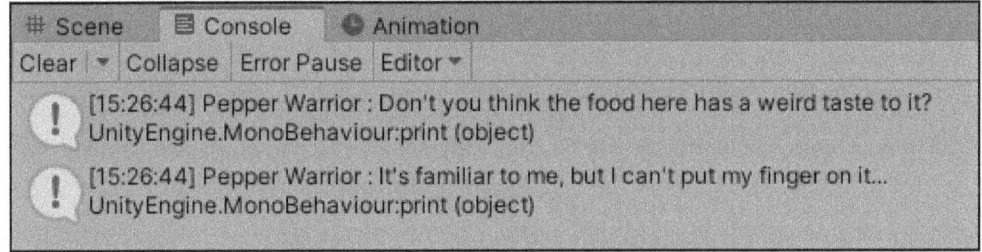

Next, you'll focus on making the dialogue system a lot more sophisticated.

Improving the dialogue manager

The Dialogue Manager serves three purposes:

- It parses each dialogue line of a conversation.
- It makes the conversation visible by passing the lines of dialogue to the **Dialogue Window**.
- It allows the player to move the conversation along.

Right now, the **Dialogue Manager** component can't do any of this yet — so that means it's scripting time! Open **RW / Scripts / Dialogue / DialogueManager** in a code editor to start improving it.

Starting a conversation

The first order of business is to add these variables below the `// Conversation` comment, above the `Awake` method:

```
private Conversation activeConversation; // 1
private int dialogueIndex; // 2
private DialogueStarter dialogueStarter; // 3
```

Here's what these will be used for:

1. This is a reference to a **Conversation** asset from which the script will read the dialogue lines.
2. The index, or the number, of the current dialogue line. For example, an index of **0** means the first line of the conversation, while an index of **5** means the sixth line.
3. A reference to the dialogue starter that called the Dialogue Manager. The script uses this reference to signal the dialogue starter that the conversation has ended.

Now, add the `ShowTextUI` method below `Move`:

```
private void ShowTextUI()
{
    answersParent.SetActive(false); // 1
    optionSelector.gameObject.SetActive(false); // 2
    continueIndicator.SetActive(true); // 3
}
```

As its name implies, this method shows the UI elements needed for displaying lines of dialogue. The dialogue window also supports questions — but since you don't have any questions yet, those UI elements get disabled:

1. Disable the GameObject that holds the UI elements for answering questions.

2. Disable the options selector cursor.

3. Show the triangular indicator at the bottom right of the window.

The next step is to add a way of showing a single line of dialogue. To do this, add the ShowLine method to the bottom of the class:

```
private void ShowLine()
{
    DialogueLine currentLine =
        activeConversation.dialogueLines[dialogueIndex]; // 1
    speakerText.text = currentLine.speaker; // 2
    lineText.text = currentLine.text; // 3

    ShowTextUI(); // 4
}
```

This method will update the **Text** UI elements of the dialogue window to show the contents of the active dialogue line. In more detail:

1. Get the current line of dialogue from the conversation and store it in currentLine.

2. Change the speaker text to show the name of the speaker found in currentLine.

3. Do the same for the text the speaker is saying.

4. Call ShowTextUI to make sure the relevant UI elements are visible.

Continue by adding this:

```
private void SetDialogueWindowVisibility(bool visible)
{
    dialogueWindow.SetActive(visible);
}
```

This method will be called to toggle the visibility of the dialogue window.

Next up is the most important method — the one that actually starts the conversation. Add this below `SetDialogueWindowVisibility`:

```
public void StartConversation(Conversation conversation,
                              DialogueStarter
  dialogueStarter) // 1
{
    playerAvatar.DisableInput(); // 2
    activeConversation = conversation; // 3
    this.dialogueStarter = dialogueStarter; // 4
    dialogueIndex = 0; // 5
    SetDialogueWindowVisibility(true); // 6
    ShowLine(); // 7
    playerInput.enabled = true; // 8
}
```

This might look like a complex piece of code, but most of it is the set up and resetting of variables to start a fresh conversation:

1. The `StartConversation` method takes two arguments: a `Conversation` asset and a `DialogueStarter` component. The references to these will be stored in the variables you added earlier.

2. This stops the player avatar from being able to move and interact with the scene. It would be kind of awkward if the player avatar walked away in the middle of a conversation, right?

3. Store the conversation in `activeConversation` for use throughout the script.

4. Save a reference to the dialogue starter for later use. The `this` keyword before the equal sign is necessary to clarify that the `dialogueStarter` on the left is the local variable, while the `dialogueStarter` on the right is the argument from the method.

5. Reset the dialogue index to the first line of dialogue.

6. Show the dialogue window.

7. Show the first line of dialogue.

8. Enable the **Player Input** component attached to the **Dialogue Manager**. Like the **Player Avatar**, the **Dialogue Manager** has its own **Player Input** component that calls the `Move` and `Interact` methods.

With this method added, it's time to test if starting a new conversation works as intended. Save this script and open the **DialogueStarter** script. Replace the `foreach` loop in the `Interact` method with this:

```
DialogueManager.Instance.StartConversation(conversation,
this); // 1
canBeInteractedWith = false; // 2
```

Instead of simply writing the dialogue lines to the console, interacting with a dialogue starter will now:

1. Call `StartConversation` on the **Dialogue Manager** and start a new conversation by passing the dialog starter's conversation and the dialogue starter itself.

2. Don't allow interactions with the dialogue starter from now on.

Save this script as well and return to the Unity editor. Play the scene and walk up to the Pepper Warrior at the table on your right again to have a chat. This time, the dialogue window will show up and show the first dialogue line of the conversation.

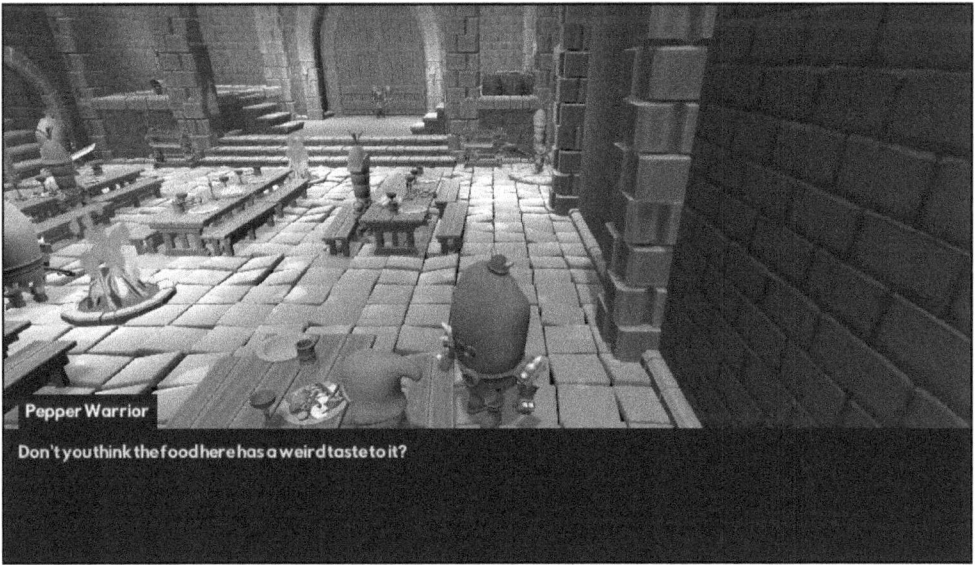

Awesome! There's still a part missing, of course, because there's no way to show the next line of dialogue, but this is already quite impressive.

Showing more lines of dialogue and ending a conversation

First, the avatar must be able to interact with the dialogue starter again once it's done talking. To achieve that, open the **DialogueStarter** script again from **RW / Scripts / Dialogue** and add the following method below `Interact`:

```
public void OnConversationEnd()
{
    canBeInteractedWith = true;
}
```

This re-enables interactions and will be called by the **Dialogue Manager** once a conversation ends. Now, save this script and open the Dialogue Manager script again.

Add the following code to the bottom of the class:

```
public void EndConversation()
{
    playerInput.enabled = false; // 1
    playerAvatar.EnableInput(); // 2
    activeConversation = null; // 3
    SetDialogueWindowVisibility(false); // 4
    dialogueStarter.OnConversationEnd(); // 5
}
```

This method makes sure everything is reset to the way it was before the conversation started. Here's what you're doing in greater detail:

1. Disable the **Player Input** component on the **Dialogue Manager**.

2. Re-enable the input of the **Player Avatar**.

3. Clear the conversation from the Dialogue Manager by setting its value to `null`.

4. Hide the dialogue window.

5. Call `OnConversationEnd` on the dialogue starter so it can be interacted with again.

The method that moves the conversation forward is next. Add this below `EndConversation`:

```
private void NormalTextInteract(DialogueLine currentLine) // 1
{
    dialogueIndex++; // 2
```

```
        if (activeConversation.dialogueLines.Length > dialogueIndex)
// 3
        {
            ShowLine();
        }
        else
        {
            EndConversation();
        }
}
```

This advances a conversation by incrementing the index of the active dialogue line, and then proceeds to check if there are more lines left. If there are, the next line is shown. If there are no more lines, the conversation ends. Here's how this is achieved:

1. The method takes a single dialogue line as an argument — which you'll use soon.

2. Increment `dialogueIndex` by **1**.

3. Check if there's a dialogue line left at this index. If there is, show the next line. If not, end the conversation.

Finally, you'll expand upon the `Interact` method to make it load new lines of dialogue. Add the following code to the `Interact` method:

```
if (!activeConversation || !context.performed) // 1
{
    return;
}

DialogueLine currentLine =
    activeConversation.dialogueLines[dialogueIndex]; // 2
NormalTextInteract(currentLine); // 3
```

Here's a rundown of what you're doing:

1. If there's no conversation loaded or the action wasn't fully performed — in other words, pressing a key or a button down and releasing it — don't do anything.

2. Load the current dialogue line into `currentLine`.

3. Call `NormalTextInteract` to actually show the line if there is one or end the conversation.

With these last lines, the Dialogue Manager is complete! Save the script and return to the Unity editor for another test run. Talk to the Pepper Warrior at the table once more and press the **Space** key to advance the conversation.

With everything in place, you'll see the next line of dialogue after the first key press and the conversation will end after the second press.

All that's left is to create more conversation assets and assign them to the NPCs in the scene. You can make the vegetable warriors funny, serious or even angry. It's all up to you! Take a look at the final project to get some ideas for the different NPCs.

To make the dialogue system even better, you can add question handling for a more interactive experience. Keep reading to learn how to do that.

Handling questions

Now that you can let the characters talk to the player avatar, it might be interesting if they can ask questions as well. This makes the conversations feel more dynamic and interesting. Every line of dialogue will have the option of becoming a question, which will prompt the player for two possible answers. Each of these answers will be linked to a different conversation asset that will be loaded by the Dialogue Manager.

By doing this, you can have long talks with NPCs that are split up in multiple conversation files.

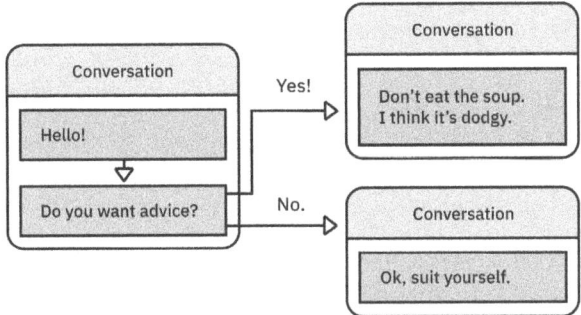

For this to work, you'll need to expand upon the existing dialogue system.

Dialogue question class

First, create a new C# script in the **RW / Scripts / Dialogue** folder and name it **DialogueQuestion**. Open the new file in a code editor and remove both the Start and Update methods. This will be another **serializable** class like DialogueLine, so replace the class declaration line with this:

```
public class DialogueQuestion
```

Next, remove all of the using directives at the top and replace them with this:

```
using System;
```

These two changes make it so DialogueQuestion is no longer a MonoBehaviour, but a regular class instead. It also makes common attributes accessible in this file. Now, make the class serializable by adding the Serializable attribute right above the class declaration:

```
[Serializable]
```

This will allow Unity to serialize the class — making instances of it editable in the editor.

Finally, add these variable declarations to the class:

```
// 1
public string firstOption;
public string secondOption;

// 2
public Conversation conversationWhenFirstOptionWasSelected;
public Conversation conversationWhenSecondOptionWasSelected;
```

Here's what these will be used for:

1. These are the possible answers to the question. For example, the first option might be "Yes" and the second one "No." The question itself will be asked via `DialogueLine`'s text variable.

2. References to the conversations that need to be activated depending on the answer that was given. The Dialogue Manager should activate `conversationWhenFirstOptionWasSelected` when the first answer is selected, for example.

Now, save this script and open the `DialogueLine` script. It needs extra variables to make use of the new `DialogueQuestion` class you just made, so add these below text:

```
public bool thisIsAQuestion; // 1
public DialogueQuestion dialogueQuestion; // 2
```

Here's a summary of their purpose:

1. This is a flag to let the Dialogue Manager know whether this line of dialogue needs to be handled as a question.

2. Information about the question, like the possible answers and what conversations they will start.

Save this script and return to the editor. Everything is now in place to start creating conversations with questions.

Setting up the editor for questions

The boss of this place is standing before the huge wooden door at the back. She's going to ask the player avatar whether he's ready to enter the arena. The player will then have the choice of answering yes or no, which will trigger another conversation. In other words, you'll need to create three conversations for the boss.

Create a new conversation in **RW / Conversations** and name it **Boss**. Now create two more conversations and name them **Boss - End** and **Boss - Not Ready**.

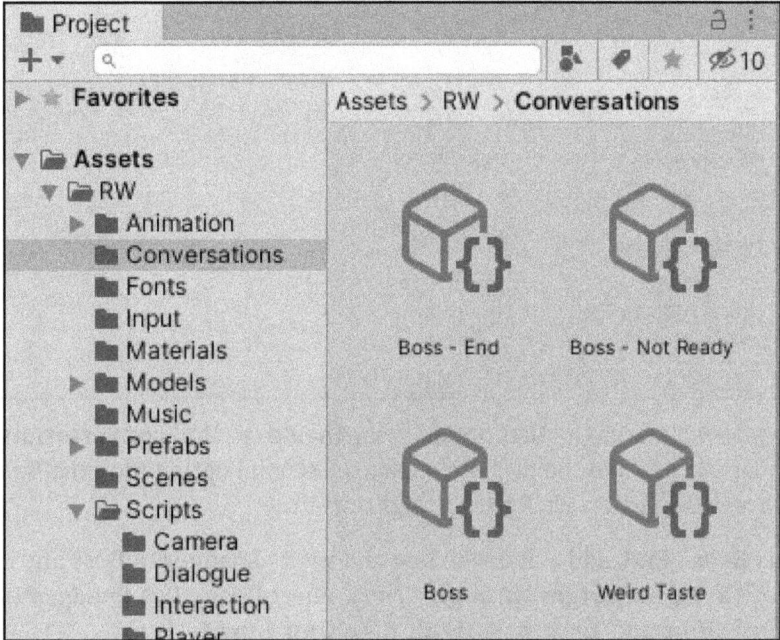

Select the Boss conversation and add a new dialogue line. Notice that there's a new checkbox now labelled **This Is A Question** and a property named **Dialogue Question** that can be expanded.

Change the value of **Speaker** to **Boss** and add "Hail warrior! Are you ready to enter the arena?" to the **Text** property. Now check the **This Is A Question** checkbox and expand the **Dialogue Question** property. Next, set the value of **First Option** to "Yes! (exit the dining hall)" and change **Second Option** to "Not yet."

As a final step, drag the **Boss - End** conversation to the first **Conversation** property and drag **Boss - Not Ready** to the second one.

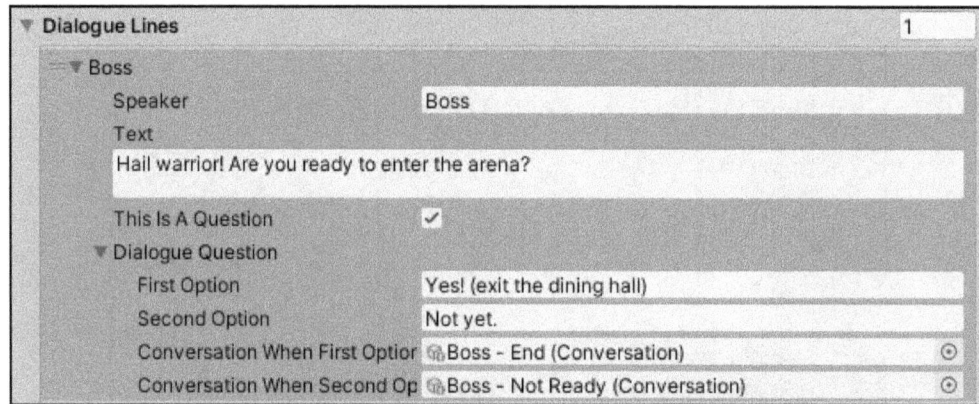

When the player chooses the first option (yes), the **Boss - End conversation** should be loaded. Likewise, when the player chooses the second option (no), the **Boss - Not Ready** conversation will start. Pretty straightforward!

Now, select **Boss - End**, add a dialogue line and set its **Speaker** to **Boss** and change its **Text** to "**Great! Step right through.**" Next, select **Boss - Not Ready**, and change its **Speaker** to **Boss** and **Text** to "**Alright, take your time.**"

The conversations are ready, but the Boss NPC still needs a **Dialogue Starter** component. Select **Interactable / NPCs / Boss** in the Hierarchy and add a **Dialogue Starter** component to it. Change its **Interaction Name** to **Boss** and change the **Interaction Verb** to **Talk to**. To complete the Dialogue Starter, drag the **Boss** conversation to the **Conversation** property.

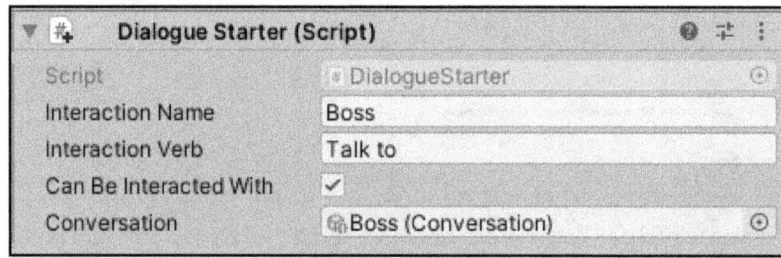

Now the avatar can go and talk to the boss lady at the back, but you won't be able to make a choice yet. All it will do is ask a question and abruptly end the conversation.

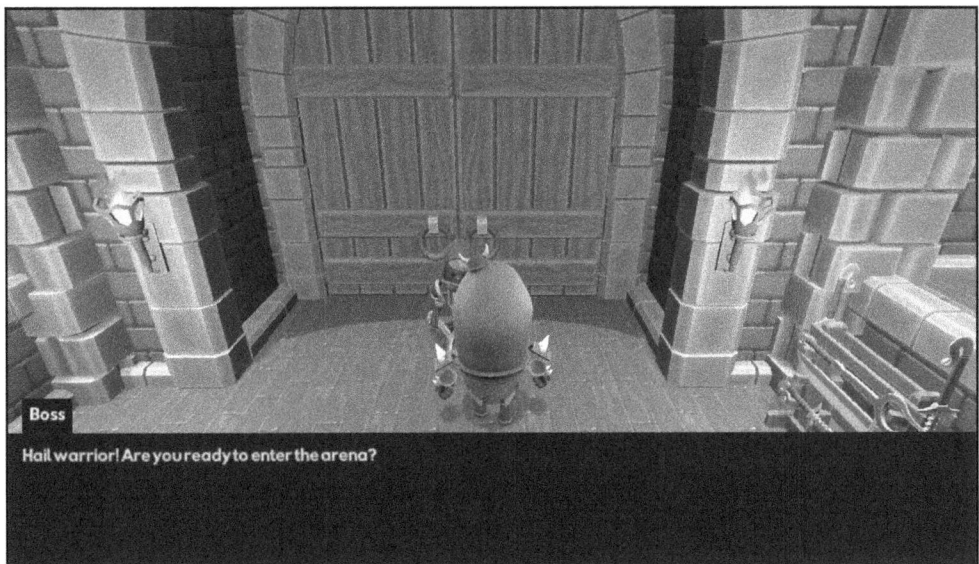

To create a realistic interaction, you'll need to do some final scripting.

Preparing the dialogue manager for questions

The dialogue manager can't differentiate between statements and questions at the moment, so it's up to you to make it smarter. This involves some more scripting, of course, so open the **DialogueManager** script from **RW / Scripts / Dialogue** in your code editor once more.

First, add this new variable below `private DialogueStarter dialogueStarter;`:

```
private bool firstOptionSelected;
```

This variable will keep track of which option is selected. Then, add the following new method below the others:

```
private IEnumerator UpdateOptionSelectorPostion() // 1
{
    yield return new WaitForEndOfFrame(); // 2

    if (firstOptionSelected) // 3
    {
        optionSelector.position =
            new Vector3(optionSelector.position.x,
    firstOption.GetComponent<RectTransform>().position.y,
    optionSelector.position.z);
    }
```

```
        else
        {
            optionSelector.position =
                new Vector3(optionSelector.position.x,
    secondOption.GetComponent<RectTransform>().position.y,
    optionSelector.position.z);
        }
    }
```

Here's what's happening:

1. This method is actually a **coroutine**, as it returns an `IEnumerator` instead of a `void`. A coroutine is a method that can spread its execution over multiple frames. More on coroutines in Chapter 11!

2. Wait to execute the following lines until the end of the frame. This gives the dialogue window a frame to settle so the correct positions of the options can be read. If you were to start to move the cursor immediately, it would appear at the wrong location because the text UI elements of the answers wouldn't be fully loaded yet.

3. This **if-statement** decides whether the option selection cursor should be moved next to the first or second options depending on the value of `firstOptionSelected`. A value of `true` will move the cursor next to the first-option text.

Next, add this method to show the question UI elements:

```
private void ShowQuestionUI(DialogueLine currentLine) // 1
{
    answersParent.SetActive(true); // 2
    continueIndicator.SetActive(false); // 3
    optionSelector.gameObject.SetActive(true); // 4
    firstOption.text = currentLine.dialogueQuestion.firstOption; // 5
    secondOption.text = currentLine.dialogueQuestion.secondOption; // 6
    firstOptionSelected = true; // 7
    StartCoroutine(UpdateOptionSelectorPostion()); // 8
}
```

This basically activates the relevant UI elements for answering questions and makes sure the position of the selection cursor is reset:

1. The `ShowQuestionUI` method takes a single `DialogueLine` as an argument to read the options from.
2. Show the GameObject that holds the answer text UI elements.
3. Hide the continue indicator at the bottom right.
4. Show the option selection cursor.
5. Set the first-option text to the first option found in the dialogue line.
6. Do the same for the second option.
7. Set the first option as the default.
8. Move the option selector cursor via a coroutine. This allows `UpdateOptionSelectorPostion` to wait a frame before moving the cursor.

Now the UI can be loaded correctly. Replace the following line in ShowLine:

```
ShowTextUI();
```

With this if statement:

```
if (!currentLine.thisIsAQuestion) // 1
{
    ShowTextUI();
}
else // 2
{
    ShowQuestionUI(currentLine);
}
```

This checks if the current dialogue line is a question before deciding which version of the UI to show:

1. If the current line isn't a question, show the regular text UI.
2. If the line is a question, show the question UI and pass the current dialogue line.

Almost there!

The `Interact` method calls `NormalTextInteract` — which is fine for regular text, but not for questions. That would just skip the question altogether and attempt to move to the next line of dialogue. To correct this, add this new flavor of the dialogue interaction method:

```
private void QuestionInteract(DialogueLine currentLine) // 1
{
    if (firstOptionSelected) // 2
    {
        StartConversation(currentLine.dialogueQuestion.conversationWhenFirstOptionWasSelected, dialogueStarter);
    }
    else // 3
    {
        StartConversation(currentLine.dialogueQuestion.conversationWhenSecondOptionWasSelected, dialogueStarter);
    }
}
```

Instead of trying to load the next line or end the conversation, this method checks which option is selected and loads a new conversation based on the choice:

1. This method accepts a single `DialogueLine` as an argument, which it uses to get a reference to the next conversation to load.

2. If the first option is selected, start the conversation linked to that option.

3. Do the same for the second option if it's selected.

Now the `Interact` method will also need some modification to use the `QuestionInteract` method. Replace the following line:

```
NormalTextInteract(currentLine);
```

With these:

```
if (!currentLine.thisIsAQuestion)
{
    NormalTextInteract(currentLine);
}
else
{
    QuestionInteract(currentLine);
}
```

This if statement checks whether the current line is a question or not. If it's not a question, `NormalTextInteract` is called. If the current line of dialogue is a question, `QuestionInteract` is called instead.

Finally, there's one more method to take a look at: `Move`. This method is called whenever the movement keys are pressed or buttons are clicked. Since there are only two options to choose from, every move action means switching between the first and the second option, which is stored in the `firstOptionSelected` variable. To add this switching logic, add the following code to `Move`:

```
if (activeConversation != null && context.performed) // 1
{
    DialogueLine currentLine =
        activeConversation.dialogueLines[dialogueIndex]; // 2

    if (currentLine.thisIsAQuestion) // 3
    {
        firstOptionSelected = !firstOptionSelected;
        StartCoroutine(UpdateOptionSelectorPostion());
    }
}
```

Here's what's going on:

1. If there's a conversation loaded and the move action was performed by pressing and releasing a key, continue running the code.

2. Get the current line of dialogue.

3. If the current line of dialogue is a question, switch the value of `firstOptionSelected`. This is done by inverting the current value of `firstOptionSelected` by using an exclamation mark before the original value. With this, `true` becomes `false` and vice versa. Next, update the position of the selection cursor to reflect this change.

That concludes the scripting for the dialogue system. Save the script and pat yourself on the back. You deserve it! Now, return to the editor, play the scene and talk to the boss at the back again.

You'll get two options to choose from, and pressing the **Space** key will continue your chat by loading another conversation asset.

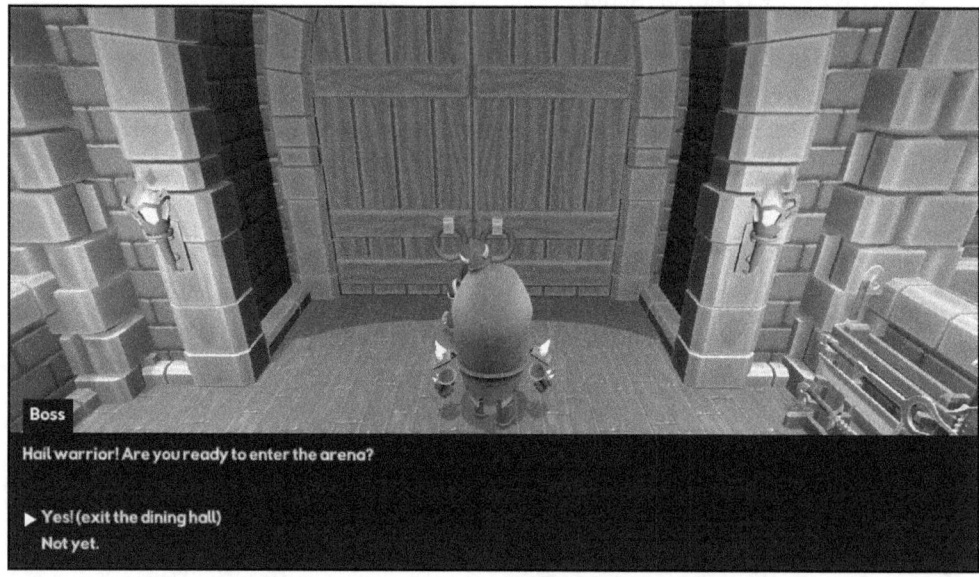

Congratulations on finishing this chapter! You'll be able to create a visual novel or another story-based game with all that you've learned up to this point. You can take your skills to the next level with the next chapter — you'll learn how to use artificial intelligence and pathfinding to make your in-game friends and foes smarter.

Key points

- A **dialogue system** allows you to speak with (non-playable) characters and make choices.

- Variables from regular classes can be edited in the Unity editor by marking them serializable using the [Serializable] attribute.

- Instances of serializable classes can be saved to and loaded from a disk or memory.

- Unity comes with a lot of built-in **property attributes** to help display your components the way you want to in the Inspector. A good example is [TextArea], which creates a multiline text field for a string variable.

- You can use a scriptable object as a data container and store it as an asset.

- Use the [CreateAssetMenu] attribute on scriptable object scripts to add them to the **Create** menu in the editor.

- Use LayerMask.NameToLayer("layer name") to get the ID of a layer.

- Test your scripts along the way by using print() to make sure what you have up until that point works.

- A **coroutine** is a method that can spread its execution over multiple frames.

Section III: Smart Enemies & the Bigger Picture

Your player shouldn't be the only smart character in a game. In this section, you learn how to use the power of Unity to automatically control enemies to make your game a challenge. You'll discover how to define where your enemies can roam and how to get them to attack!

You'll also see how to control multiple cameras so the player doesn't miss seeing a thing. Finally, learn how to reuse weapons and enemies once they've been expended so you can reduce the resources your game requires.

The game in this section takes place in an arena. Hurry! There's a battle about to begin!

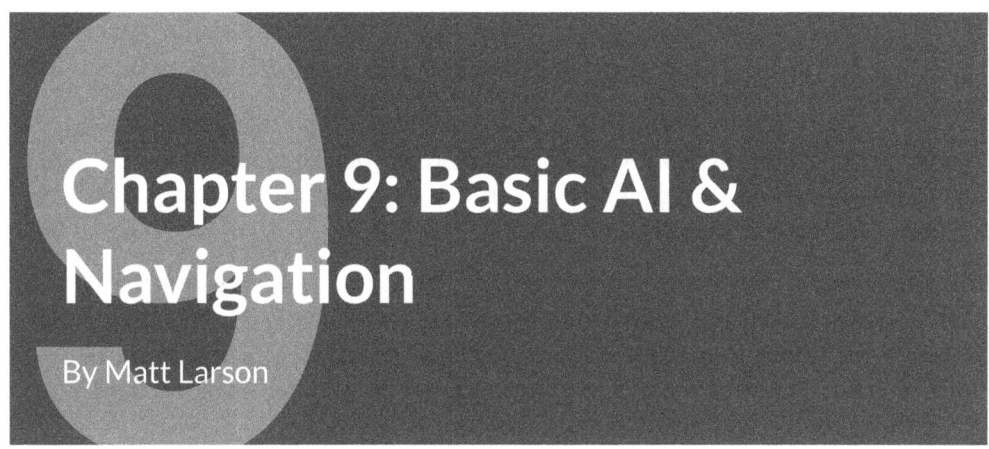

Chapter 9: Basic AI & Navigation

By Matt Larson

Introduction to the Arena

This chapter is the first installment in the three-part adventure arc of **veggie combat**! Can you survive as one tank against an army of mad veggie gladiators armed with cutlery???

You begin with a starter project containing an arena filled with veggie spectators eagerly awaiting the combatants. By the end of this chapter, you'll have added some point-and-click navigation and basic enemy AI to the scene.

Are you afraid of an unlimited army of veggie gladiators? Not when you're driving a tank!

First, you'll need to learn how to add a basic navigation AI to your games through the Unity **Navigation System**. Through this system, you can create agents that are able to navigate the geometry of a scene through the generation of navigation meshes — or simply **NavMeshes**.

This movement system is the perfect choice for a variety of games where the dominant mechanic is not the coordination of the player, but rather the strategy of exploring and interacting with a complex world of objects. Top-down adventure games and turn-based strategy games are both excellent examples of mechanics where the Unity Navigation system is a great fit.

Navigation

Navigation in Unity is automatically handled by intelligent agents that find the shortest paths on NavMeshes. NavMeshes are data structures composed of polygons, where there are no barriers between points within a given polygon. Paths across a map are found by stepping between the polygons of the NavMesh structures. Overall, the NavMesh simplifies the geometry of objects in the scene to less varied surfaces that face upwards.

NavMesh Agents calculate the shortest possible paths over the NavMesh surface to reach a destination from their current position. Unity runs the **A* shortest path algorithm** to search over the NavMesh graph for shortest paths and remove less efficient routes quickly.

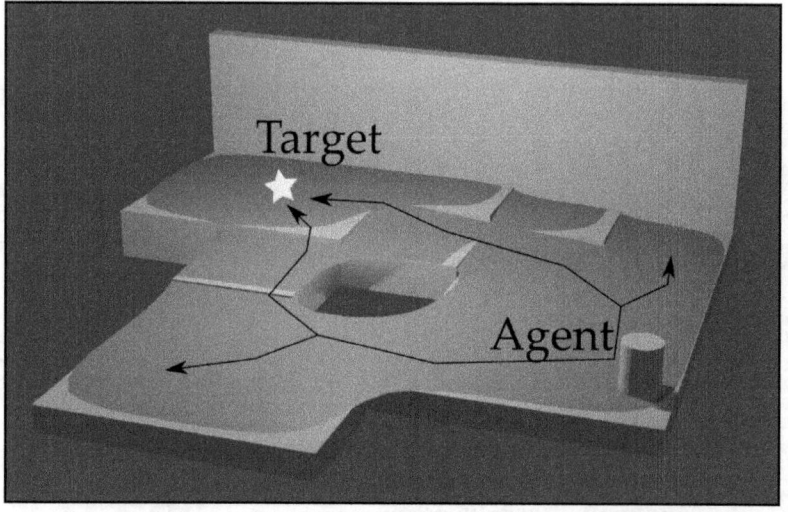

Building a NavMesh

Building a NavMesh is done through a process called **NavMesh Baking**, where all the geometry of the scene is analyzed and GameObjects and terrains are processed to make a simplified surface that can be transversed by a NavMesh Agent. Shortest paths are calculated over this surface using algorithms such as the A* pathfinding algorithm.

Open the starter project for this chapter in Unity. Then, open the **RW / Scenes / Arena** scene. You'll begin this game by converting your tank into an agent that can navigate around the arena:

1. From the top menu, choose **Window ▸ AI ▸ Navigation** to make a navigation pane appear in the right side panel.

2. In the Hierarchy, select the **Scene ▸ Arena-Floor** GameObject of the Arena scene.

3. Click the **Navigation** pane and make sure the **Navigation Static** indicator under the **Navigation ▸ Object** tab is checked. This ensures the arena is included in the NavMesh baking process.

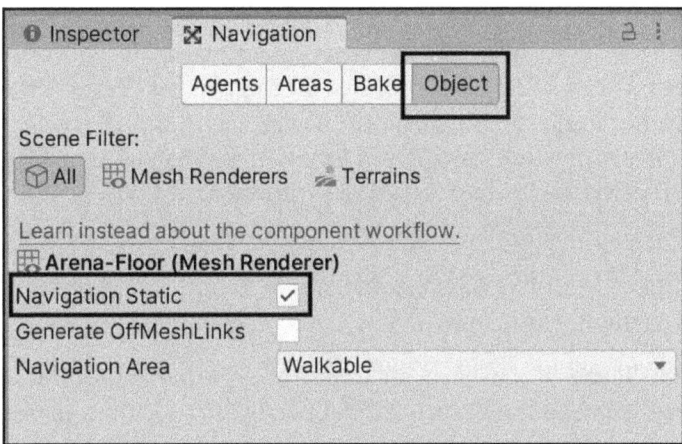

4. Switch to the **Navigation ▸ Bake** tab and click the **Bake** button to generate a static NavMesh describing the floor of the arena.

The bake settings adjust how the surface is created to match the size of a NavMesh Agent, which can make it easier or harder to reach surfaces or climb inclines. **Agent Radius** defines how close the agent center can get to an edge of a surface such as a wall or a ledge. The **Agent Height** can be adjusted to make it easier to reach the spaces raised off the ground. The **Max Slope** can be adjusted to make it possible to navigate up steeper angles and ramps in the surfaces. Finally, the **Step Height** defines whether the agent can step over an obstruction.

> **Note**: What is "Baking"? When you pre-run calculations in the Unity Editor and save the results to disk, this process is called baking. Unity loads the baked data at runtime, and having this precalculated data reduces the performance cost at runtime. You'll similarly hear of "Baking Lighting," which is another way to perform a one-time calculation for lighting effects rather than constantly recalculating while the game is running.

In the **Project** pane, your **RW / Scenes** folder now includes an **Arena / NavMesh** asset for the generated mesh.

Look back at the **Scene** window, and make sure the **NavMesh Display / Show NavMesh** is enabled. You'll see the areas defined by the NavMesh in blue. If the blue NavMesh isn't displaying, check that the **Gizmos** button is enabled at the top of the scene window. Notice the pit in the center of the arena is not part of the navigable area. The steep cliff of the pit in the center of the map defines an edge to your NavMesh, while the walls of the arena form the other boundaries.

Configuring a player NavMesh Agent

The NavMesh Agent component enables characters to utilize the baked NavMesh to find pathways to a target and avoid obstacles. It's time to make your first moving NavMesh Agent to be guided by point-and-click mouse input of the new Unity Input System.

Find and select the **Tank** prefab in the **RW / Prefabs** folder, and from the Inspector view select **Open Prefab** to view the tank.

Then, select **Add Component** and choose **NavMesh Agent**. This is the fundamental unit that will drive the AI of the tank to be able to navigate your mesh.

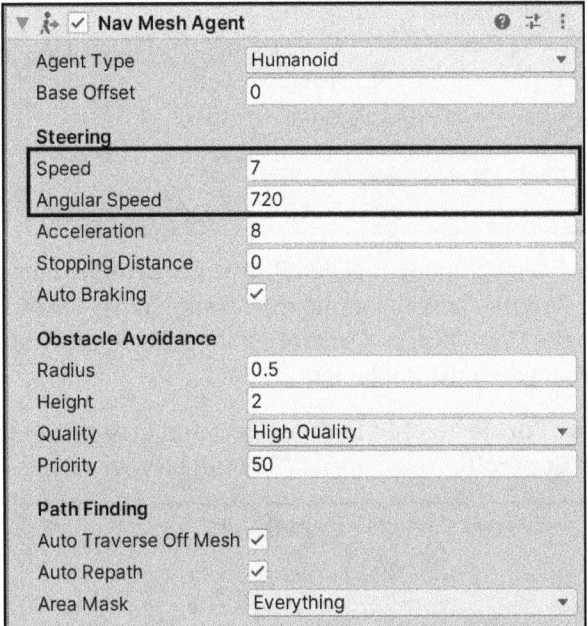

Take a quick look at the **NavMesh Agent** component in the inspector, which configures how pathfinding for the agent behaves and how the agent will avoid obstacles. The **Speed** controls how fast the agent will travel along its path, while the **Angular Speed** determines how quickly the agent will rotate at turns. **Acceleration** determines how quickly the agent will speed up, while the **Stopping Distance** configures how close to the target the agent will stop. The **Obstacle Avoidance** parameters will determine how far from obstacles the agent needs to be in any path.

Adjust the **Steering** section to increase the **Speed** to **7** and **Angular Speed** to **720**. These options make the tank more responsive and faster to turn to new positions.

The tank prefab still needs another script to adapt input from the player to actions taken by the NavMesh Agent. Add another component — the **Player Input** — from the new Unity Input System. Set the **Actions** to a pre-defined Input System action called **MyActions**.

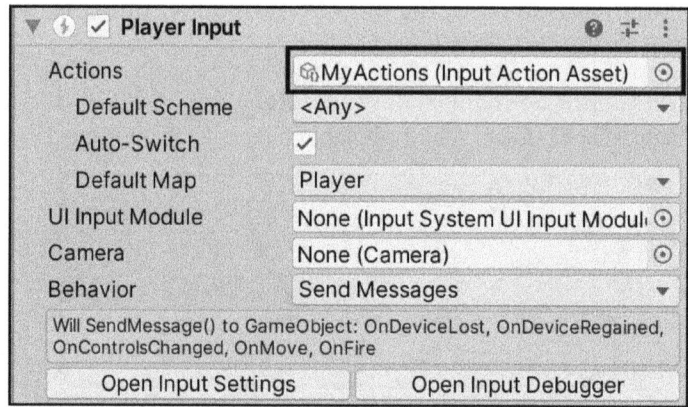

Last, add the predefined component called **Player Controller**. This script needs additional logic to describe how the input system should trigger the moves of the tank around the arena floor. **Player Controller** should also provide actions such as firing projectiles that you must implement.

Find **RW / Prefabs / ForkProjectile** in the project and drag this to the **Projectile** field in the **Player Controller** component. This will be your ammo.

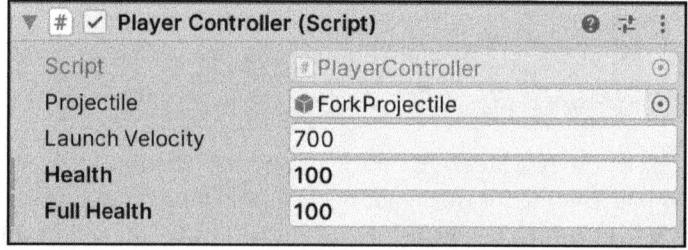

Now for some animation!

Game logic

Look at the Hierarchy view of the tank prefab. Your tank prefab is actually constructed of a hierarchy of different 3D models — from the wheels all the way to the cannon. As an animating effect, you'll allow the cannon to freely move and target enemies to fire the projectile. You'll implement the **PlayerController** script logic next to allow this.

Setting a destination from Input System

The first thing you need to do is to get the tank to move. The goal is to convert a position of the mouse to a 3D location to direct the tank as a navigation target.

Open the **PlayerController** script and find the OnMove method. OnMove is the expected name for the action handler to be called any time there's a mouse click, as defined by the MyActions Input System profile.

Add the following logic to OnMove:

```
RaycastHit hit; // 1
Debug.Log("Try to move to a new position");

// 2
if (Physics.Raycast(Camera.main.ScreenPointToRay(
                       Mouse.current.position.ReadValue()),
                   out hit,
                   100))
{
    agent.destination = hit.point;  // 3
    Debug.Log("Moving to a new position");
}
```

Going through this:

1. You define a RaycastHit object which you'll use to store a point that you want the tank to move towards.

2. Camera.main.ScreenPointToRay is a method provided by the Unity API that takes a 2D coordinate (x, y) of the where the mouse is on the screen, and converts this to a ray from the camera position forward into the 3D scene. The Physics.Raycast method traces the path of the ray until it encounters an object in the scene where it calculates and returns the 3D coordinates (x, y, z) of this point in the RaycastHit object.

3. You set `agent.destination` to this point. When you do this, the NavMesh Agent will begin to find a path and move towards it.

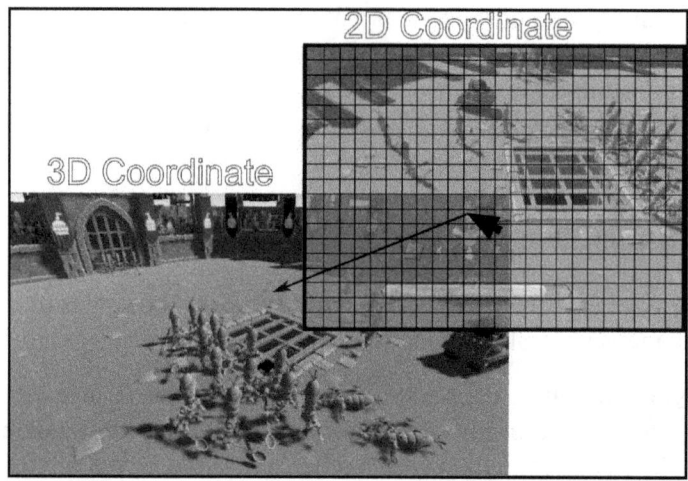

Essentially, the 3D coordinate becomes the new destination for the tank. The NavMesh Agent AI will then use the A* algorithm to find the shortest path on the baked NavMesh to reach the target.

Save your script and go back to the Unity Editor. Click **Play** on the scene to give the movement a try. Click anywhere in the arena and watch the tank head in that direction!

What's really neat is that if you click a point on the other side of the pit, the tank will move around it to reach the new destination. Remember that the pit is not part of the NavMesh, so the tank can't go over that part of the scene!

Setting aim from Input System

Return to the **PlayerController** script and find the `OnFire` method stub. Fill in the logic for the projectile firing with this:

```
// 1. On a mouse click, get the mouse current position
float x = Mouse.current.position.x.ReadValue();
float y = Mouse.current.position.y.ReadValue();

// 2. Ray trace to identify the location clicked.
Ray ray = Camera.main.ScreenPointToRay(new Vector3(x, y,
            Camera.main.nearClipPlane));

// 3. Raycast to hit the surface, turn turret to face.
RaycastHit hit;
if (Physics.Raycast(ray, out hit))
{
    Vector3 target = hit.point;
    target.y = cannonHorizontal.transform.position.y;
    cannonHorizontal.transform.LookAt(target);
}

// 4. Find the direction forward of the cannon
Vector3 forward = cannonVertical.transform.forward;
Vector3 velocity = forward * launchVelocity;
Vector3 velocityHand =
    new Vector3(velocity.z, velocity.y, velocity.x);

// 5. Instantiate a projectile and send it forward
Transform cannon = cannonVertical.transform;
GameObject fork =
    Instantiate(projectile, cannon.position, cannon.rotation);
fork.GetComponent<Rigidbody>().AddForce(velocity);
```

Here's what's happening:

1. You first identify the x and y positions where the mouse was clicked.

2. To find what is being clicked, you convert from screen coordinates to a ray along the camera direction to find hits.

3. You use the transform `LookAt` method to determine how the turret needs to rotate to aim at this target.

4. You use the turret cannon barrel to determine the angle the projectile needs to launch from and the vector of a velocity to apply to the projectile as movement.

5. You finally instantiate your prefab of the projectile, and send it shooting forward with the velocity.

Save your script and play the game again. This time, try right-clicking to launch your projectile. Forks away!

> **Note**: If you look at the top level of the Hierarchy as you play the game, you'll notice that each fork you fire is added as a separate GameObject to the scene. A more optimized way to handle this would be to use **Object Pooling**. You'll learn more about this in the coming chapters.

Enemy AI and NavMesh Agents

Next, you'll incorporate NavMesh Agents to provide automated movements for some enemies.

Find the **RW / Prefabs / Warrior_Carrot** prefab in the Project view, and drag it into your scene. Adjust the position so that the warrior carrot is at **X:0, Y:0, Z:10**, standing right next to the pit.

If you play the scene, the enemy carrot will animate in an idle pose — but it won't do much because it doesn't have any other attributes. So now you'll make this enemy chase after the tank!

Attached to the **Warrior_Carrot** is both a configured NavMesh Agent component and a script called **Enemy Controller**.

To get started, open up the **Enemy Controller** script in your editor. The enemy has three possible states: Ready to chase the player, Attacking the player or Dead:

```
// 1. States
enum States { Ready, Attack, Dead };
```

You'll find the Update method with some empty blocks of code for handling these states. Implement the chasing the player action first by adding the following to the state == States.Ready block:

```
// 1. Set the destination as the player
agent.SetDestination(player.transform.position);
characterAnimator.SetFloat("Speed", agent.velocity.magnitude);

// 2. Stop when close and animate an attack
if (agent.remainingDistance < 5.0f)
{
    agent.isStopped = true;
    characterAnimator.SetBool("Attack", true);

    state = States.Attack;
    timeRemaining = 1f;
}
else
{
    // 3. Stop attacking and allow movement
    agent.isStopped = false;
    characterAnimator.SetBool("Attack", false);
}
```

Here's what you're doing:

1. First, you set the destination for the **Nav Mesh Agent** component to the current player position.

2. When the enemy approaches the player (within a distance of 5 in this case), you stop moving the NavMesh Agent and enable an animation for the enemy attack motions by changing the state to Attack.

3. The last section will exit the attack animation state if the player moves away and enables the enemy to repeat the chase.

Now, complete the action by finishing the `state == States.Attack` block:

```
timeRemaining -= Time.deltaTime;
if (timeRemaining < 0)
{
    state = States.Ready;
    if (Vector3.Distance(player.transform.position,
            gameObject.transform.position) < 5.0f)
    {
        player.GetComponent<PlayerController>().
                DamagePlayer();
    }
}
```

This keeps the enemy attacking the player for a brief amount of time before beginning to chase again.

Save your script, and play your scene!

Wow, those Carrot Warriors are pretty vicious! It's a good job you're in a tank!

The last bit of enemy logic is to allow triggering colliders to eliminate the enemies. These colliders could be the projectiles or even the tank itself. Open the **EnemyController** script again and go to the stub for `OnTriggerEnter` and add this to the `if (state != States.Dead)` block:

```
characterAnimator.SetBool("Death", true);
Destroy(gameObject, 5);
state = States.Dead;
agent.isStopped = true;
```

Save the script and run the scene again, and now your tank can fire at and run over the enemy carrot warrior. How satisfying!

Game state

To fully finish the game design, you'll implement waves of Carrot Warriors to battle against. You'll also track the player's health as the attack happens.

Create an empty GameObject named **Game** in your Arena scene. Add the script called **Game State** to this GameObject using **Add Component**.

Open the script in your editor, and you'll see this contains a simple state machine with the four states: **Countdown**, **Fight**, **Battle** and **Lose**. The **GameState** script updates the GUI to provide a countdown and a health bar that reflects your tank damage. It also defines the start of the game and — when the player loses — its end.

The `UpdateGUI` method provides feedback on the **Canvas** overlay:

```
void UpdateGUI()
{
    switch (state)
    {
        case States.Countdown:
            int timer = (int) Math.Ceiling(timeRemaining);
            MessageBar.text = timer.ToString();
            break;
        case States.Fight:
            MessageBar.text = "Fight!";
            break;
        case States.Battle:
            MessageBar.text = "";
            break;
        case States.Lose:
```

```
            MessageBar.text = "You Lose!";
            break;
    }

    HealthBar.sizeDelta = new Vector2(735 *
  player.GetComponent<PlayerController>().GetPercentHealth(), 65);
}
```

Depending on the value of state, the MessageBar will update to display new information.

You need to first assign the relevant components to the public fields.

Go back to the Unity Editor and view the **Game State** script component in the Inspector. Now, attach each of the GUI objects to the appropriate fields in **Game State**: Drag the **Canvas / Text** GameObject from the Hierarchy to the **Message Bar** field of **Game State** in the Inspector, then drag the **Canvas / Frame / Bar** health bar to the **Health Bar** field of **Game State**.

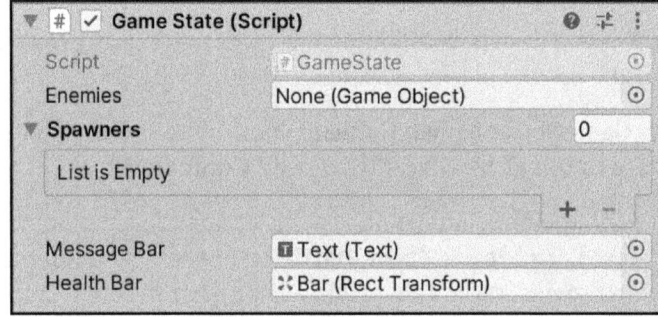

Now, if the player's health falls to zero, **Game State** enters the losing state and updates the GUI with the relevant message.

Play the game, and you'll see a countdown. Given enough time, the single enemy player will take away all your health and the game will display the "You Lose!" message.

One enemy is not a real challenge, though, so it's now time to implement the spawning of waves of the carrot army!

Adding the enemy waves

The enemy waves spawn at the gates of the arena. Each of the **Scene / GateWall** GameObjects has a component **GateSpawner** that can instantiate a crowd of **Warrior_Carrot** enemies. You need to connect each of these into the **Game State** to provide spawn locations for the enemies.

Before that, you need to disable any NavMesh Agents until the enemies are spawned at the gates.

Open the **EnemyController** script, and add this to the bottom of the Awake method:

```
agent.enabled = false;
```

This will ensure the agents don't show up until you ask them to. This happens in the Enable method.

Save the script then head back to the Unity editor. Now, select the **Game** GameObject and view the **Game State** component script in the Inspector view. Click the **Lock** button in the upper right to keep this component in view.

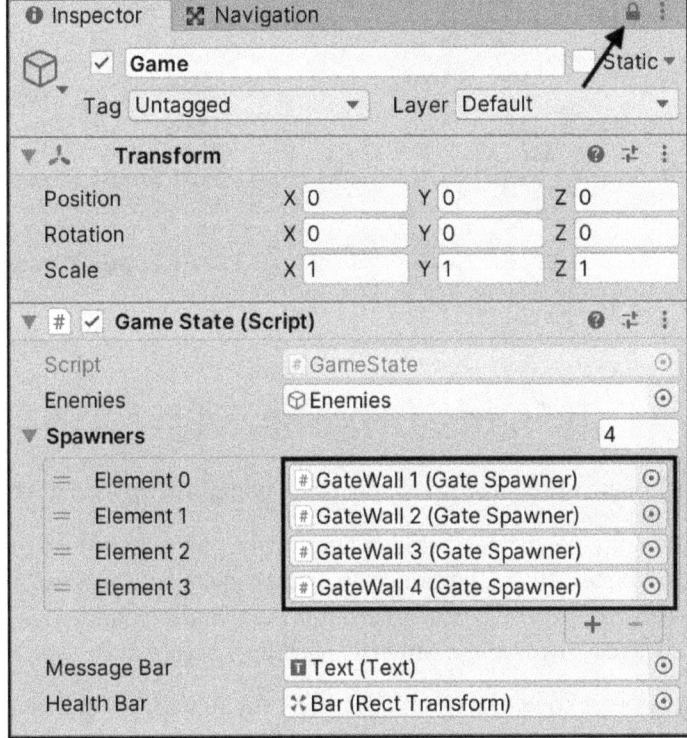

Click the + button under the **Spawners** list four times and drag each of the four **Scene/GateWall** GameObjects of the scene into the list to add each as a potential spawning location.

Next, you need to assign the parent for all these enemies. This is simple — just assign **Enemies** to the **Enemies** field in the **Game State** script.

Once you've completed mapping the fields, you can delete the sole warrior carrot you added earlier from the scene hierarchy. He's served his purpose.

Now click **Play** to battle it out in the arena against an army of carrots!

This concludes the project on the arena.

Common pitfalls with NavMesh Agents

While NavMesh Agents provide out-of-the-box navigation, they do have limitations:

1. Unity can be quite picky if a NavMesh Agent isn't on the NavMesh or within a minimum distance. This will produce errors in the console and navigation functions won't work. The best workaround when adding characters to a NavMesh is to reposition them onto the NavMesh before activation.

2. If an agent appears to get stuck or blocked by small inclines and walls, increase the NavMesh Agent size or adjust the allowed angle for navigation to enable the characters to overcome the heights you want them to.

Key points

1. The Unity **Navigation System** provides advanced pathfinding intelligence.
2. **Window ▸ AI ▸ Navigation** enables the Unity Navigation panel.
3. Bake a NavMesh for a selected GameObject to create a navigation geometry.
4. GameObjects can be marked **Navigation Static** to allow them to be baked into the NavMesh.
5. A component called the Nav Mesh Agent must be added to a GameObject to provide pathfinding and obstacle-avoiding intelligence.
6. You can create complex behaviors using a NavMesh Agent by calling its API from your **MonoBehaviour** scripts.
7. The **Navigation System** is a great way to build enemy AI that can intelligently march around a field, chase after targets and avoid obstacles.

Where to go from here?

In this chapter, you learned about using the Unity **Navigation System** to implement point-and-click navigation and some basic enemy AI.

You can experiment with the features to dig deeper into the subject. For example, you can add some obstacles with the **NavMesh Obstacle** component. When these exist as moving objects, the NavMesh Agents will attempt to avoid them, and when they are stationary, these objects will carve out regions of the NavMesh.

For dynamically changing NavMeshes and more advanced uses, the AI Navigation package (https://docs.unity3d.com/Packages/com.unity.ai.navigation@1.0/manual/index.html) provides additional tools.

You can also learn more about the Unity **Navigation System** and pathfinding with the raywenderlich.com tutorial Pathfinding with NavMesh: Getting Started tutorial (https://www.raywenderlich.com/16977649-pathfinding-with-navmesh-getting-started).

Chapter 10: Advanced Camera Controls With Cinemachine

By Matt Larson

The camera is your portal into your game so don't underestimate how much good camera control can contribute to the feel of it. However, properly implementing complex camera behaviors isn't trivial. It's easy to go wrong. The Cinemachine plugin provides a turnkey solution for all your camera needs. Time to explore Cinemachine and take the veggie battles to the next level!

Introduction

Cinemachine is a package provided in the Unity Registry. It offers a complete solution to managing multiple cameras and complex camera behaviors.

Don't reinvent the wheel by attempting to build custom camera scripts to control the camera in your games! Cinemachine handles all of the responsibilities via **Virtual Cameras** to allow you to build multiple camera views — each with unique and complex logic — to follow GameObjects and aim at targets. Cinemachine provides out-of-the-box solutions for 3rd-person-following cameras, orbiting cameras and many more.

Open the Chapter 10 starter project in Unity and begin by loading the **RW / Scenes / Arena** scene. Before working with the advanced camera components, you need to add the Cinemachine package via the top menu: **Window ▸ Package Manager**. Choose **Packages: Unity Registry** from the drop-down and select **Cinemachine**.

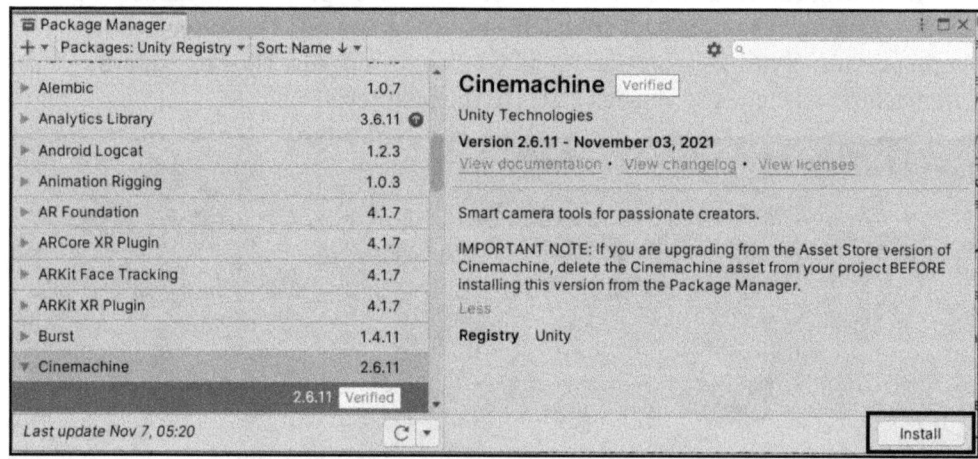

Select **Install** to add the package. After it's added to the Unity project, a new top menu named Cinemachine is immediately added to the Unity Editor.

Cinemachine Components

Cinemachine coordinates multiple camera views through a central hub called the **Cinemachine Brain. Virtual Cameras**, also called **vcams** for short, provide means to customize the behaviors of your camera views and assign special camera locations in your scenes.

Cinemachine Brain

The **CinemachineBrain** is a component script that acts as the connector between multiple **vcams** and a single active **Main Camera** GameObject.

Select the **MainCamera** GameObject in the Hierarchy, and add a component called **CinemachineBrain** via the Inspector. The GameObject should have its **Tag** assigned to **MainCamera**.

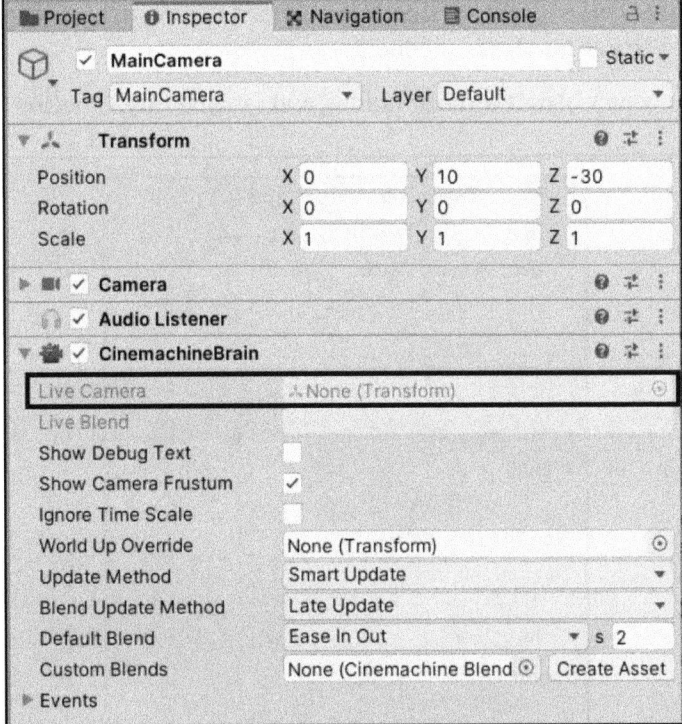

The **Live Camera** field is currently inactivate and assigned to **None**. When there are vcams present in the scene, this field is automatically assigned a virtual camera.

The CinemachineBrain will transition smoothly between different vcams using **Blends** that determine how to animate the transition. Animations between any two vcams can be modified by assigning **Custom Blends**, otherwise a **Default Blend** will apply to any camera transition.

Virtual Cameras

You'll start by adding some Virtual Cameras to the scene to provide different in-game views.

Create an empty GameObject in your scene named **VirtualCameras** to hold all the cameras you'll now create.

Next, add your first Virtual Camera from the top menu: **Cinemachine ▸ Create Virtual Camera**. This will add a GameObject named **CM vcam1**, which will contain a **CinemachineVirtualCamera** component.

Move this into your **VirtualCameras** holder, and rename the GameObject to **Zoom vcam**.

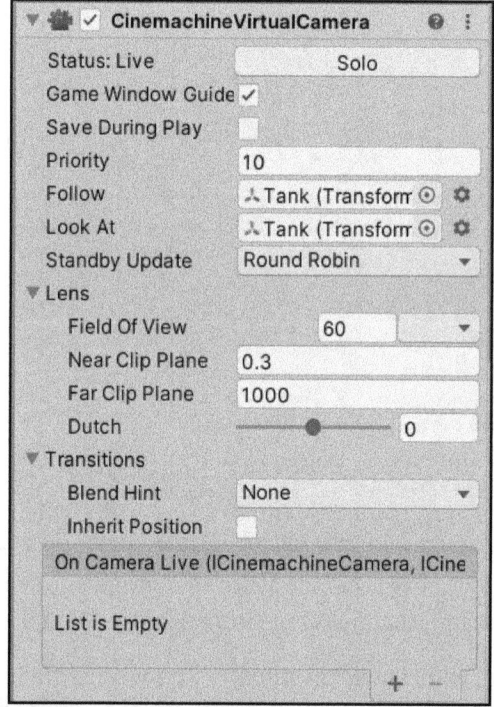

View **Zoom vcam** in the inspector, and assign the **Tank** to both the **Follow** and **LookAt** items. Those targets assign the vcam to position and aim at the tank. Until you customize it further, the vcam will be positioned inside the tank.

You'll fix that first. Expand the **Body** section in the inspector:

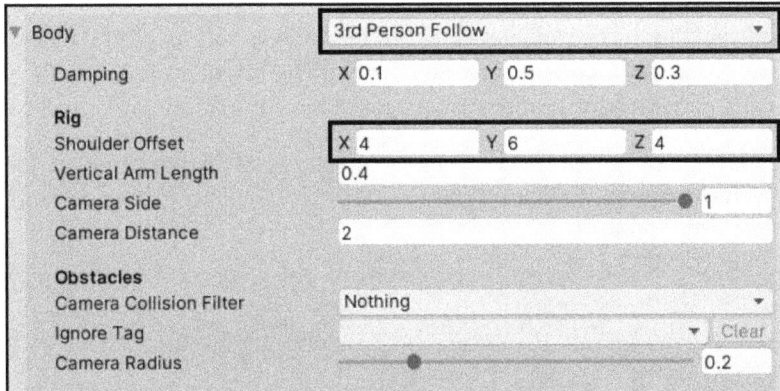

The **Body** section controls the behavior of the Virtual Camera in the scene. Here, set this to **3rd Person Follow** to have a trailing 3rd-person camera view that remains close to the player. Set the **Shoulder Offset** to **(X:4, Y:6, Z:4)** to place the camera at a comfortable angle and distance from the tank.

Now, expand the **Aim** section:

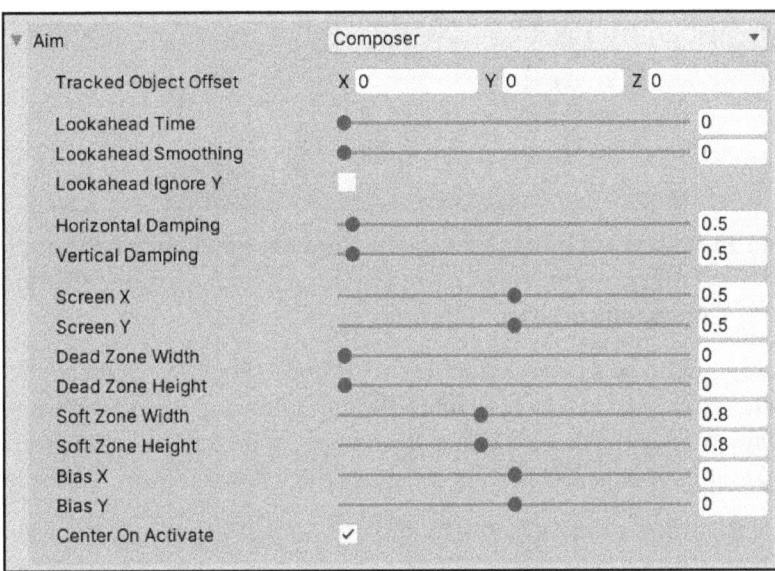

The Aim section controls how the camera responds to follow the **LookAt** target you provided above. The **Composer** type keeps a single **Look At** target in the camera frame. As a comparison, if you changed the type to **Group Composer**, this could instead keep a group of enemies or other GameObjects with the view.

The additional properties allow you to fine-tune how the vcam aims at the target —
such as **Lookahead**, which attempts to predict where the target will be for a leading
shot; **Damping**, which controls how quickly the camera settles on the object of
interest; and **Dead/Soft Zone** sizing, which gives the target an area to move around
in without the camera continuously fidgeting to keep it exactly in the center.

Select the **MainCamera** again and observe that the **Live Camera** field is now
assigned to the **Zoom vcam** virtual camera. This is the highest-priority (and only!)
vcam active in the scene.

Now, create another **vcam** by duplicating the **Zoom vcam**. Rename the duplicated
GameObject to **Follow vcam**. View this in the inspector, and expand the **Body**
section of its **CinemachineVirtualCamera**.

Since this is going to be a camera that loosely follows the player, increase the Body's
Damping to **(X:2, Y:1, Z:2)** to have more slack in following the player. **Damping**
specifies how quickly the camera reacts to changes, and increasing the positional
values makes it behave as if it was a slower, heavier camera following the player.

Change the **Rig**'s **Shoulder Offset** to **(X:0, Y:10, Z:-12)** to position the following
camera directly behind the tank.

In the **CinemachineVirtualCamera**, decrease the **Priority** field to **5**, then select the
MainCamera, and observe that the **Zoom vcam** with a higher priority of 10 has
taken control of the camera. Now return to the **Follow vcam** and increase **Priority**
to **15**.

Play the scene.

You'll see the game already has a better feel because the **Follow vcam** camera provides a third-person view that smoothly realigns with the tank.

Gate Camera

Again, duplicate the **Zoom vcam** and rename the GameObject to **Gate vcam**. Set the **Follow** and **Look At** targets to **GateWall 1**.

In this camera, change the **Body** to be an **Orbital Transposer**, and set **Binding Mode** to **Lock To Target With World Up**. Then, set the **Follow Offset** to **(X:1, Y:8, Z:8)**. The **Orbital Transposer** sets the **vcam** relative to the direction the target is moving or facing, and you'll use this to position the gate camera in front of the spawn point. The **Heading** should be assigned to **Target Forward**.

Note: Cinemachine is designed to query user input by the standard Unity `Input.GetAxis(name)`, which is incompatible with the Unity **Input System** used in this book. To avoid a conflict with accessing the old-style input API, clear the **Input Axis Name** under the **X Axis** section. When you do want to query user input affecting the cameras in Cinemachine, you can add a component **CinemachineInputProvider** to the **vcam** GameObject to override the standard input source.

To check that the camera will view the **GateWall**, raise its **Priority** to a value of **20**, and then select the **MainCamera** again to see what it's looking at - this will be the GateWall GameObject. Now, set the **Priority** of **Gate vcam** down to **1** since it shouldn't be the highest priority.

Next, you'll integrate these different cameras into the game!

Transitioning between cameras with scripting

Each virtual camera in the scene has a priority value; the camera which has the highest priority for the scene will be assigned to the Unity Camera. In order to change the active camera by a script, you simply need to change which camera has the highest priority.

The `GameState` class controls the flow of the game, and so you need to change this script so that when key events happen, such as when enemies appear or the tank gets destroyed, you redirect to the relevant camera to show the action.

Open the **RW / Scripts / GameState** script in an editor. At the top of the script, add a new import, just below the others:

```
using Cinemachine;
```

Then, inside `GameState`, add the following properties:

```
public CinemachineVirtualCamera zoomCamera;
public CinemachineVirtualCamera playerCamera;
public CinemachineVirtualCamera gateCamera;
```

These will represent the different camera views in the scene.

Now, at the bottom of the class, implement the `ActivateCamera` method:

```
public void ActivateCamera(CinemachineVirtualCamera camera)
{
    zoomCamera.Priority = lowPriority;
    playerCamera.Priority = lowPriority;
    gateCamera.Priority = lowPriority;
    camera.Priority = highPriority;
    camera.MoveToTopOfPrioritySubqueue();
}
```

This resets all the vcams to a low priority and then sets the specified virtual camera to the highest priority, causing the **CinemachineBrain** to make this the active view.

`MoveToTopOfPrioritySubqueue()` ensures this vcam has priority over any other vcams that happen to have the same priority value — which is a good practice when you want to make a vcam the live camera.

Now, call your new method by adding this to the end of `Reset()`:

```
ActivateCamera(zoomCamera);
```

When the game starts, the camera will begin zoomed-in on the target of the `zoomCamera` — in this case, the player's tank.

To show the first enemies as they appear at a gate, you need to switch to the `gateCamera` **vcam** when they first spawn. In the `Update()` method, find the `if (state == States.Fight)` clause, and, within the block, add the following after the call to `g.SpawnEnemies(5)`:

```
ActivateCamera(gateCamera);
```

After the enemies have spawned, you need to change back to the **vcam** that follows the player. Still in the `Update()` method, find the `if (state == States.Battle)` clause, and, at the top of the block, add the following:

```
ActivateCamera(playerCamera);
```

Save your changes and return to the Unity Editor.

Inspect the **Game** GameObject. Assign the **Zoom vcam** GameObject to the **Zoom Camera** field and **Follow vcam** to the **Player Camera**. Last, assign the **Gate vcam** to the **Gate Camera**.

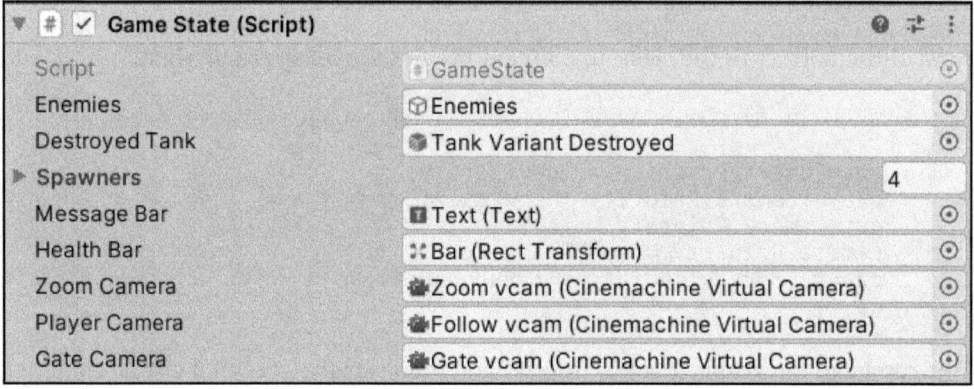

Run your game now, and you'll see the **vcams** transition between the **Follow vcam** and a **Gate vcam** as the first enemies are introduced.

However, you'll see the animated transition to the gate **vcam** is too slow. This animation between the **vcams** is controlled by a **Blend**, and you can customize the behavior of the camera transitions under the **MainCamera**.

Inspect the **MainCamera**, and set the **CinemachineBrain**'s **Default Blend** to **Cut**.

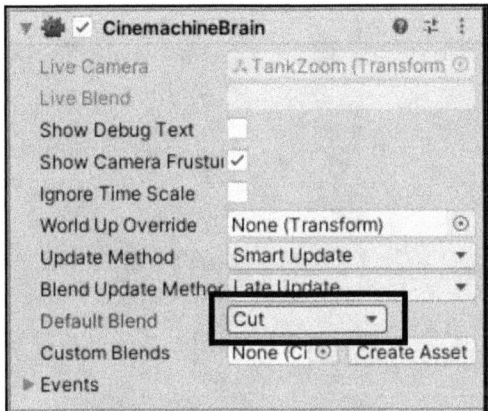

When you run the scene again, the transition is instantaneous between the different **vcams**.

Tank destruction

A neat effect you can introduce is to show the tank being destroyed when the battle is lost.

Go back and edit the **GameState** script again, and add the following to the Update() method just after the line state = States.Lose;:

```
// Hide player.
player.SetActive(false);
ActivateCamera(zoomCamera);
UpdateGUI();

// Replace with destroyed tank.
DestroyedTank.transform.position = player.transform.position;
DestroyedTank.transform.rotation = player.transform.rotation;
DestroyedTank.SetActive(true);
```

This code is executed when the player's health becomes less than zero, meaning they're dead! It swaps the **Tank** prefab with a set of models with colliders and rigidbodies. The individual parts will collapse upon the activation of the GameObject in the scene and show as a quick destruction of the tank. As this happens, the camera switches to zoom in on the damaged tank.

Save your changes and switch back to the Unity Editor. Play the scene and watch as the camera transitions to highlight the destruction of the tank!

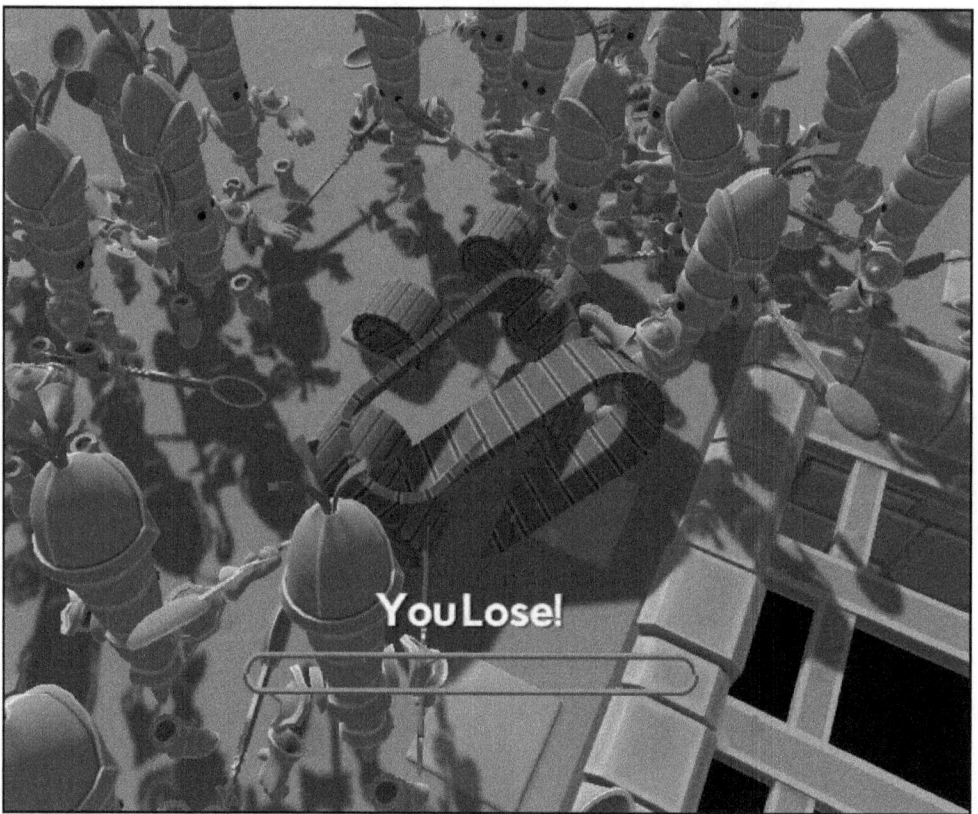

Challenges

If you want to go further with the Cinemachine system, try these challenges:

1. Implement a **Blending property** to change the behavior of the animation transitions between your cameras in the arena. Try building more complex **Custom Blends** for camera transitions.

2. Explore adding special effects to the cameras — including using an **Impulse** to add a camera shake that responds to in-game events. Add a **Cinemachine Collision Impulse Source** to the **Tank** GameObject, and add a **Cinemachine Impulse Listener** to the main **TankFollow** virtual camera. Can adding camera shakes on collisions enhance the immersion of the battle?

3. Experiment with using **vcams** to control the camera during a dialogue between two characters. Add two characters with nearby **vcam** instances aimed at their heads and `Priority` value 0. When a character speaks a line of dialogue, increase the **vcam** to the highest priority to create a cinematic cut to the speaker.

Key points

1. **Cinemachine** is a package that provides easy-to-use camera controls.

2. **Virtual Cameras**, or **vcams**, are customizable cameras representing different views in your scene.

3. **CinemachineBrain** is a component that should be assigned to your **Main Camera**. It determines the active **vcam** view based on the highest priority and configures how camera transitions behave.

Chapter 11: Asynchronous Functions, Coroutines & Object Pooling

By Matt Larson

Introduction

The veggie gladiators are pouring through the gates! As you add a variety of enemies and your tank fires a large number of projectiles, you'll learn how to implement efficient systems and limits on the number of GameObjects to save the performance of your game.

Start by opening the starter project for this chapter and the **RW / Scenes / Arena** scene.

Play the game and fire several projectiles. You'll see the accumulation of GameObjects in the Hierarchy.

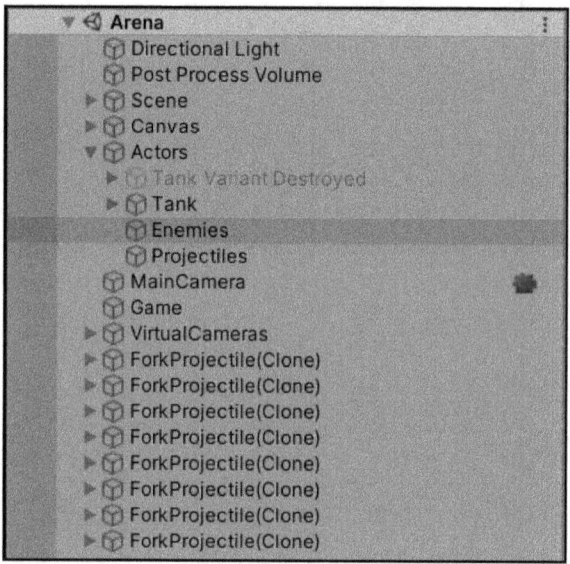

Timed destruction of GameObjects

You need mechanisms to clean up the **Hierarchy** from the projectiles and enemies after they expire. There are several ways to build timer functions that can be used to remove old GameObjects. You'll explore two patterns for writing asynchronous timer functions: **coroutines** and **async/await**.

Synchronous and asynchronous functions

When you write code, you're giving your game a set of instructions to run. It will complete those instructions in the order they're written. This is called synchronous programming. It works well because you can determine what your game will do next.

However, it's not so good when you want something to happen over a period of time or frames. For example, if you were to write something like this:

```
while (transform.position != someTargetPosition)
{
    MoveTowards(someTargetPosition);
}
```

The code in the while loop would be called multiple times in the same frame — or "tick" — until your object had moved to where you wanted it to be. But to the user, it would appear as if it happened instantly.

Asynchronous methods are run on their own independent paths — so they don't block the main flow of your game. You can even run multiple asynchronous tasks at the same time.

Understanding coroutines

In Unity, you can write coroutine methods for your asynchronous code. A coroutine must be called using StartCoroutine(MyCoroutine);, and the coroutine needs to be an IEnumerator method. At the end of each frame, Unity will return back to the MonoBehaviour and continue execution at the statement immediately after the statement beginning with yield return.

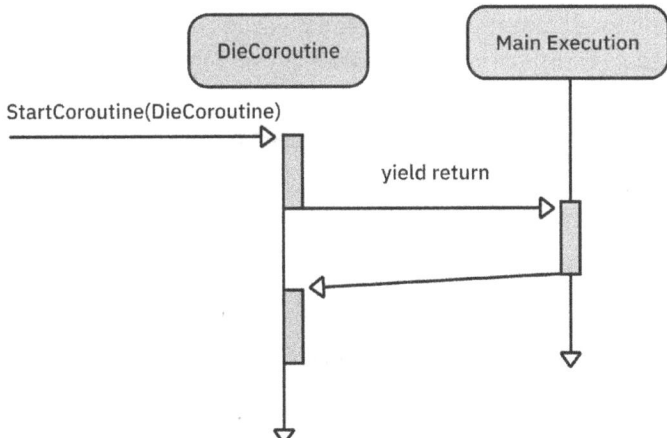

It's time to write your first coroutine method to remove an enemy GameObject whenever an enemy is killed. Open the **EnemyController** script from the **RW / Scripts** folder. Within the class, add the following method:

```
IEnumerator DieCoroutine()
{
    // 1. Delay for 5 seconds.
    yield return new WaitForSeconds(5);
    // 2. Destroy the GameObject
    Destroy(gameObject);
}
```

Here's what you're doing:

1. When you use a `yield` instruction, you're saying to the `IEnumerator`, "OK, we're done for now. Come back later." You can specify when to return using built-in methods such as `WaitForSeconds` or `WaitForEndOfFrame`.

2. In this case, after the wait provided by `WaitForSeconds(5)` has occurred, execution is returned back to the next instruction after the `yield`, where you destroy the GameObject.

Calling this coroutine when an enemy is defeated will therefore allow a delay for the enemy death animation before the enemy GameObject is destroyed.

To do that, find the method `OnTriggerEnter`, and at the start of the block `if (state != States.Dead)`, add the following:

```
StartCoroutine(DieCoroutine());
```

When a character is killed by a projectile or tank, the coroutine will now be called and enemies will be removed from the scene after a delay of 5 seconds after their death. The coroutine provides the asynchronous behavior of handling the timing while the gameplay can proceed in parallel.

Save your changes, head back to the Unity Editor and play the scene.

A new alternative: Async/Await

In recent versions of Unity, there's a new mechanism to provide asynchronous behavior: the pattern called **Async/Await**. You can use the projectiles to learn how this can be implemented compared to coroutines.

With the **Async/Await** pattern, you create an async method that includes an instruction — Task.Yield(). These are quite similar to the IEnumerator and yield return statements from the coroutine pattern.

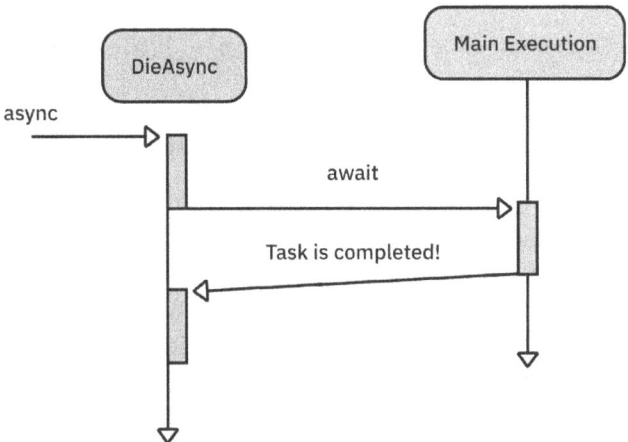

The keyword async defines a method that can run asynchronously. Put the async between the access modifier (public, private, etc.) and the return type.

Open the **RW / Scripts / ProjectileBehaviour** script and add the following method to the class:

```
public async void DieAsync()
{
    // 1.
    await Task.Delay(2000);
    // 2.
    Destroy(gameObject);
}
```

Compare this with the coroutine function above:

1. Instead of the yield, you have an await instruction that acts on a Task, which in this case provides a delay for 2000 milliseconds (2 seconds). The Task is a class that represents a single operation that can run asynchronously.

2. After the Task asynchronously completes, execution continues to the Destroy call to remove this projectile GameObject.

You need to start your async function after the projectile is instantiated, so open the **RW / Scripts / PlayerController** script and find the `OnFire()` method. Towards the bottom of this method, add the following to the bottom of the `if (projectile)` block:

```
projectile.GetComponent<ProjectileBehaviour>().DieAsync();
```

Save all your changes in your scripts and run the scene. Fire some projectiles and after 2 seconds, the timed calls to `Destroy` clean up the used projectiles.

> **Note**: Which pattern should you use? If you prefer the style of the coroutine, feel free to use it, but often the async/await pattern is a better option. In many ways, coroutines were a precursor to async/await. The biggest advantage of async/await is its overall simplicity and common approach to asynchronous code in C# outside of Unity. Either mechanism in Unity will asynchronously run your code on the main thread of the game avoiding conflicts that could occur with asynchronous multithreading.
>
> One of the advantages of async/await is that it allows you to return a value — which you can't do with an `IEnumerator` method. If you need to stop your asynchronous methods from outside of the method, there are built-in functions for coroutines such as `StopCoroutine`, however, there aren't any easy built-in methods for async/await.
>
> To read more about coroutines, check out the Unity Official Documentation (https://docs.unity3d.com/Manual/Coroutines.html). And, to learn more about Asynchronous Programming in Unity, check out this great tutorial on raywenderlich.com (https://www.raywenderlich.com/26799311-introduction-to-asynchronous-programming-in-unity-3d).

Object pooling

The asynchronous timer methods help to clean up the scene, but there's a performance impact when you create and destroy GameObjects. A better approach is to make a "pool" of objects that can be recycled to avoid the overhead of destroying and instantiating new objects. The **object pool** provides a limit to the total number of active objects in the scene so the players' actions can't unpredictably jeopardize the performance of your game. Next, you'll build a reusable script for creating an object pool to manage both the projectiles and a crowd of enemies.

How to implement object pooling

You can construct an object pool by completing the **RW / Scripts / ObjectPool** script. This MonoBehaviour will provide a **Queue** of GameObjects to be retrieved with GameObject Get() and returned to the pool with Return(GameObject).

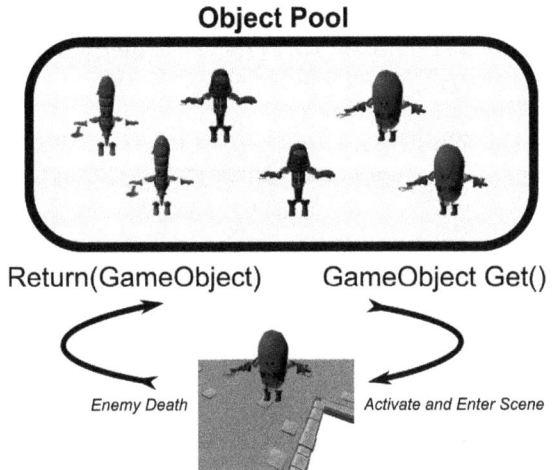
Object Pool

Return(GameObject)   GameObject Get()

Enemy Death   Activate and Enter Scene

Before you can create a generic ObjectPool class, there are certain rules that any poolable GameObject must consider. If you open the **RW / Scripts / IPoolable** interface, you see it defines the methods any poolable GameObject should implement in a component script:

```
public interface IPoolable
{
    // 1.
    void Reset();

    // 2.
    void Deactivate();

    // 3.
    void SetPool(ObjectPool pool);
}
```

A **C# interface** like this sets the **basic rules** that scripts must follow to:

1. Implement a method that returns it back to a ready state in Reset().

2. Implement a method that defines what happens when it goes back to the pool in Deactivate().

3. Provide a helper method to track what pool it belongs to.

To use the `IPoolable` interface, your class must inherit it. For example, if you look at `ProjectileBehviour`, you'll see that it does just that:

```
public class ProjectileBehaviour : MonoBehaviour, IPoolable
```

Once you state this, the class must implement the interface's methods. So in this case, it needs to have methods called `Reset()`, `Deactivate()`, and `SetPool(ObjectPool pool)` defined. Stubs for these methods have already been added to `ProjectileBehaviour` and `EnemyController`.

Later, you'll update these methods to follow the rules above so that the `ProjectileBehaviour` and `EnemyController` are ready for action.

Complete the ObjectPool

First, create the methods that will provide a reusable object pool for either type of GameObject.

Open the **RW / Scripts / ObjectPool**. The class has pre-defined variable called `pool`:

```
private Queue<GameObject> pool = new Queue<GameObject>();
```

This is a `Queue` of GameObjects that contains a "first-in, first-out" queue of any reusable GameObject.

To add objects to the `pool` queue, add the following to the `Add(GameObject anObject)` method:

```
// 1.
IPoolable poolable = anObject.GetComponent<IPoolable>();
if (poolable != null)
{
    // 2.
    pool.Enqueue(anObject);
    poolable.SetPool(this);
}
```

Going through this:

1. First check if the supplied GameObject has the necessary `IPoolable` component script.

2. If it does, put it into the `pool` queue to be used later.

Now to request a poolable GameObject from the queue. Add the following to the
Get() method stub, above the `return null;` statement:

```
// 1.
if (pool.Count > 0)
{
    // 2.
    GameObject toReturn = pool.Dequeue();
    toReturn.GetComponent<IPoolable>().Reset();
    return toReturn;
}
```

1. Check if the pool has any members.

2. If so, reset the state of the pool member so it's ready to be used, and return it.

You now need a way to put a GameObject back in the pool, Add the following to
Return(GameObject anObject):

```
// 1.
IPoolable poolable = anObject.GetComponent<IPoolable>();
if (poolable != null)
{
    // 2.
    poolable.Deactivate();
    Add(anObject);
}
```

1. First check if this the supplied object is an IPoolable member.

2. If so, deactivate the poolable object, then add it back to the pool.

The last method you need to write is a helper to construct a pool from a set of
prefabs. You'll use this to create a pool of projectiles or various enemies. Add the
following to the Awake() method:

```
// 1.
for (int i = 0; i < PoolSize; i++)
{
    // 2.
    GameObject poolMember = Instantiate(Prefabs[i %
Prefabs.Length],
                                        transform);
    // 3.
    poolMember.SetActive(false);
    Add(poolMember);
}
```

This method will build a pool by instantiating one or more example prefabs provided by the array of `Prefabs`.

Going through this:

1. The number of objects in the pool will be determined by the `PoolSize` variable. So loop around for that number of times.
2. Instantiate the next prefab from the `Prefabs` array. This uses **modular arithmetic**; just as you can count 24 hours on a clock face without using a number beyond 12, this allows you to count the full pool size without extending beyond the length of your `Prefabs` array.
3. Make the pool member inactive in the scene before adding it to the pool.

Save your changes and head back to the Unity editor.

Creating an object pool for projectiles

Find and select the empty **Actors / Projectiles** GameObject in the Hierarchy and add the component script **Object Pool**. Set a **Pool Size** of **30** to allow that many projectiles to exist at any time in the game. Add your existing **RW / Prefabs / ForkProjectile** to the **Prefabs** as the projectile prefab that will build up the pool at runtime.

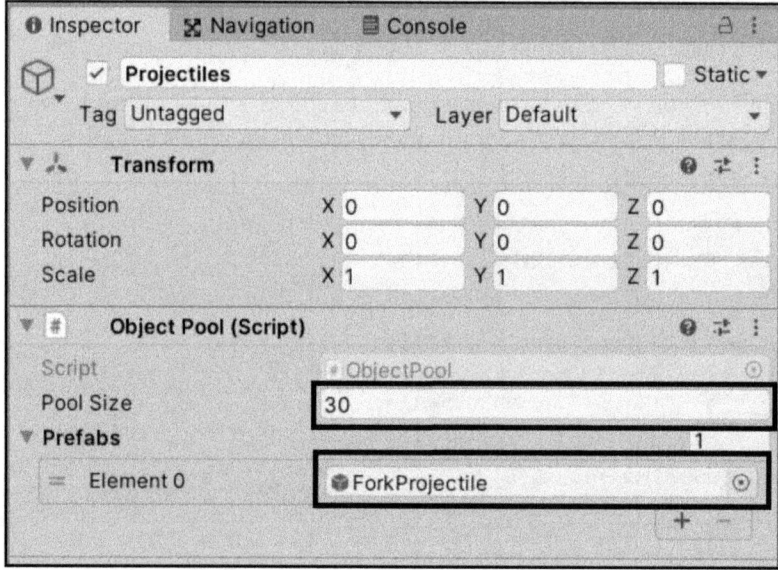

The **ForkProjectile** already has a component **ProjectileBehaviour**, but you need to define what happens when a projectile is reset and when it's deactivated upon returning to a pool.

Open the **RW / Scripts / ProjectileBehaviour** script.

In `DieAsync()`, replace `Destroy(gameObject);` with:

```
if (ProjectilePool)
{
    ProjectilePool.Return(gameObject);
}
```

This will now return the GameObject to the pool instead of destroying it.

The `Reset()` method needs to provide a ready-to-use projectile and is called automatically when requesting a GameObject with `ObjectPool.Get()`. This method needs to clear the velocity of the projectile and keep it active for a couple of seconds before it's returned to the pool automatically.

Add the following to the `Reset()` method:

```
// 1.
gameObject.SetActive(true);
gameObject.GetComponent<Rigidbody>().velocity = new Vector3(0, 0, 0);
// 2.
DieAsync();
```

Going through this:

1. To reactivate a projectile, make the GameObject active and clear its velocity.

2. Start the async method to return it back to the pool.

Finally, you need to implement the `Deactivate()` method that will be called by `ObjectPool.Return(GameObject)` when returning the projectile to its pool:

Add the following to `Deactivate()`:

```
gameObject.SetActive(false);
```

This simply sets the GameObject inactive to hide it from view and stop all motion.

Save your changes. You've now completed the major logic for the projectile pool — ready now to reuse, reduce and recycle those projectiles!

Updating the projectile launch

The next change needed for **ProjectilePool** is to pull GameObjects from the **ProjectilePool** instead of instantiating them.

Open the **RW / Scripts / PlayerController** script and replace the line `public GameObject Projectile;` with the following:

```
public ObjectPool ProjectilePool;
```

Next, in `OnFire()` replace `GameObject projectile = GameObject.Instantiate(Projectile);` with:

```
GameObject projectile = ProjectilePool.Get();
```

This retrieves a ready-to-use **ForkProjectile** that can fire from the tank.

Since the projectile now starts the `DieAsync()` coroutine as part of the `Reset()` pool method, you can also remove `projectile.GetComponent<ProjectileBehaviour>().DieAsync();` from the `if (projectile)` block of `OnFire()`.

Save your changes and head back to the Unity editor. Select **Actors / Tank** in the Hierarchy, and in the **Player Controller** component in the Inspector, assign the **Projectiles** GameObject to the **Projectile Pool** field:

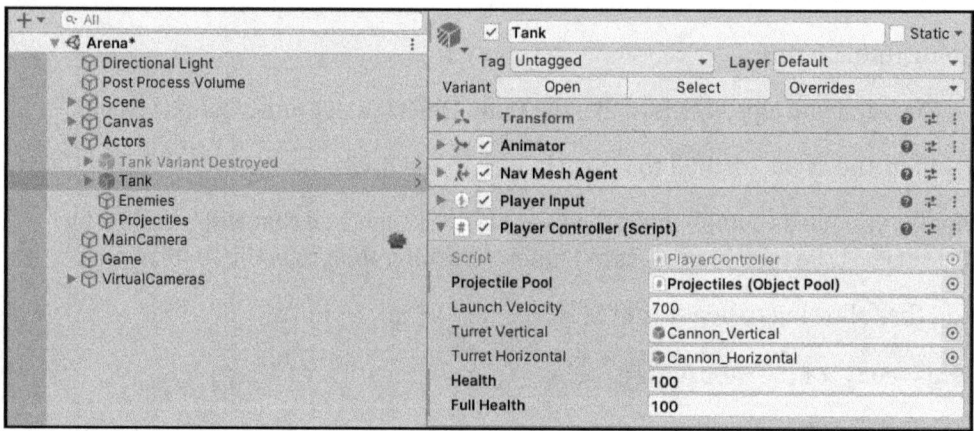

Save your scene. Play it and observe that **ForkProjectiles** now fill the **Projectiles** GameObject and become activated and inactivated as they're fired by the tank and returned back to the pool.

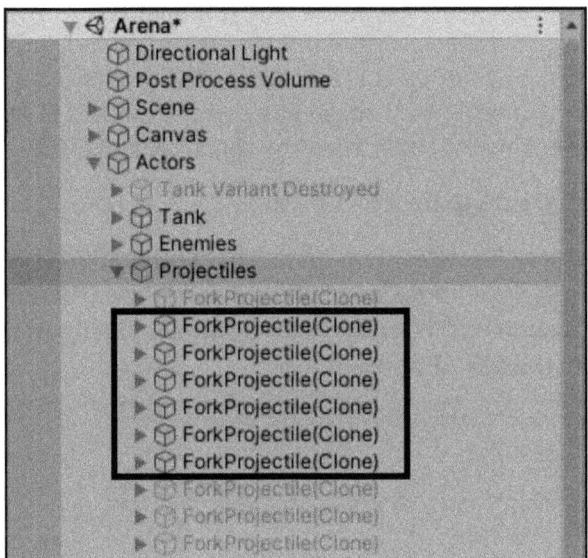

Creating an object pool for the enemies

Creating a pool of different varieties of enemy gladiators is even easier now that the `ObjectPool` is defined.

Open the **RW / Scripts / EnemyController** script and in `DieCoroutine()`, change `Destroy(gameObject)` with:

```
if (EnemyPool)
{
    EnemyPool.Return(gameObject);
}
```

This is the same as what you did for the projectiles earlier.

It's critical to reset the enemy state when obtaining an enemy from the pool when calling `ObjectPool.Get()`, so add the following to the `Reset()` method:

```
state = States.Ready;
characterAnimator.SetBool("Death", false);
```

This resets the enemy to be ready for battle.

Now, add the following to `Deactivate()`:

```
agent.isStopped = true;
gameObject.SetActive(false);
gameObject.GetComponent<NavMeshAgent>().enabled = false;
```

Remember that when a GameObject is returned to the pool with `ObjectPool.Return(GameObject)` the `Deactivate()` method is called. So this is where you hide the enemy by inactivating the character and disable its navigation.

Save the script and go back to the Unity editor.

Find the empty **Actors / Enemies** GameObject in the Hierarchy and add the **Object Pool** component to it. Set a **Pool Size** of **50**, and assign the **Warrior_Carrot Variant**, **Warrior_Pepper Variant** and **Warrior_Potato Variant** prefabs to the pool by dragging them from the **RW / Prefabs** folder.

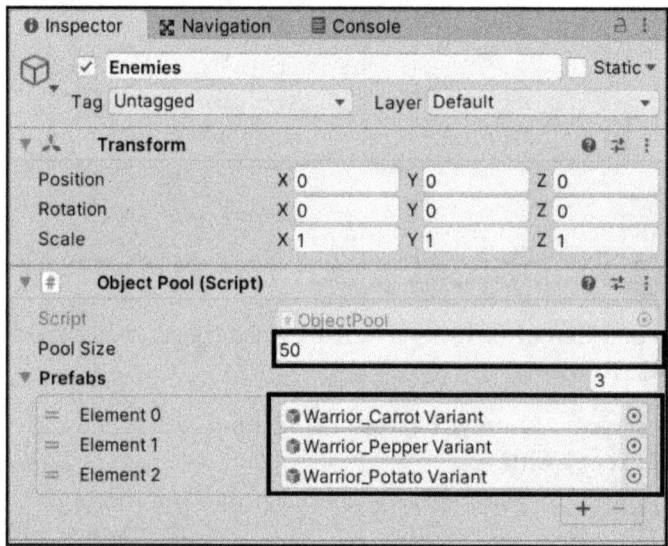

Lastly, open the **RW / Scripts / GateSpawner** script. Here, you again need to replace the GameObject variable with an `ObjectPool` variable.

At the top of `GateSpawner`, replace `public GameObject Enemy;` with:

```
public ObjectPool EnemyPool;
```

Now, in `SpawnEnemies()`, use your new variable by replacing `GameObject enemy = Instantiate(Enemy, Gate.transform.parent);` with:

```
GameObject enemy = EnemyPool.Get();
```

Save your changes, and in the Unity editor, select all four of the **GateWall Variant** GameObjects in the Hierarchy, find their **Gate Spawner** component, and assign all to have the **Enemies** GameObject in the Hierarchy to the **Enemy Pool** field in the component.

Now, play the scene and you'll see a varied attack force of slow potatoes, carrots and spicy peppers!

Within the **Enemies** container, the same enemies are being reactivated and recycled to use in the scene.

Congratulations! You've made the game more complex with new enemies, and you've mastered efficiency with **asynchronous operations** and **object pooling**!

Key points

1. **Coroutines** and **async/await** are two ways you can implement asynchronous operations for timed delays to actions.

2. **Object Pools** are a reusable mechanism for managing large numbers of GameObjects in a scene — such as Projectiles, Enemies and other spawnable elements. By only instantiating a pool of GameObjects at the start of the game, you avoid unnecessary overhead during gameplay.

3. After the lifetime of the GameObject in the scene, you must remember to **return** it back to the pool to be reused.

4. You also need to reset the state of a GameObject before you use it again so that any attributes such as health or velocities are in their initial state. Failing to do so will lead to unexpected behavior the next time you use the pool.

Continue to the next chapter to see what becomes of all the defeated veggie gladiators and what's cooking down below!

Section IV: Cooking Up Animations

Animation adds so much more interest and fun to games, and Unity has a wealth of tools and techniques to help you add the right effects. This section first introduces tween animations - an effective way to get objects to move from one place to another. It then goes on to cover more advanced animation principles that allow your characters to animate in different ways while in different states.

You'll then look at using scriptable objects as data containers to make more efficient use of memory and increase your game's responsiveness.

The action in this section takes place in the kitchen, where Chef is cooking up some interesting dishes...

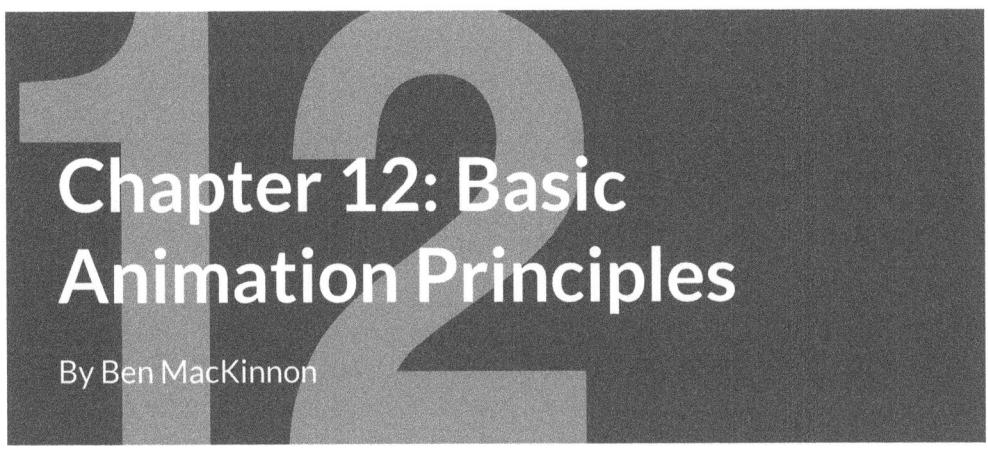

Chapter 12: Basic Animation Principles

By Ben MacKinnon

Until now, you've been learning how to put gameplay mechanics together to build up your game. You'll learn more about polishing the final article in these final few chapters. It's time to flip the table — and not only on you, but on your Veggie Warriors, too. :]

In this chapter, you'll learn the basics of animation in Unity. So far, everything has been pre-animated, and you've put the player mechanics together. Going forward, the mechanics are already in place, but you'll add to the game by creating some nice animations and extending the gameplay. For this, you'll look at a new game environment - the kitchen! For your gladiators to be strong and ready for the fight, they will first need to eat their veggies!

Introduction to Unity animation types

Just like there are many ways to peel a vegetable — whether it's a trusty peeler, a new-fangled machine or the edge of a blunt knife — there are many ways you can animate objects in Unity.

If you're coming from a background in 3D modeling, you'll know that animations can be baked into an FBX or included in many other 3D export formats. Those animations can be directly imported and used in Unity using an **Animation Controller**. You'll get to that later. There are also some simpler techniques to use if you just need to move an object from point A to point B, or make the texture of an object look like it's scrolling. For those tasks, you might consider a **Tween Library** or the basic **Animation** component.

Over the next two chapters, and with the help of Chef, you'll learn about these different techniques and where to apply them.

Introducing the kitchen

You might be wondering what happened to all those Veggie Warriors that fell in battle against the tank. Well, you're about to find out. Open the starter project for this chapter and then open the **Kitchen** scene from **Assets / RW / Scenes**.

It doesn't look like much just now, but before long you'll have this place sending meals out to help prepare those warriors for battle.

As for the ingredients, click **Play** in the editor and you may see a few familiar faces pop up in the scene.

> **Note**: The functionality for this game is already set up. The objective is for Chef to take the ingredients, wash them, chop them and place them on a plate, before picking up the plate and sending it to the "pass" - the table at the bottom of the screen with the arrows on. Even though nothing animates at the moment, you can already do all this with the following controls:
>
> **W, A, S, D,** - Move Chef around.
>
> **Space** - Pick up ingredient / plate or place ingredient on plate.
>
> **Ctrl** - Perform Wash / Chop action.

Fortunately for Chef, that tank is pushing all the defeated warriors down the grate in the center of the arena, and they're falling straight into his kitchen. A never-ending supply!

> **Note**: That supply is actually an **Object Pool** — similar to the one you learned about in the previous chapter.

At the moment, the vegetables — or Ingredients, as Chef likes to call them — are just appearing up in the air. Your first task is to get them to fall into the troughs below, ready for Chef to collect.

In other words, you need to get the Ingredients from point A to point B.

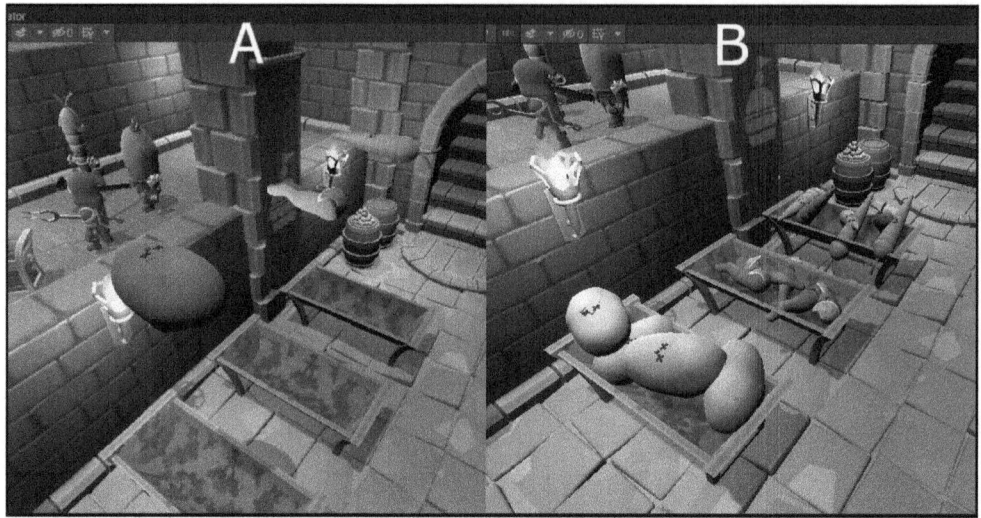

Deciding on how to animate your GameObjects

There are many ways to animate GameObjects inside of Unity. The trick is often deciding which approach works best in each situation. You have to consider some of the following facts:

- Does the animation need to be complex?
- Does the animation need to transition between various states?
- Is the animation a looping movement?
- Is the animation always between the same values?

Answering these kinds of questions will help you decide what method to use. If the answer for either of the first two questions is yes, odds are you're dealing with some sort of character animation. These would likely be imported with your 3D models, and then built up using an **Animation Controller**. More on that in the next chapter.

For a looping animation, such as a spinning coin or perhaps a scrolling texture, you would want to consider the **Animation** component. More on that later in this chapter.

The Animation component would also work if your animation was always between two fixed values. As you may have spotted from the images above, the **Ingredients** are all appearing in the same locations, but need to end up in slightly different positions (and rotations) inside the trough.

This is your *from A to B* process. You know where the GameObjects start, and you know where they need to end, but you need to be able to describe what happens in between. This process is often referred to as **tweening**.

Building a tween library

Tweening is a very common method of creating animations in Unity. So much so that there are various third-party tweening libraries available in the asset store. Some of the most popular include DOTween (https://assetstore.unity.com/packages/tools/animation/dotween-hotween-v2-27676) and LeanTween (https://assetstore.unity.com/packages/tools/animation/leantween-3595). Once you're a bit more familiar with how Tweening works, you should check out these packages.

However, for what you need to achieve in the Kitchen scene, you don't need a full tweening package. You'll need just *one* method call and your scene will come alive.

Filling the trough

In the Hierarchy, find one of the **Troughs** under the **Interactables** parent GameObject. Select it and take a look at the **PickupArea** component. You'll see three key things have been set up:

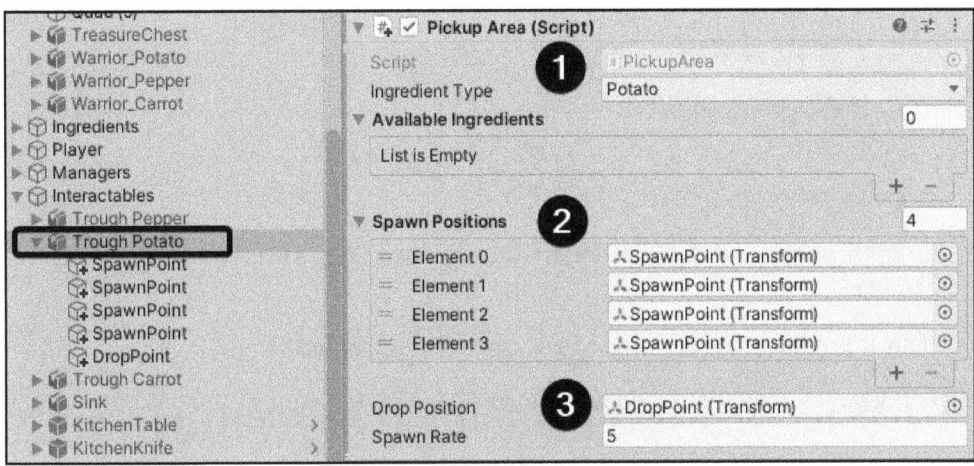

1. The type of **Ingredient** that falls into this trough.
2. A **List** of **SpawnPositions** as **Transforms**.
3. The **DropPosition**, also stored as a **Transform**.

The **DropPosition** is where the Ingredients currently appear when they spawn into the scene. The **SpawnPositions** are where you *actually* want them to be. So let's get them from A to B.

Open the **PickupArea** script by double-clicking on the script component or finding it in **Assets / RW / Scripts**. Navigate down to the **Spawn** method.

```
private void Spawn()
{
    // 1
    if (availableIngredients.Count < spawnPositions.Count)
    {
        // space for more ingredients
        // 2
        IngredientObject newIngredient
            = IngredientPool.Instance.Fetch(ingredientType);
        if (newIngredient != null)
        {
            // 3
            availableIngredients.Add(newIngredient);
            // 4
            newIngredient.transform.parent = transform;
            // 5
            newIngredient.Lerp(
                dropPosition,
                spawnPositions[availableIngredients
                                    .IndexOf(newIngredient)],
                0.5f);
        }
    }
    // 6
    timeSinceSpawn = 0;
}
```

There's a lot going on in here:

1. First, check to see if the number of available ingredients is less than the trough can hold.
2. If so, try to fetch another ingredient from the **IngredientPool**.
3. If you got an ingredient, add it to the available ingredients.

4. Then, **parent** it to the trough. This means changing the location of the GameObject in the Hierarchy programmatically. Take your new Ingredient and make it a child of the trough. That way, you can deal with its position and rotation *relative* to the trough. In Unity, **transforms** have a `localPosition` and `localRotation` for this purpose.

5. After that, call the **Lerp** method passing the `dropPosition` and next available `spawnPosition`.

6. Finally, in all cases, reset a timer that called the `Spawn` method.

You won't need to edit any of this code, but the one line that's worth noting is that last one inside the second `if` statement:

```
newIngredient.Lerp(
    dropPosition,
    spawnPositions[availableIngredients.IndexOf(newIngredient)],
    0.5f);
```

Lerp logic

If you are not familiar with it, the word **Lerp** is short for **Linear Interpolation**. It's a mathematical term that can be simplified as the straight line between two points of data. Using this line, you can work out any position between these two points.

In Unity you can use **Lerp** to help animate any number of things. You can say, "given the values *a*, *b* and the interval *t*, you can find any value *t* distance between *a* and *b*."

$$\text{lerp}(a, b, t) = \underbrace{a}_{\text{Start}} + \underbrace{(b - a)}_{\text{Distance from A to B}} * \underbrace{t}_{\text{Percentage}}$$

And in Unity, *a* and *b* could be just about any value. Alpha, Color, Position, Rotation, Audio Volume — the possibilities are nearly endless, so long as you're willing to work out the math! Math doesn't always need to be hard, though. Consider *a* and *b* just to be simple float values. Say, **1** and **3**. If you wanted to Lerp between *a(1)* and *b(3)* by **0.5**, you'd get the answer **2**.

- 1 + (3-1) * 0.5
- 1 + (2) * 0.5
- 1 + 1

Or, you can also consider it on a graph:

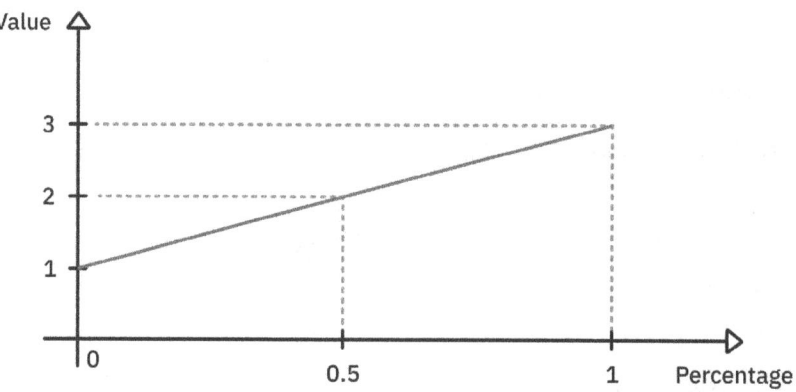

But the Lerp method is already there, you say. Technically, yes it is. But take a closer look. Navigate to that Lerp function. Hover over the text in Visual Studio (or the editor of your choice), hold down **Control** or **Command** and **Left-Click**. This will take you to where this method is defined. Or, if your editor isn't smart enough, you can open the **Tween** script from inside the **Assets / RW / Scripts** folder.

You'll end up at this method:

```
public static void Lerp(this MonoBehaviour m,
                    Transform from,
                    Transform to,
                    float time)
{
    m.transform.position = from.position;
    m.transform.rotation = from.rotation;

    m.StartCoroutine(Lerp(m.transform, to, time));
}
```

The signature of the method should look familiar. You're asking to **Lerp** something **from** one Transform **to** another over **time**. But if you're observant, you'll notice this isn't the only **Lerp** method in the class, and you can see that this method calls another **Lerp** method from within.

Look at the method signatures — the variables inside the parenthesis — and you'll see each one is different. This technique is called **Overloading** and is useful when you want different ways to carry out the same action.

It's a great way to keep your code DRY:

- Don't
- Repeat
- Yourself

The first Lerp in Tween is taking just the **from** and **to** variables, combining them with a fixed **duration** of one second, and calling the second Lerp method. The second Lerp method adjusts the **position** and **rotation** of the object you want to animate, to the same as **from**, and then calls the final Lerp method via a **Coroutine**.

Creating the Lerp function

> **Note**: You're going to use **Coroutines** and **IEnumerators** again here. If you want a quick refresher on them, please review the previous chapter.

As mentioned above, the third **Lerp** method in the **Tween** script is an **IEnumerator**, and this is where you will actually get your objects to move. Here's the code at present:

```
private static IEnumerator Lerp(Transform transform,
                                Transform target,
                                float time)
{
    yield return null;
}
```

The method takes three pieces of information:

1. A reference to the **Transform** you want to move.
2. Another reference **Transform** of where you want to move to.
3. An amount of **time** that you want the transition to last.

You're going to harness the power of the Coroutine to run the Lerp method over time, so the first thing you need to do is keep track of the time. Add the following to the method:

```
float elapsedTime = 0;
```

Next, add this:

```
Vector3 startPos = transform.position;
```

This saves the position that the object is initially starting from.

You now need to wrap all the code that will change values over time in a **loop**. Wrap the existing `yield return null;` statement in a `while` statement, like this:

```
while (elapsedTime < time)
{
    yield return null;
}
```

The `while` loop will execute *while* the elapsed time is less than the transition time. Putting the `yield` instruction inside the loop allows the rest of the game to continue running, and tells the system to come back to the coroutine in the next update.

At the moment, the `while` loop won't actually ever stop looping because you haven't updated `elapsedTime`. So to do that, add the following before the `yield` instruction:

```
elapsedTime += Time.deltaTime;
```

`Time.deltaTime` is a really useful Unity variable. It gives the amount of time that has passed between the previous frame and the current one. This allows you to make smooth calculations over time. By incrementing `elapsedTime` with this delta, `elapsedTime` will eventually reach the value of `time`, so the loop will exit.

Now, in order to actually *move* the object, you might have been worrying about some complex 3D vector math. Well, fear not! Unity has some nice built-in utility functions for you to use. You'll never guess the name of the one you're going to use. :]

Add this line inside the loop, above where you increment `elapsedTime`:

```
transform.position = Vector3.Lerp(startPos, target.position,
time);
```

All this lerping around is getting tedious.

Yes, yes. But would you rather have to write out the vector math?

If you hover over the `Vector3.Lerp` call, you'll see that it returns the value from a familiar equation.

> Vector3 Vector3.Lerp(Vector3 a, Vector3 b, float t)
> Linearly interpolates between two points.
>
> Returns:
>   Interpolated value, equals to a + (b - a) * t.

However, if you run this as it is now, it still won't work how you want it to. And that's because you're using the **time** value wrong.

Think back again to the earlier description of the Lerp function.

$$\text{lerp}(a, b, t) = a + \underbrace{(b - a)}_{\text{Distance from A to B}} * \underbrace{t}_{\text{Percentage}}$$

(Start)

Your *t* needs to be passed as a *percentage*. You'll need to calculate the percentage of time that has passed since you began your Lerp, and then move your object *that far* between *a* and *b*.

Over time, your object's position is going to move, so you need that reference to where it began in order to work out where it should be at any given *t*.

Change the **Vector3.Lerp** call to use a percentage of time.

```
transform.position = Vector3.Lerp(startPos,
                                  target.position,
                                  elapsedTime / time);
```

Finally, add the following to the bottom of the method, after the `while` loop:

```
transform.position = target.position;
```

Once the loop is finished, you make sure the position is set to the correct final position.

Phew, that was a lot. But don't worry — that's 90% of the coding you need to do for this chapter!

Dropping the veggies into the troughs

Save your changes and return to the Unity editor. Click **Play** and watch as the Veggies now fall into the troughs. Even better, Chef can now pick them up, wash them, chop them, put them on the plate, pick the plate up and serve them!

All that lerping around really paid off!

There's just one small issue left. The ingredients are all lying the same way in the troughs. And they, *ahem*, look a little dodgy when Chef picks them up.

The good news is that you can fix this with just three more lines of code.

Go back into **Tween** script again, and revisit the **Lerp IEnumerator**. Notice that you're passing **Transform**s into this method, which means that along with the position data, you also have access to the rotation data.

Below the line where you cached the startPos, add the following:

```
Quaternion startRot = transform.rotation;
```

Just as Vector3 has its own Lerp method, so does Quaternion. Following the Vector3.Lerp call, add the following line:

```
transform.rotation = Quaternion.Lerp(startRot,
                                     target.rotation,
                                     elapsedTime / time);
```

Finally, make sure the correct rotation is set at the end of the method, just after you set the final position.

```
transform.rotation = target.rotation;
```

Save your changes and return to the Unity editor.

Click **Play** once more and see how the animations come to life now as the veggies rotate and move between each interaction.

Congratulations! You just built your first tween library. And it's already been put to use in no less than 10 places throughout the game. This really shows the power and versatility of using such a library.

Setting up a basic animation

Sometimes you might want a very simple looping animation just to bring life to a scene. Take a look at the serving table in the scene. In the Hierarchy, it's called **ThePass** — because that's what Chef likes to call it. Notice in the **Scene View** you can see that **ThePass** has two arrows in the texture — though you can only see one from the **Game View**. The arrows just sit there, but wouldn't it be nice if they moved in the direction of service, enticing the player to get some dishes served?

This is the perfect example of setting up a simple looping animation using Unity's **Animation** component, and some basic keyframe set-up, too.

Introduction to the Animator component

Expand **ThePass** to reveal its children, and navigate down to the **Arrow** child GameObject.

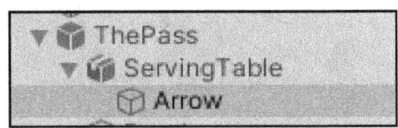

Have a look at the Inspector view for the Arrow GameObject. Notice that it has an **Animator** component already, but the **Controller** field doesn't have a value yet.

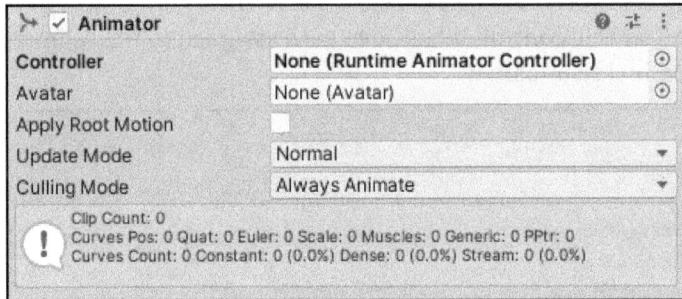

With the **Arrow** GameObject still selected, open the **Animation** window by selecting **Window ▸ Animation ▸ Animation** from the top menu. You'll see the following window open in the editor, prompting you to create a new **Animation Clip**.

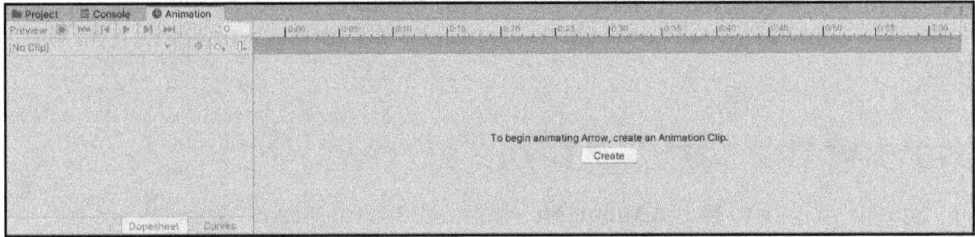

Click the **Create** button to create a new Animation Clip. Save it in the folder **Assets / RW / Animations** with the name **Arrows_Scroll**. Now go check that folder and see that two new files are in there — **Arrow.controller** was automatically created.

Double-click to open the file, and Unity will open the **Animator** window.

What you see here is an Animation Controller that calls the **Arrows_Scroll** Animation Clip that you just created. Select the **Arrow** GameObject in the Hierarchy again, and see that this controller has been auto assigned to the Animator component you looked at earlier.

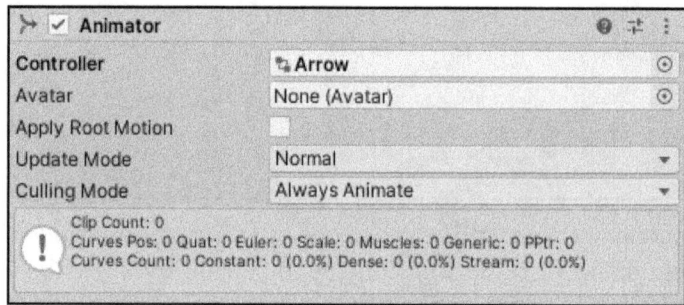

Great! Unity has done all the hard work for you. You'll learn more about the Animation Controller in the next chapter, but for the scrolling arrows this is all you need.

Moving the serving table arrows

OK, time to go back to that **Animation** window. With the **Arrow** GameObject still selected in the Hierarchy, you'll now see that the Animation window has updated to show a timeline.

It will also have your new **Arrows_Scroll** animation selected in the drop-down.

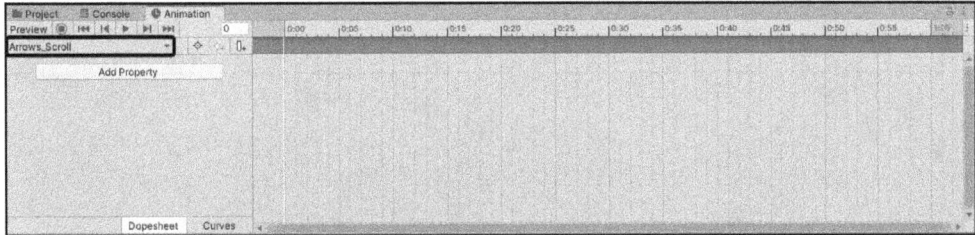

To animate the arrows texture on ThePass, you can use a very simple technique with the **Shader** on the **Material** — the **UV Offset**.

With the **Arrow** GameObject still selected, look in the Inspector and find the **Material** at the bottom of the view. Make sure it's expanded so you can see all the information there. Under the **Main Maps** section, you'll see two **Vector2** fields — one for **Tiling** and one for **Offset**.

Hover your mouse over the **Y** label for offset (not the number field, but the actual label), and notice the mouse pointer changes to a drag arrow. **Click and drag** slowly to the right, and you'll see the number start to change. Watch what happens to the texture of the **Arrow** GameObject in the **Scene View** as you do so.

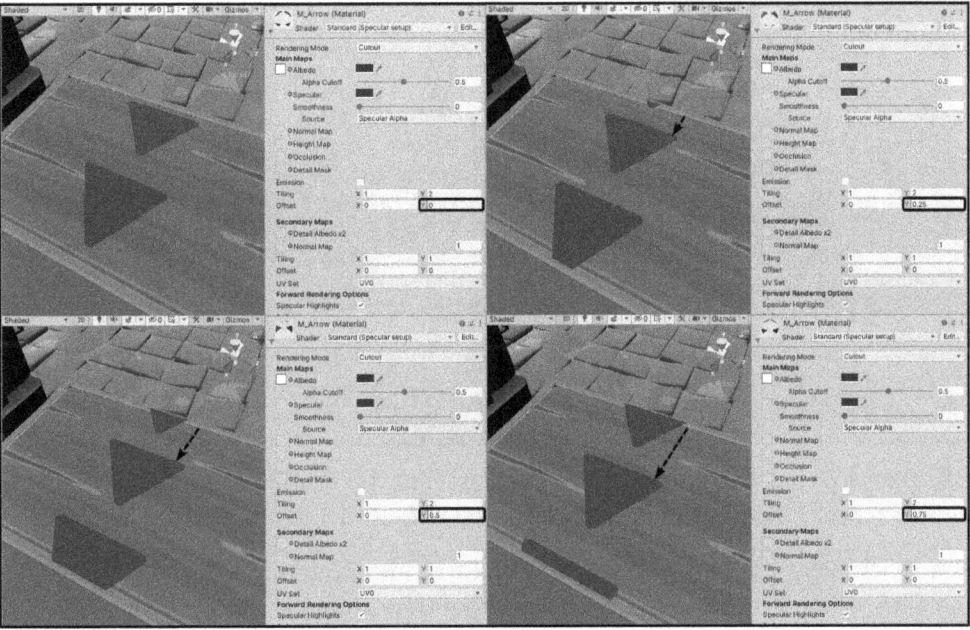

OK, so all you need to do is make the offset change automatically! Set the **Offset Y** back to **0**. Take a mental note of how it looks. Now set the **Offset Y** to **1**. How does it look now?

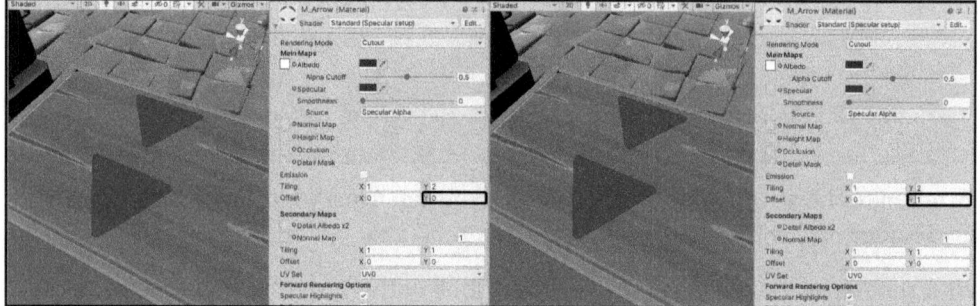

It looks as if nothing has changed. That's because the Arrow texture is a repeating texture. In fact, you can also see that the **Tiling Y** value is set to **2**. That's why you can see two arrows on ThePass. If you switch the **Tiling Y** to **1** you can see that it doesn't look very good.

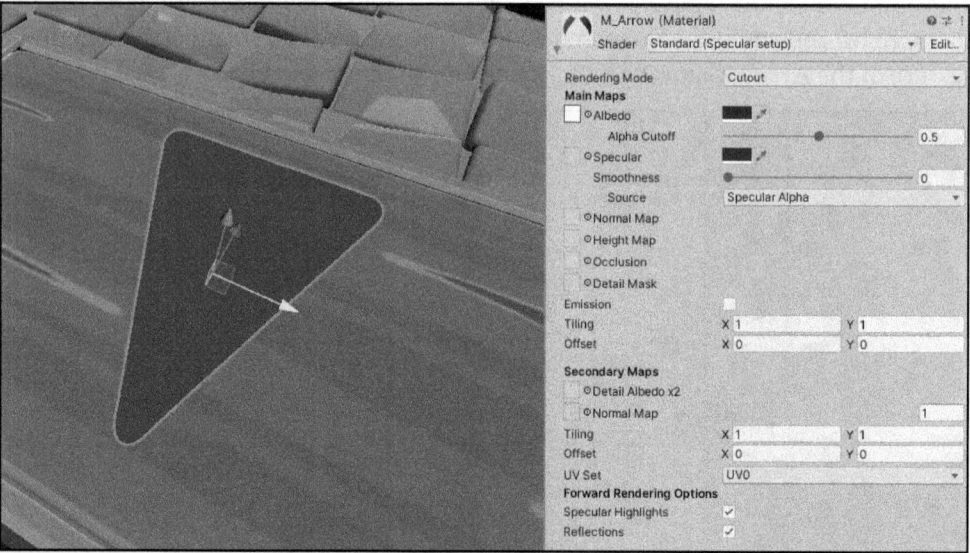

OK, time to put all this knowledge to good use. Put the **Tiling** and **Offset** back to how they began. **Tiling** should be **{ 1, 2 }**, and **Offset** should be **{ 0, 0 }**.

Head back over to the **Animation** window. **Click and drag** on the **Time Ruler** at the top of the window to place the **PlayHead** (that thin white line) at the **1:00** mark. This will also update the **Frame Counter** to **60**.

Then, click the **Record** button to prepare the Animation window for recording. Notice that the Timer Ruler and the Record button now highlight red to show you are in recording mode.

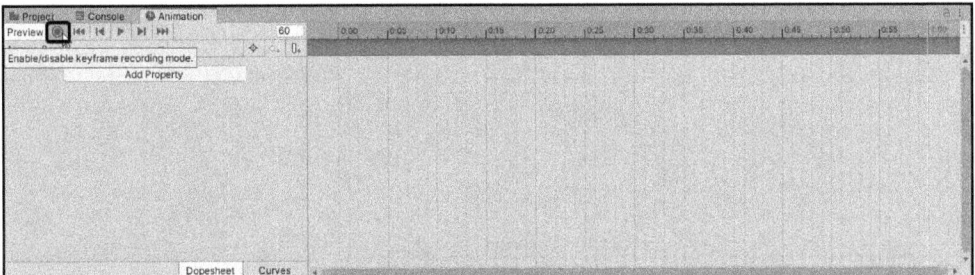

With the recording state active, go back to the material once more and change the **Offset Y** to **1**. Notice these fields are also highlighted in red to show that they are now part of the recording.

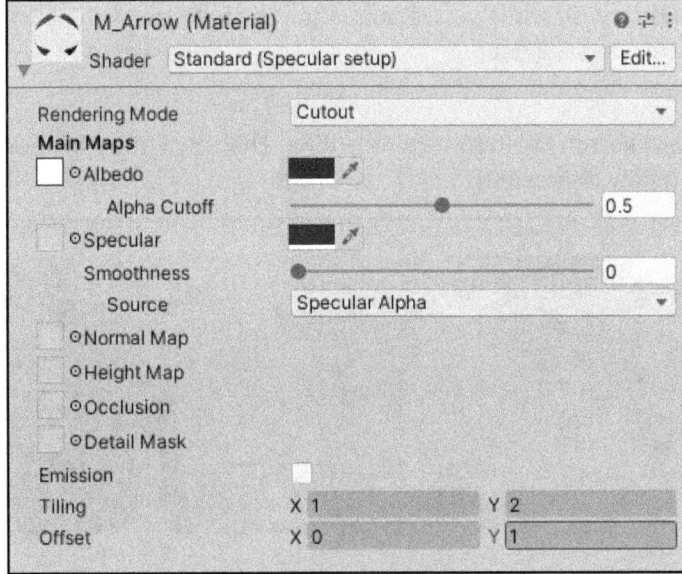

And if you check back over in the Animation Window, you can see these properties have now been added. Because you set the **Playhead** to the one-second mark earlier, you now have a **Keyframe** added at this position, with the values you just entered.

A keyframe has also automatically been created at the beginning of the animation, which holds the default values from the scene.

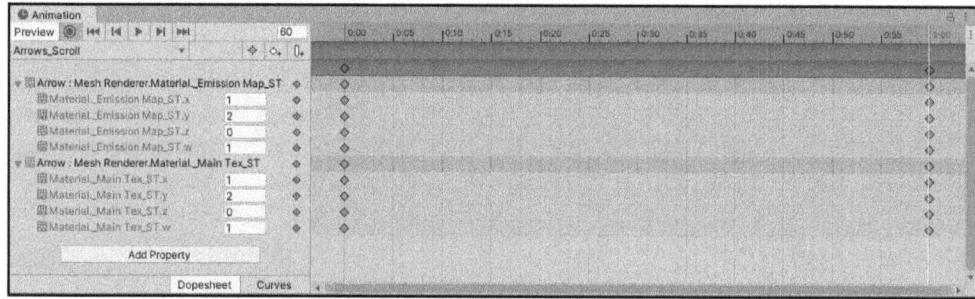

> **Note**: You can see that two properties have been added to the timeline, even though you only changed one value. That's because of the type of material used for the arrows. It's a **Specular** material, meaning it creates its own **Emissive** lighting. So while you're animating the texture, you're also animating the Emission Map.

Click the **Record** button again to stop recording. Then click the **Play** button in the **Animation** window to preview.

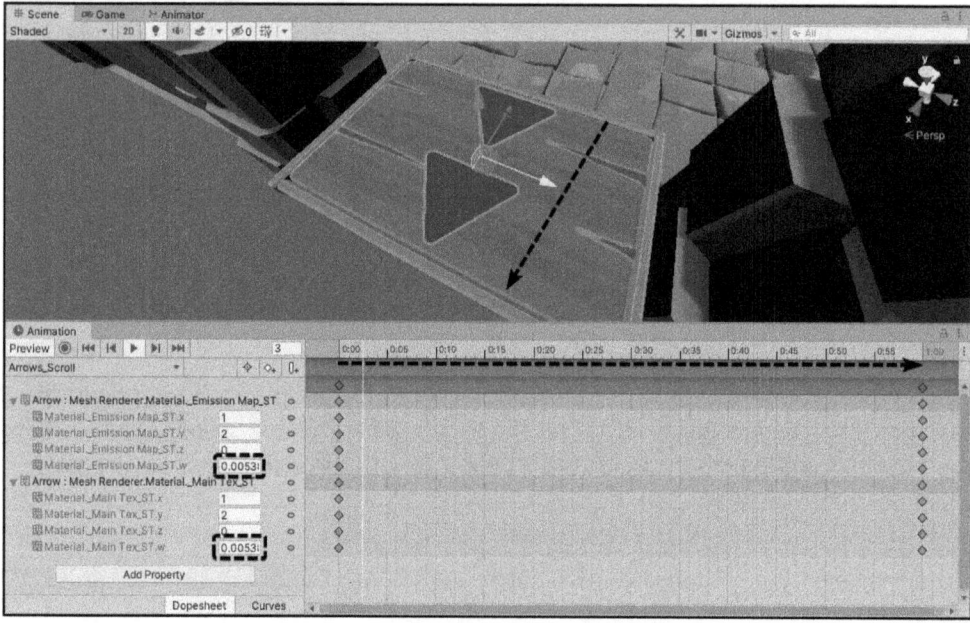

There you have it! Animating arrows. Only, it still doesn't look right, does it? That's because by default, the animation uses an **Ease In-Out** style. You need to change this to a **Linear** style so that it looks like a single, smooth, looping motion.

Modifying animation curves

It's time to take a look at the other view inside the **Animation** window. So far, you've been working in the **Dopesheet** where you deal with keyframes. Now you need to switch over to the **Curves** editor.

Click on the **Curves** tab at the bottom left of the **Animation** window. By default, you probably won't be able to see the curves very well.

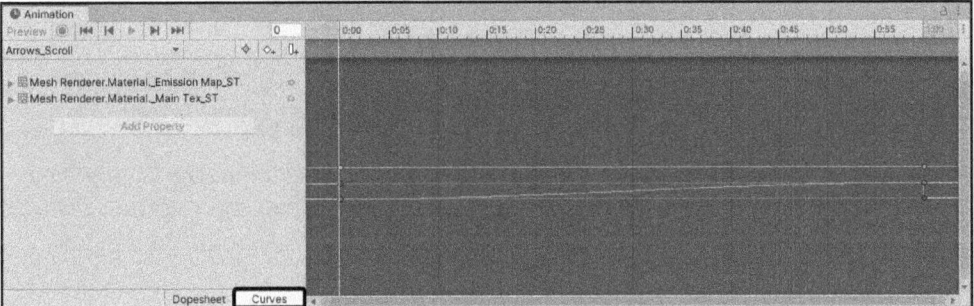

To see more clearly, expand the **Mesh Renderer.Material._Main Tex_ST** object and select the **w** value. Then, using the **mouse wheel** to zoom in, and **Shift + mouse wheel** to zoom in the vertical only, get yourself into a better position to see the curve for the animation.

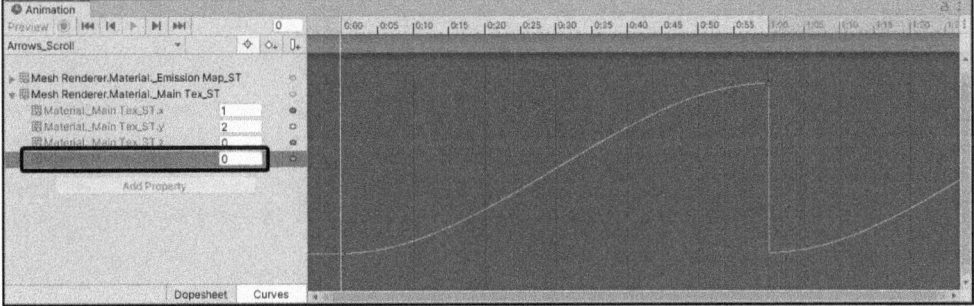

As you can see, the value change starts off slow, picks up pace and then slows down again as it reaches its final value — like a train pulling away from one station and slowing down into the next. This is known as **Ease In-Out**.

You can also see on the graph that there are still the key frames at zero and at one second. **Click** on the key at **1:00** and you'll see a handle appear. You can use these handles at any keyframe to manipulate how the curve looks. Double-clicking on the curve will also add new keyframes for you to manipulate. Right-clicking on a key will bring up a context menu. Use that to delete any extra keys you made, and then right-click on the keyframe at **1:00**. Select **Both Tangents ▸ Linear**.

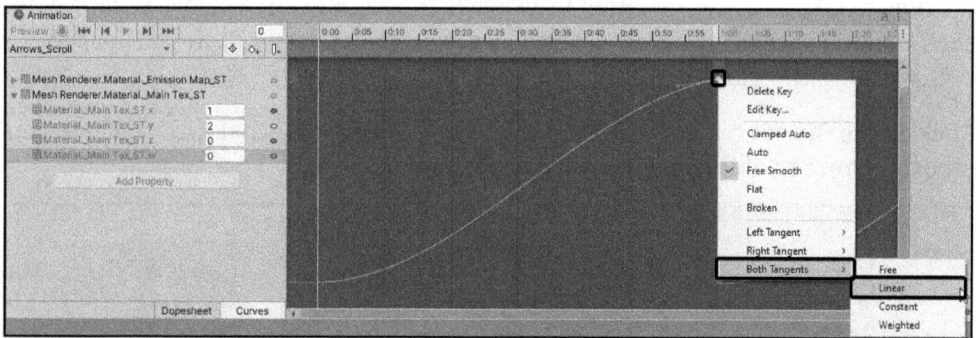

Now do the same with the first key frame and you'll end up with a straight line — a **Linear** animation. Once it's done, make sure the **Arrow** GameObject is still selected in the Hierarchy, and click the **Play** button once more in the **Animation** window.

You'll see the arrow texture looping steadily across the pass.

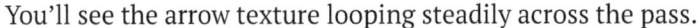

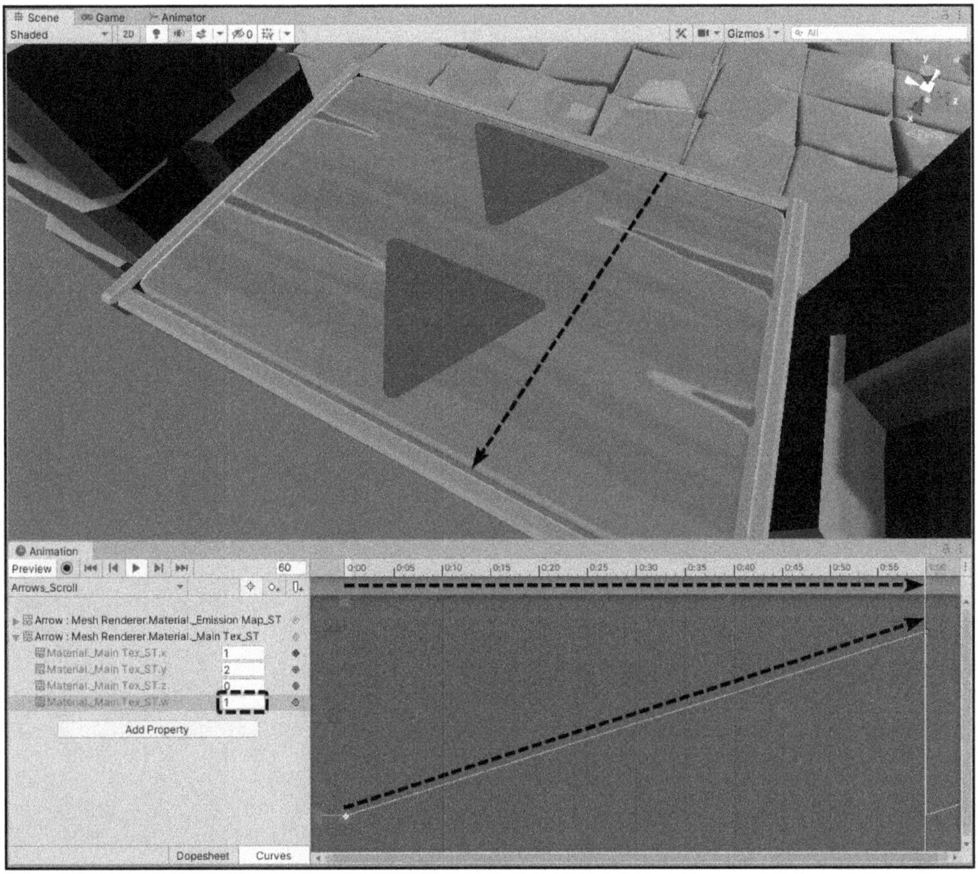

Marvelous. Chef can't wait to start serving those meals!

Key points

- Unity has many different ways to build animations.
- Always think about what approach is best for your situation.
- Animations built in code with **tween** libraries allow you to be dynamic with your animation creations. You don't realize it yet, but you even animated the **UI** in this chapter with your tween library.
- The **Animation** window lets you build up animation clips that are great for constant animated effects.
- The **Curve** editor lets you create all kinds of varied animations.

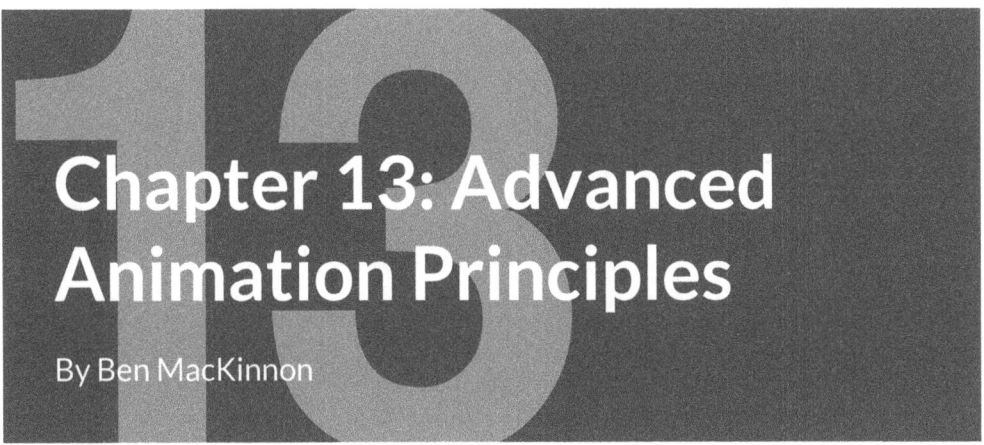

Chapter 13: Advanced Animation Principles
By Ben MacKinnon

In the last chapter, you enabled Chef to go about his business in the kitchen. With the help of the tween library, ingredients drop into the trough now. Chef can pick them up, wash them, chop them, place them on the plate and serve them.

But Chef himself is stuck in the same pose throughout.

Fortunately, Chef came prepared with his own set of animations!

Open the starter project for this chapter, then open the **Kitchen** scene from **Assets / RW / Scenes**.

Take a look in **Assets / RW / 3D / Chef / Animations** and you'll find a collection of animations that were imported with the 3D model. Click the arrow to expand one of them, then select the icon that looks like a **moving triangle**.

You'll be able to play a preview of the animation in the Inspector window.

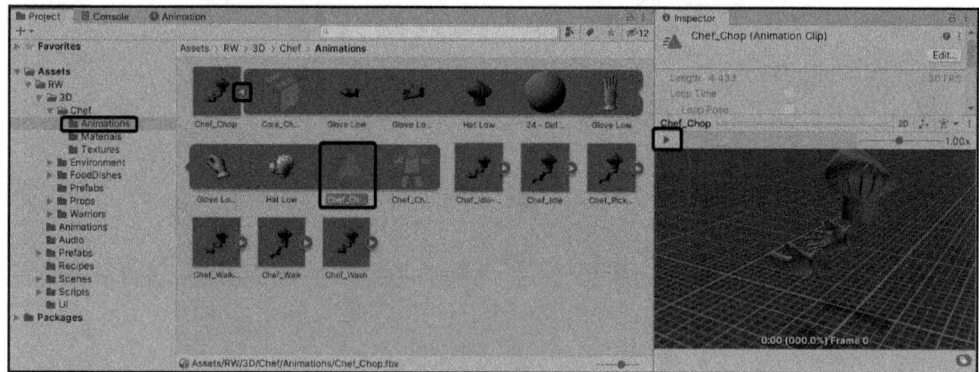

You have animations for all the following states:

- Chop
- Idle
- Idle-Hold
- Pick Up
- Walk
- Walk-Hold
- Wash

In this chapter, you'll learn how to build up an animation state system using the **Animator Component**, including how to transition between states, and different ways to trigger the transitions.

Animator component

In the previous chapter, you created an **animator controller** for the arrow scrolling animation. It triggered the scrolling animation, which remained in the same state forever. However, the animator controller is a lot more powerful than that.

If you recall, the animator for the arrows looked like this:

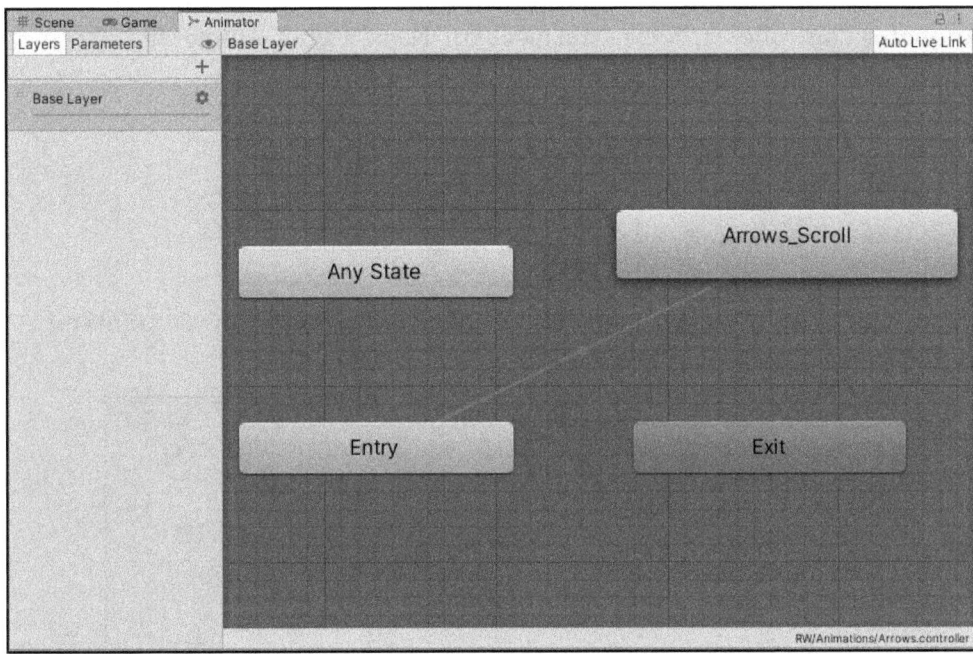

By the end of this chapter, you will have created an animator that looks like this:

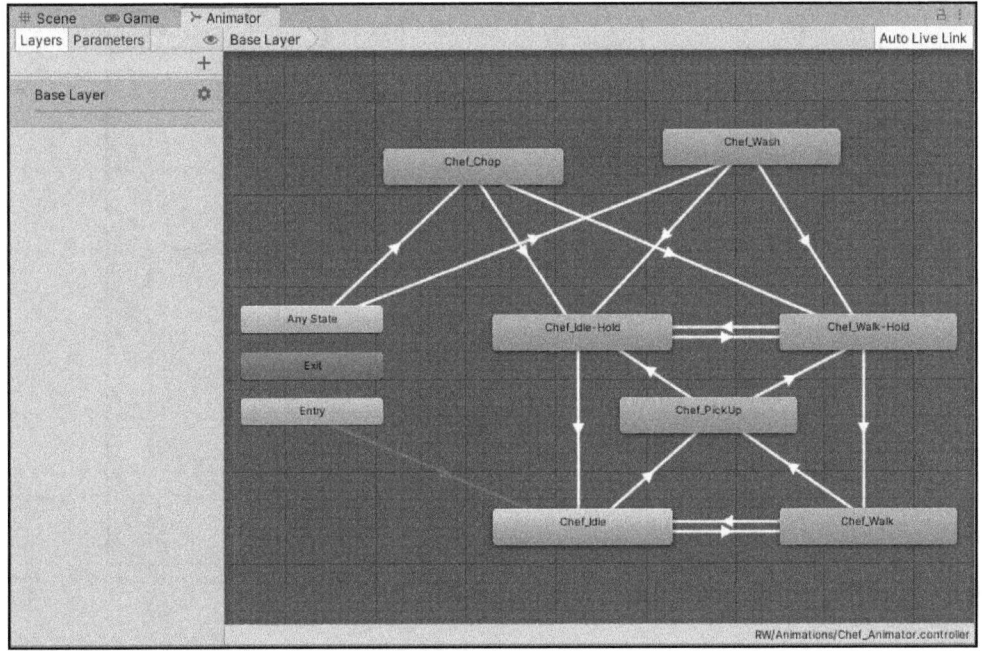

First things first. You need to create the new animator controller. Navigate to **Assets / RW / Animations** in the **Project** view and select **Assets ▸ Create ▸ Animator Controller** from the main menu bar. Name it **Chef_Animator**.

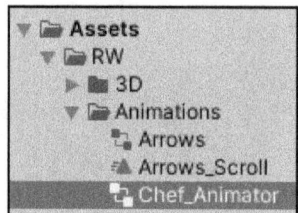

Then, in the Hierarchy view, assign this new animator controller to the **Animator** component on Chef under **Player / Chef**.

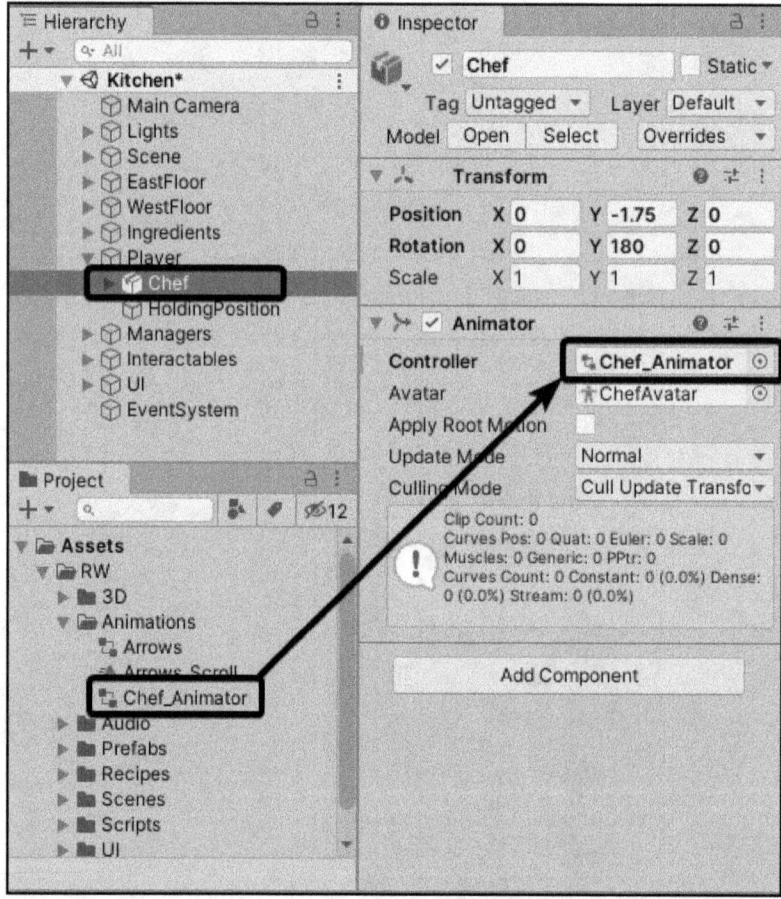

Save the scene. Chef is now ready to be animated.

Importing the animations as states

The animator controller is currently empty. Well, it has three default states: **Entry**, **Exit** and **Any State** (depending on your editor layout, you might have to zoom out a bit to see all three). These states alone don't provide any animations. So the first task is to create some states that Chef *does* need.

Double-click the **Chef_Animator** to open it in the **Animator** window. Then right-click inside the grid area to bring up the context menu and select **Create State ▸ Empty**.

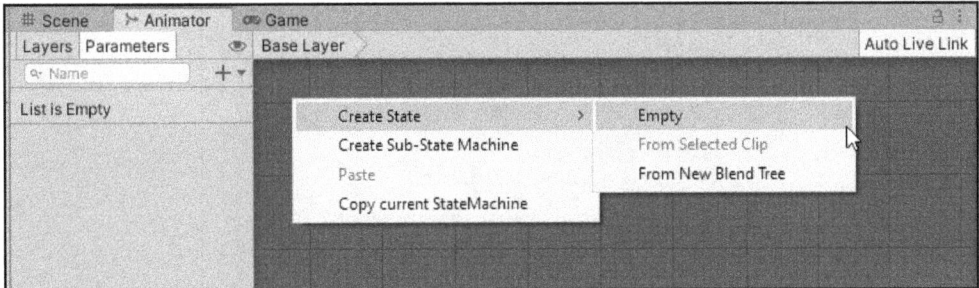

The new state will be created and will automatically become the default state. It highlights in orange to show this, with an arrow coming from the **Entry** state to the new one. Rename the new state **Chef_Idle** and assign the **Chef_Idle** clip to the **Motion** parameter.

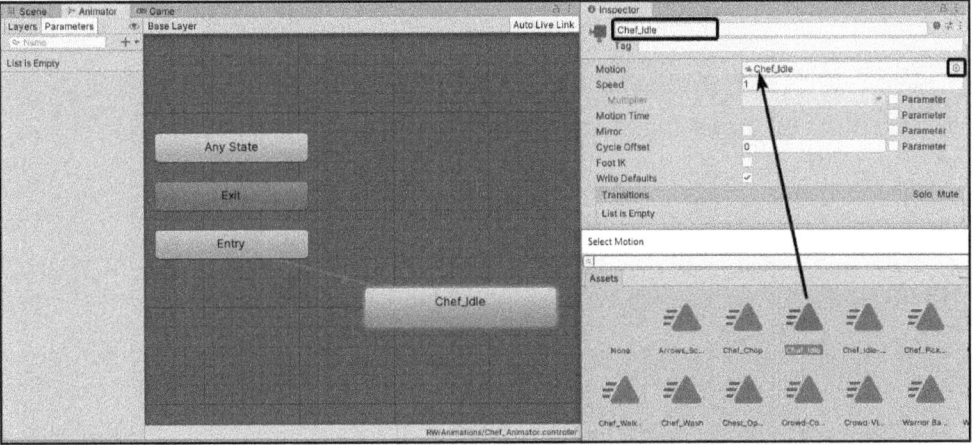

This is already enough to animate Chef! Click **Play** and you can see that Chef now bobs up and down a little while he waits on you as you set up the rest of the animator.

There are a lot of animations to set up, so it's time for a shortcut. You may have recognized the icons in the last step as those you took a peek at in the beginning of this chapter. That little dashing triangle is the symbol for an **Animation Clip**, and rather than creating new states and then assigning clips, you can bring clips directly into the Animator window.

Navigate to the **Project** view and use the filter button to filter for **Animation Clip**.

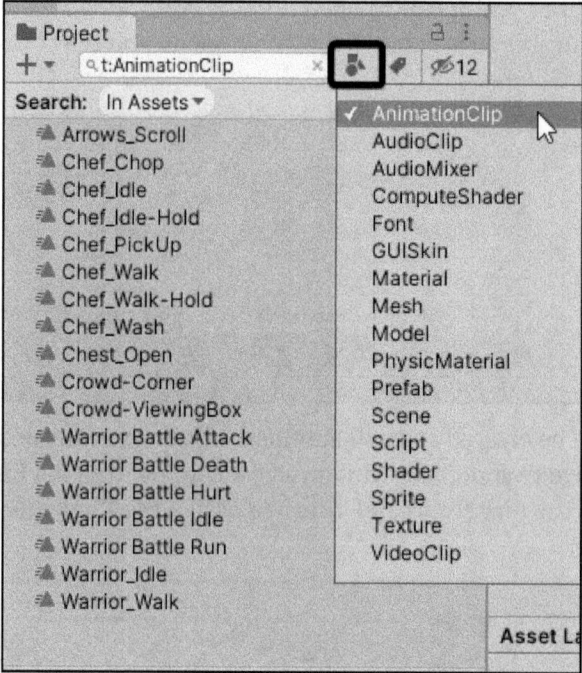

Now select the following clips and drag them into the **Animator** window:

- Chef_Idle-Hold
- Chef_PickUp
- Chef_Walk
- Chef_Walk-Hold

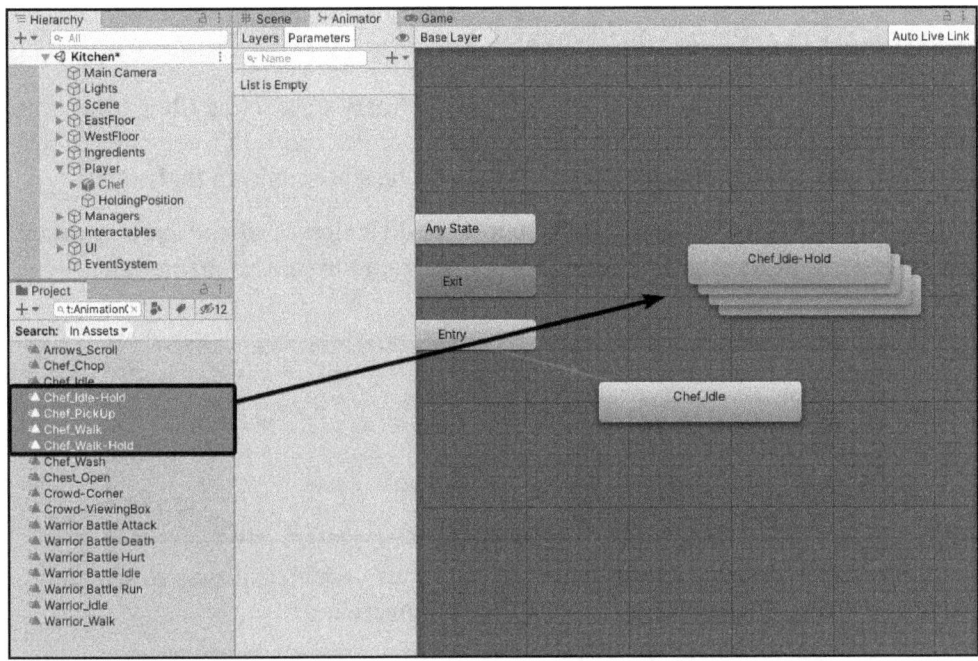

This creates new states — already named and with the animation clips already assigned.

Space out the new states so that you can see them better. Make a X shape with them, with **Chef_Walk** to the right of **Chef_Idle** and **Chef_Idle-Hold** and **Chef_Walk-Hold** above them. Put **Chef_PickUp** in the middle of them all.

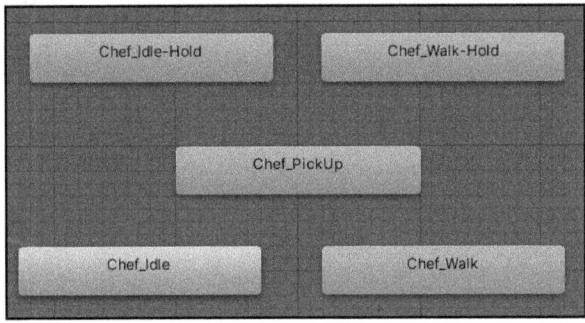

Now you have the beginning of an animation system. It's time to get Chef moving!

Animator transitions

Notice there's already a transition arrow from the **Entry** state to the **Chef_Idle** state. In order for the state to change throughout the animator controller, you need to set up **transitions** in each possible direction so that one state could go to the next.

In order to make a new transition, all you have to do is right-click the state you want to transition from, then select **Make Transition** from the context menu that appears.

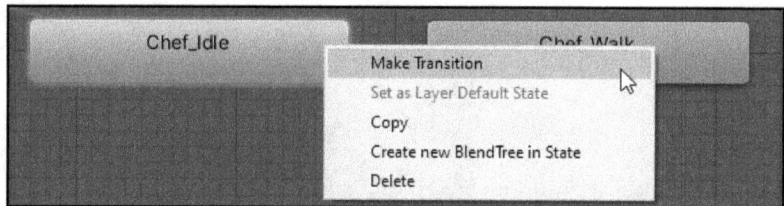

You'll then have an arrow line attached to your mouse, which will snap to any state you hover over. Left-click the state you want to transition to.

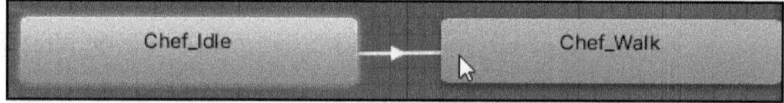

To start with, right-click **Chef_Idle** and select **Make Transition**, then hover over **Chef_Walk** and left-click it to select the transition destination.

Once you've created the transition, left-click on the arrow to bring up a preview of the animation in the Inspector.

You'll see all the settings associated with the transition, as well as a preview of how the two animations blend together.

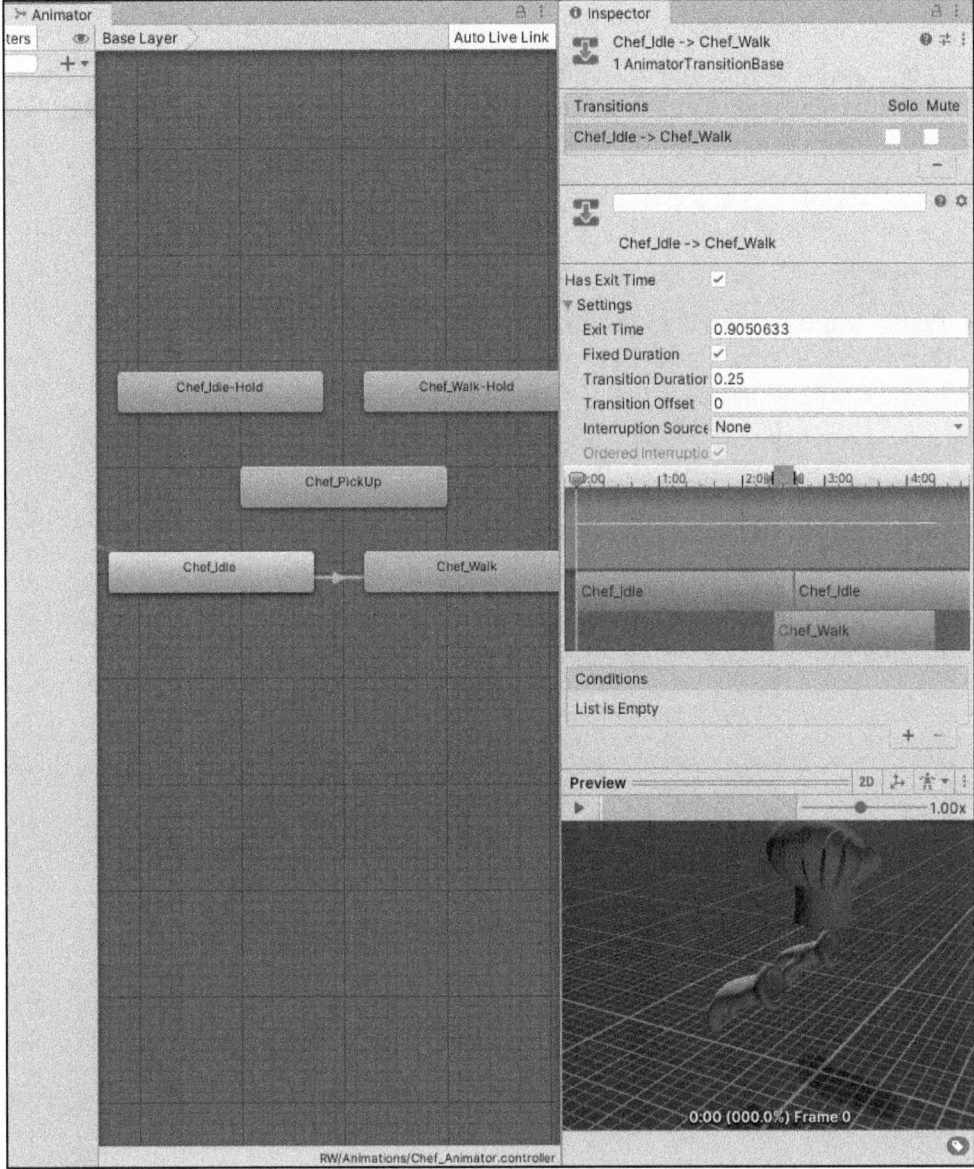

Take a look at what each of the settings does:

- **Has Exit Time** is used when you automatically want a state to end and move to the next state.

- **Exit Time** is the time the previous state must have played before the next state is evaluated. For example, you may want a player to finish their jump animation before they can move into an attack animation.

- **Fixed Duration** If this is checked, then **Transition Duration** is evaluated as seconds. If it's unchecked, then the transition is evaluated as a fraction (0-1) of the animation.

- **Transition Duration** is controlled by **Fixed Duration**. It's represented on the timeline as the area between the two blue markers.

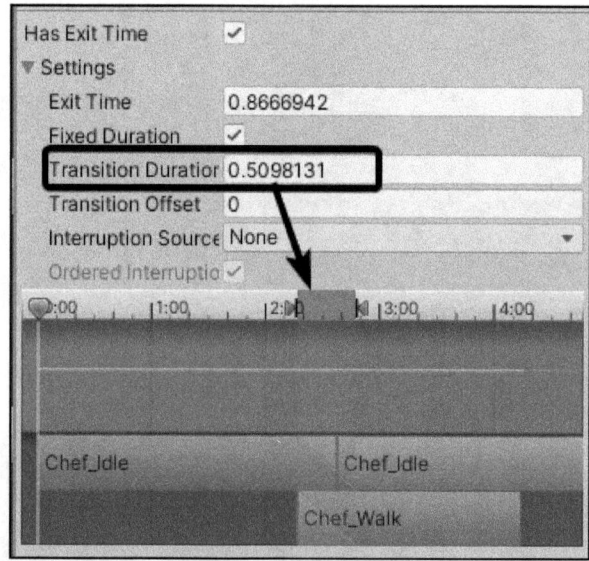

- **Transition Offset** is the offset of the animation that the next state should start at. For example, setting this to 0.5 would make the animation start half way through its clip.

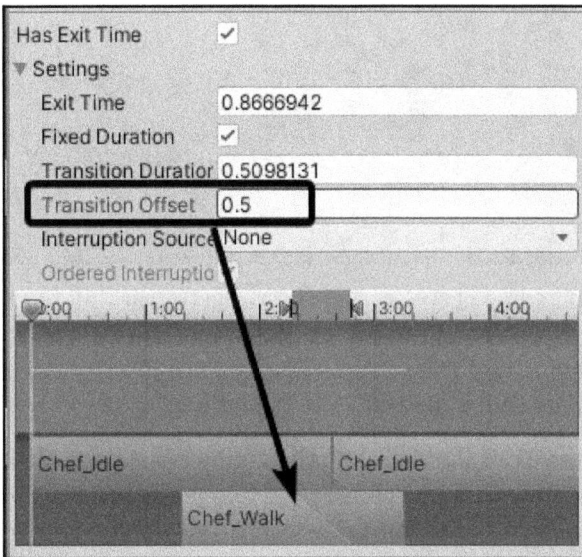

- **Interruption Source** comes into play on the occasion that more than one state could possibly transition to the next. Using the interruption source, you can dictate the priority of animation states. However, states that transition from **Any State** will always be added first in the queue.

With all that in mind, it's time to build some transitions! Get ready, because there are a few steps to complete here. The first step is to create each transition you need.

1. You should already have a transition from **Chef_Idle** to **Chef_Walk** from earlier.

2. Add a transition in the other direction — from **Chef_Walk** back to **Chef_Idle**.

3. Repeat these steps with the **Hold** states, with transitions going back and forth between **Chef_Idle-Hold** and **Chef_Walk-Hold**.

4. When Chef puts something down, he needs to return to the Idle/Walk state. Add a transition from **Chef_Idle-Hold** back to **Chef_Idle**.

5. And another from **Chef_Walk-Hold** to **Chef_Walk**.

Once you've completed all these steps, your animation state map will look like this:

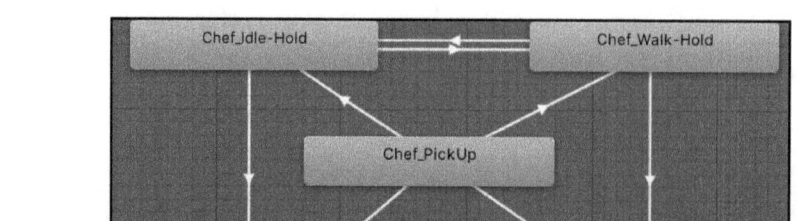

Now it's time to edit some of the settings for these transitions. Each of these state changes, with the exception of the two coming out of **Chef_PickUp**, are going to be triggered by user input, and you want them to happen instantly. Go through each of the transitions and **uncheck** the **Has Exit Time** field.

Finally, you want the **Chef_PickUp** state to happen the second the user presses the **space bar**. As such, you want any previous state to be interrupted by the **Chef_PickUp** state. Change the following transitions to have **Interruption Source** set to **Next State**.

1. **Chef_Idle-Hold** to **Chef_Idle**

2. **Chef_Walk-Hold** to **Chef_Walk**

3. **Chef_Idle** to **Chef_Walk**

4. **Chef_Walk** back to **Chef_Idle**

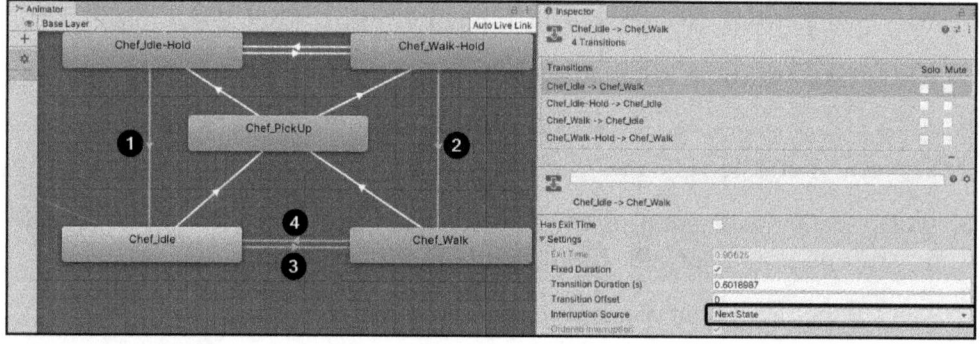

This way, no matter what state the player is in, when they press **Space** to pick up something, the **Chef_PickUp** animation will play instantly. These decisions on how to prepare the settings of an animator controller are key to making your gameplay as responsive as possible.

Speaking of responsive, you have so far set up the *how* of animation transitions. But before it can be tested, you need to set up the *when* and *why*.

Animator parameters

In order to change the states in your animation, you need a way for the user input that's already captured in code to be passed to the animator controller. As you know from the previous chapter, there's already code in here to make Chef walk around and pick up ingredients. So all you need to do is add a connection from those pieces of code to the animator controller.

The first thing you'll need is a way to transition between the walking and idle states. In the **Animator** window, click the **Parameters** tab, and then click the + button.

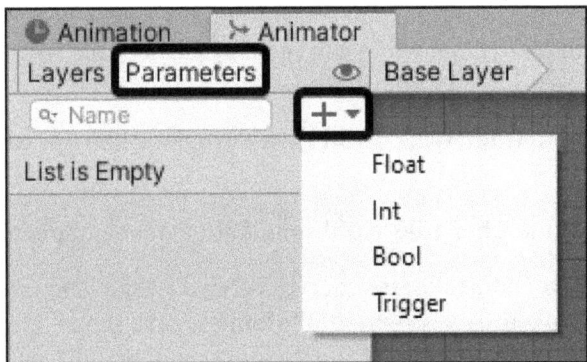

As you can see, there are a few options available here. The first three are value-related parameters: **float**, **int** and **bool**. These can be set from code, so long as there is a reference to the **animator** component. You'll get to the last trigger in the next section.

Float Condition

Add a **float** parameter and call it **Speed**. Then, select the transition between **Chef_Idle** and **Chef_Walk**. In the Inspector, find the **Conditions** list and add a new condition. The new **Speed** parameter will be selected by default. Set the value to **Greater** than **0.1**.

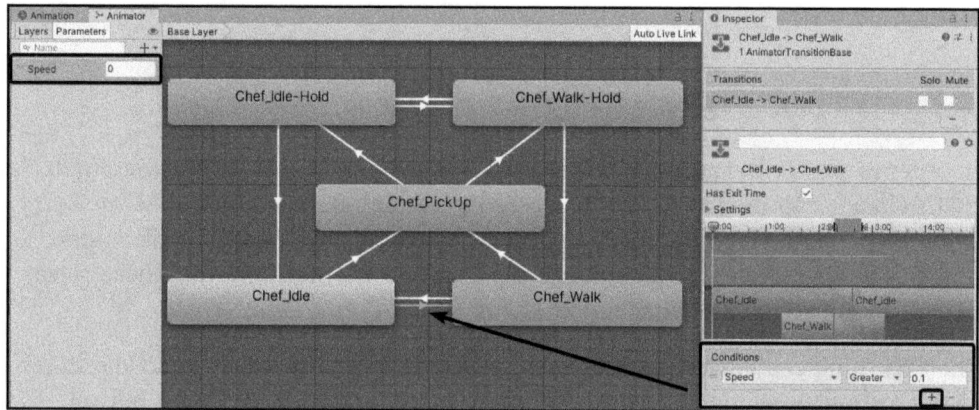

Now, select the reverse transition, and add the condition again — but this time set the value to **Less** than **0.1**. And while you're here, do the same with the transitions between **Chef_Idle-Hold** and **Chef_Walk-Hold**.

1. **Chef_Idle-Hold** to **Chef_Walk-Hold** should trigger when **Speed** is **Greater** than **0.1**.

2. **Chef_Walk-Hold** to **Chef_Idle-Hold** should trigger when **Speed** is **Less** than **0.1**.

Now that the animator controller is set up to receive a value and trigger transitions, all that's left is to have the code send that information to the animator controller.

In the Hierarchy, select the **Player** object and take a look at the **PlayerController** component.

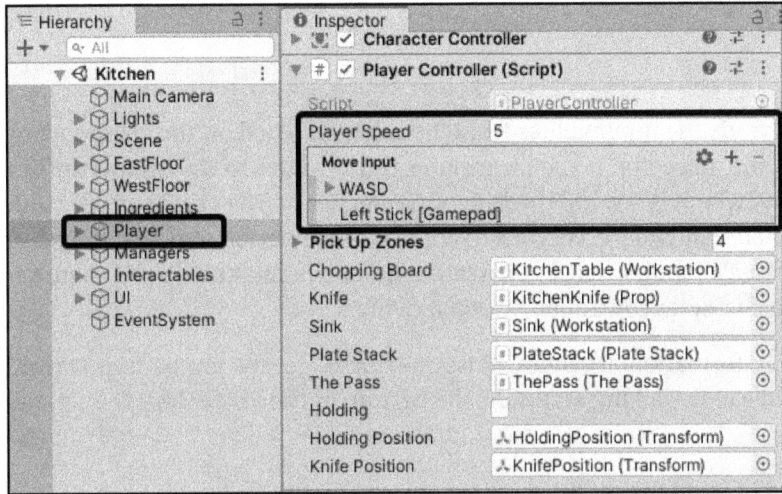

You can see at the top of this component are two values of interest.

1. **Player Speed**: A **float** value.

2. **Move Input**: An **InputAction** that defines the controls to move Chef.

Open the **PlayerController** script, and navigate down to the **FixedUpdate** method:

```
private void FixedUpdate()
{
    if (moveInput.enabled)
    {
        Vector3 move =
            new Vector3(-moveInput.ReadValue<Vector2>().y,
                0,
                moveInput.ReadValue<Vector2>().x);
        if (move.magnitude > 0.01f)
        {
            Vector3 targetForward =
                Vector3.RotateTowards(transform.forward,
                    move,
                    6.238f *
Time.fixedDeltaTime,
                    2);
            controller.Move(playerSpeed
                * Time.fixedDeltaTime
                * move);
            transform.forward = targetForward;
        }
        else
```

```
            {
                controller.Move(Vector3.zero);
            }
        }
    }
```

This code reads the input values from the controls listed on the component that you can see in the inspector. It then translates those values to the **Character Controller** component, which is also on the **Player** GameObject. The character controller has a Move method that takes a **Vector3** to control the direction in which the player should move. If there's input, a value is passed to that Move method. And if there's no input, it tells the character controller to stop moving.

Using this information, it requires just one line to get the animations transitioning between Idle and Walking states. At the bottom of the **FixedUpdate** method, add this line:

```
animator.SetFloat("Speed",
                  controller.velocity.magnitude / playerSpeed);
```

Take a look at what's happening here:

1. `animator` is a reference to the animator component.

2. `SetFloat` is a method that allows you to set values for parameters in the animator controller.

3. `"Speed"` is the parameter you set up earlier.

4. `controller.velocity.magnitude / playerSpeed` is a way for you to calculate how much the player is moving.

OK, so there may have been a small white lie there. There's a *little* extra code required, and that is to set up the `animator` reference.

Scroll up to the top of the **PlayerController** class. Underneath the declaration for the **CharacterController**, you need to add a new reference for an **animator** component.

```
private Animator animator;
```

Then, scroll down to the Start method. There, you'll see that the **CharacterController** reference is assigned. Below that, add this line to assign the reference for the new **animator**.

```
animator = GetComponentInChildren<Animator>();
```

Save your script and head back to the Unity editor. Click **Play** and walk around in the scene. You'll see Chef's hat start to bob from side to side as he walks around. Select **Player** / **Chef** in the Hierarchy with the **Animator** window open, and you'll be able to see the animation states transition in real time. Since you added a threshold of **0.1** for **Speed**, this transition will only happen when Chef moves fast enough!

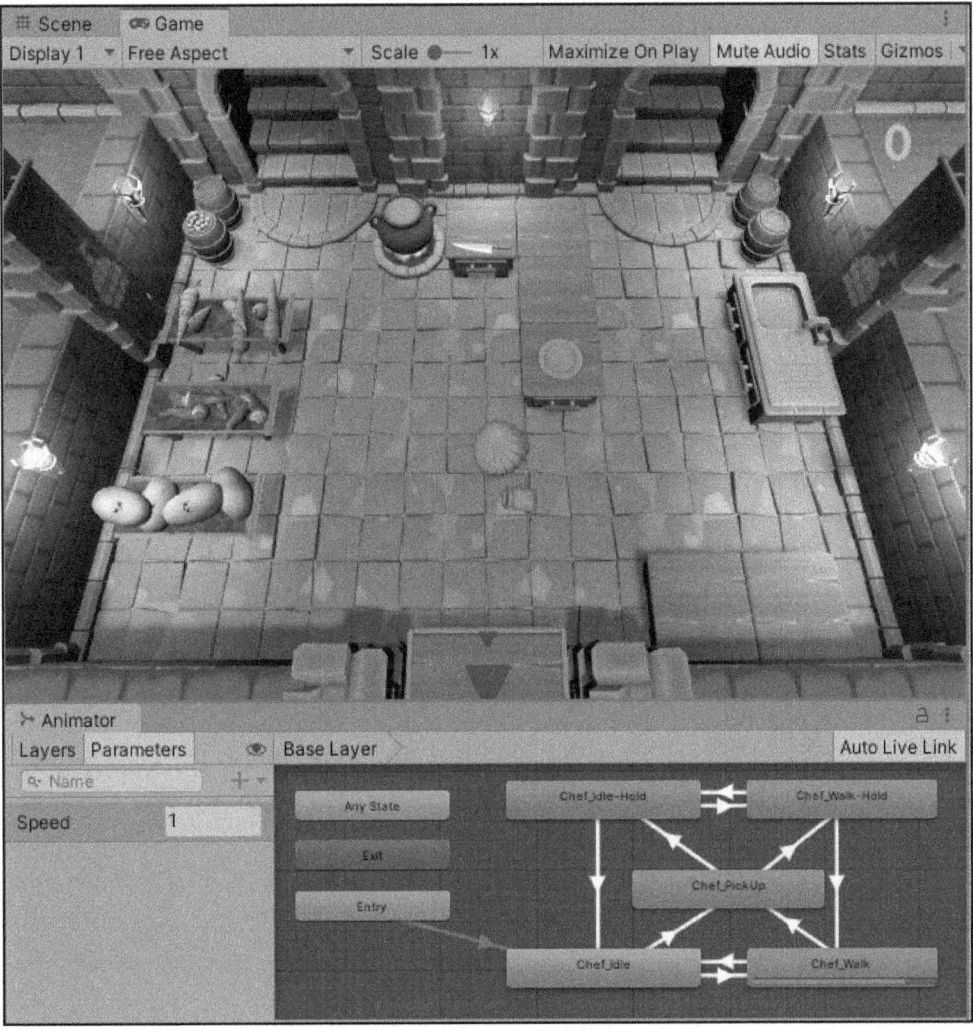

Boolean Condition

Now that you've seen how to set up parameters and transition conditions, and how to change them from the game code, it's a straightforward process to toggle Chef's holding animations.

Head back into **Animator** window and make sure you have stopped the game. **Add** a new **parameter** — this time a **bool** named **Holding**.

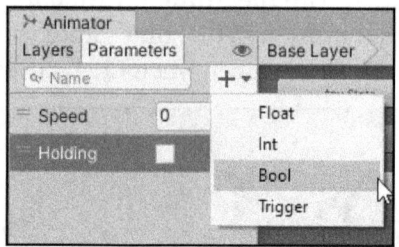

It's set to **false** by default, which is what you want. Now, you need to set up the conditions that are affected by this new parameter. Add conditions to the following transitions:

1. **Chef_Idle** to **Chef_PickUp** should trigger when **Holding** is **true**.
2. **Chef_Walk** to **Chef_PickUp** should trigger when **Holding** is **true**.
3. **Chef_Idle-Hold** to **Chef_Idle** should trigger when **Holding** is **false**.
4. **Chef_Walk-Hold** to **Chef_Walk** should trigger when **Holding** is **false**.

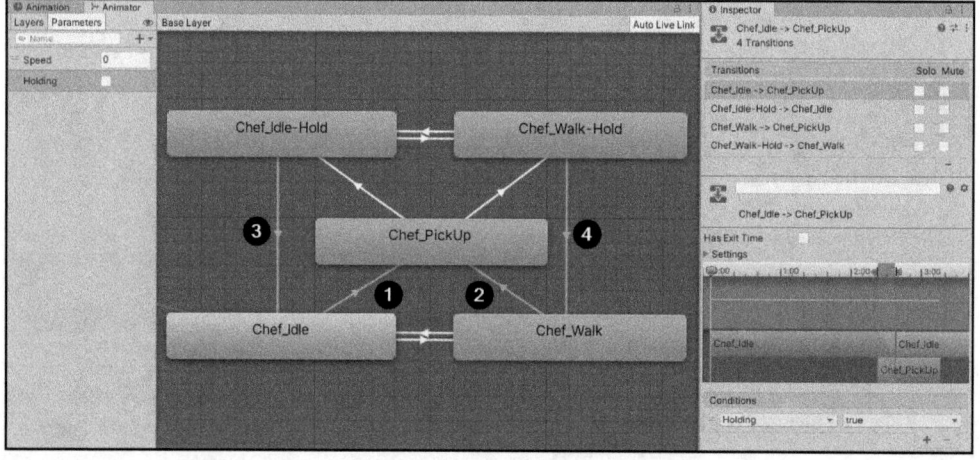

> **Note:** Remember that where a transition has a condition, **Has Exit Time** should be **unchecked** in the settings.

With the conditions set up, it's time to get back into the code to trigger the changes. Open the **PlayerController** script once more. As you know, Chef is already programmed to pick up ingredients, wash them, chop them, put them on a plate, pick up the plate and put it on ThePass. At the top of the PlayerController class, you'll find a number of variables that help control all of these states. This one is of particular interest:

```
// state for holding something or not
[SerializeField]
private bool holding;
```

This **bool** is already set up to switch states depending on if Chef is holding a plate, an ingredient or nothing at all. In your code editor, right-click the variable **holding** and select **Find All References**. Doing so will show that the state changes at **four** points in the code.

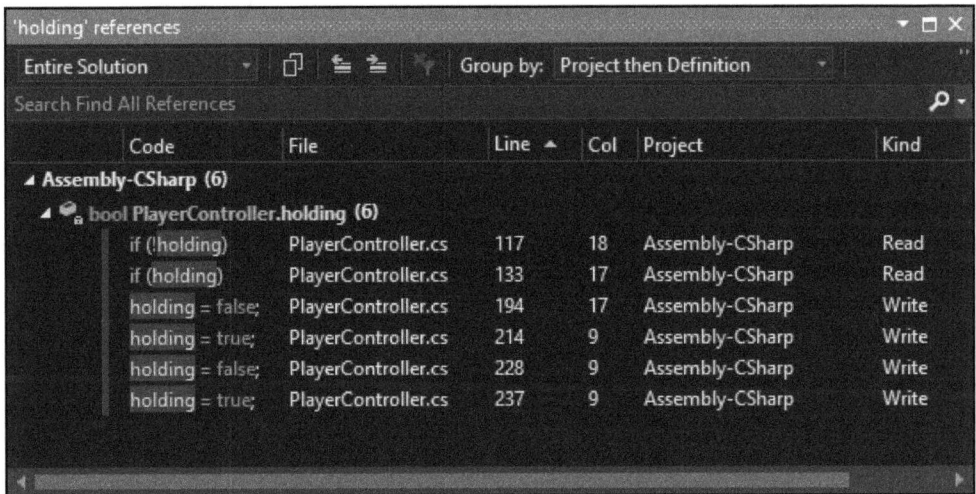

> **Note:** If your code editor doesn't have this option, you can always just use **Find** to find where these lines are.

Click each of the references where the **holding** variable gets set to **true/false**. There should be an empty line after each left for you to add in the following statement:

```
animator.SetBool("Holding", holding);
```

As before, this line is passing a variable over to your animator controller:

1. `animator` is the reference to the animator component.
2. `SetBool` is a method that allows you to set values to parameters in the animator controller.
3. `"Holding"` is the parameter in the animator controller that you added earlier.
4. `holding` is passing the current state from code.

> **Note:** You've added this four times already. If you have trouble finding them, they were in the following methods:
>
> `CheckPass` - inside the second `if` statement.
>
> `TakeIngredient` - before the final call to `ToggleMovement();`.
>
> `SetIngredient` - as the final line of the method.
>
> And `TakePlate` - again as the final line of the method.

Save the script and head back to the Unity editor. Click **Play** once more and go to pick up an ingredient using the space bar.

Chef's hand will now animate to grab those ingredients ready for preparing delicious meals for the Veggie Warriors!

Animator triggers

The Chef animations are almost complete. But if you remember from when you first looked at them, you have two more that have yet to even be added to the animator controller. Chef needs to be able to **Wash** and **Chop** the ingredients. Unlike the walk and holding states though, these are actions that are triggered and then play out for a set duration. This is where the **Trigger** parameter and **Has Exit Time** come into play.

But first, you need to add these animations to the animator controller. Find the **Chef_Chop** and **Chef_Wash** animations using the same trick as earlier, and **drag** them onto the **Animator** window. Space them out near the top of the existing graph.

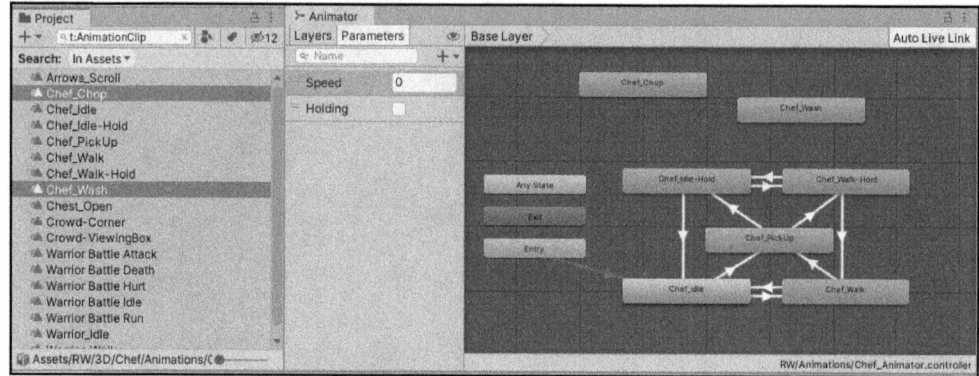

The player will trigger these animations by pressing the **Ctrl** key when near the sink or chopping board. In either case, it doesn't really matter what animation state Chef was in — you need him to transition to washing or chopping right away. This is the reason for the **Any State** state.

Add two new transitions from **Any State** to the new **Chef_Chop** and **Chef_Wash** states.

When Chef is finished washing or chopping, he takes the ingredient back into his hands. So, you need transitions going from the new states back to the holding states. Add four more transitions:

1. From **Chef_Chop** to **Chef_Idle-Hold**.

2. From **Chef_Chop** to **Chef_Walk-Hold**.

3. From **Chef_Wash** to **Chef_Idle-Hold**.

4. And from **Chef_Wash** to **Chef_Walk-Hold**.

Then final graph will look like this:

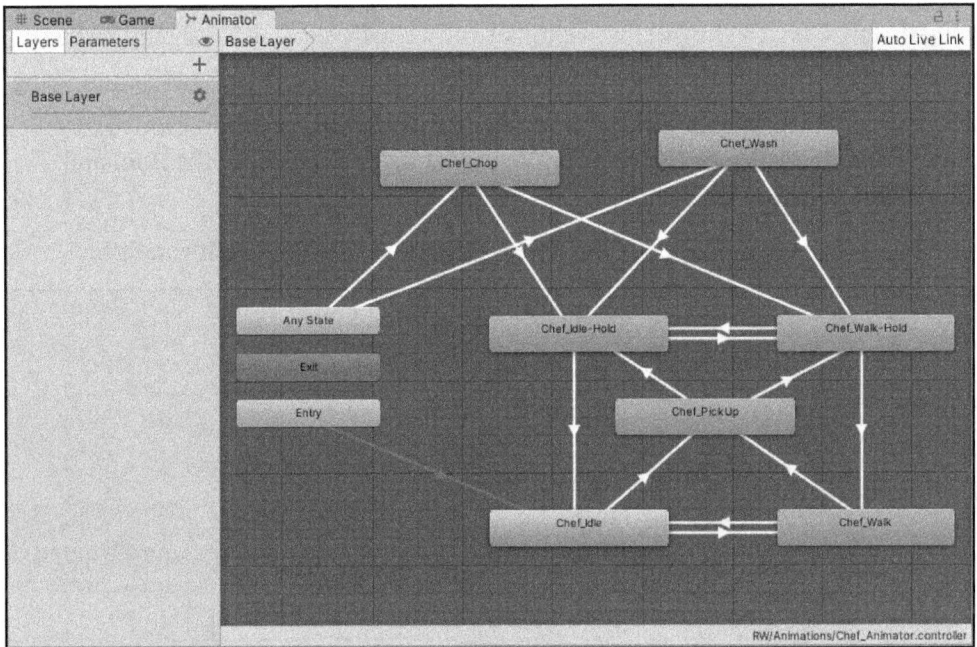

New transitions have **Has Exit Time** checked by default, so you don't need to change any of the settings for the transitions coming out of **Chef_Wash** and **Chef_Chop**. This means the wash and chop animations will play their duration, and then return to the Chef holding animations.

But you do still need to set up how the wash and chop states are triggered. For this you need two new parameters. Add two new parameters in the **animator**. Both should be **triggers**. Name them **Wash** and **Chop**.

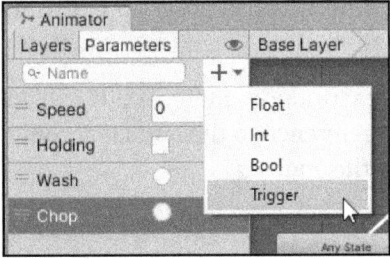

Triggers work differently than the other parameter types. They are for one-shot settings. When the trigger is set on, a transition using that trigger will take place immediately. The trigger will then automatically be off, ready to fire again. This is perfect for the actions you need to create here.

For the **Any State** to **Chef_Chop** transition, add the **Chop** condition. Notice that there is no other value or choice after the trigger like there was for the **Bool** and **Float** conditions you used earlier.

Similarly, for the **Any State** to **Chef_Wash** transition, add the **Wash** condition.

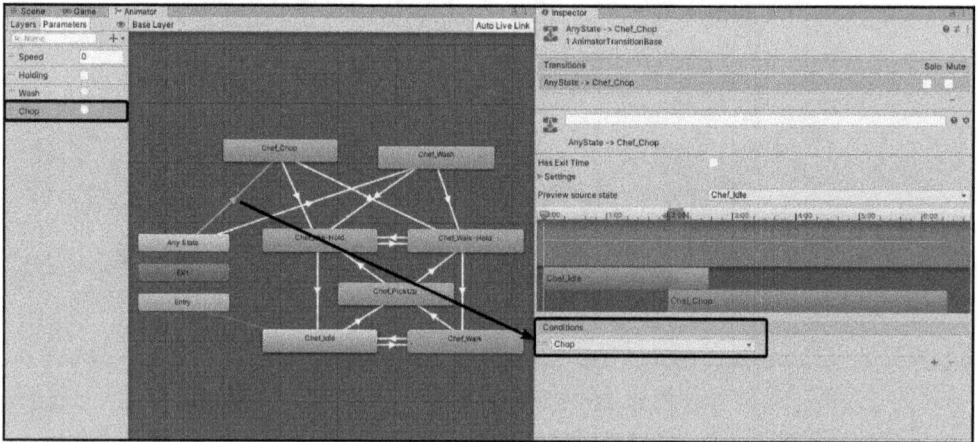

Now you know what's coming next. It's time to add some code to trigger the triggers!

This time however, you'll do something a little different. You have two state transitions that need to be triggered from code, and each needs to be triggered from a different action. You *could* write some code around each of these actions in the player controller. However, the sink and the chopping board each already have a component called **Workstation** which exposes an **OnInteract** event in the inspector. You use this to trigger the animations when Chef interacts with these workstations.

Open the **PlayerController** script once more. You'll still add some code there because there's already the reference to the animator component. Add the following method to the class toward the end:

```
public void SetAnimationTrigger(string name)
{
    animator.SetTrigger(name);
}
```

This method simply takes a **string** name of an animation trigger, and triggers it on the **animator** component. As it's a **public** method, it'll be exposed to you in the editor. **Save** the script and head back into the Unity editor.

In the Hierarchy, select the **Interactables / Sink** GameObject. Then in the Inspector, within the **Workstation** component, click the + to add a new listener to the `OnInteract` object. **Drag** the **Player** GameObject into the field, then from the dropdown list, select **PlayerController ▸ SetAnimationTrigger (string)**. Then, type **Wash** into the field.

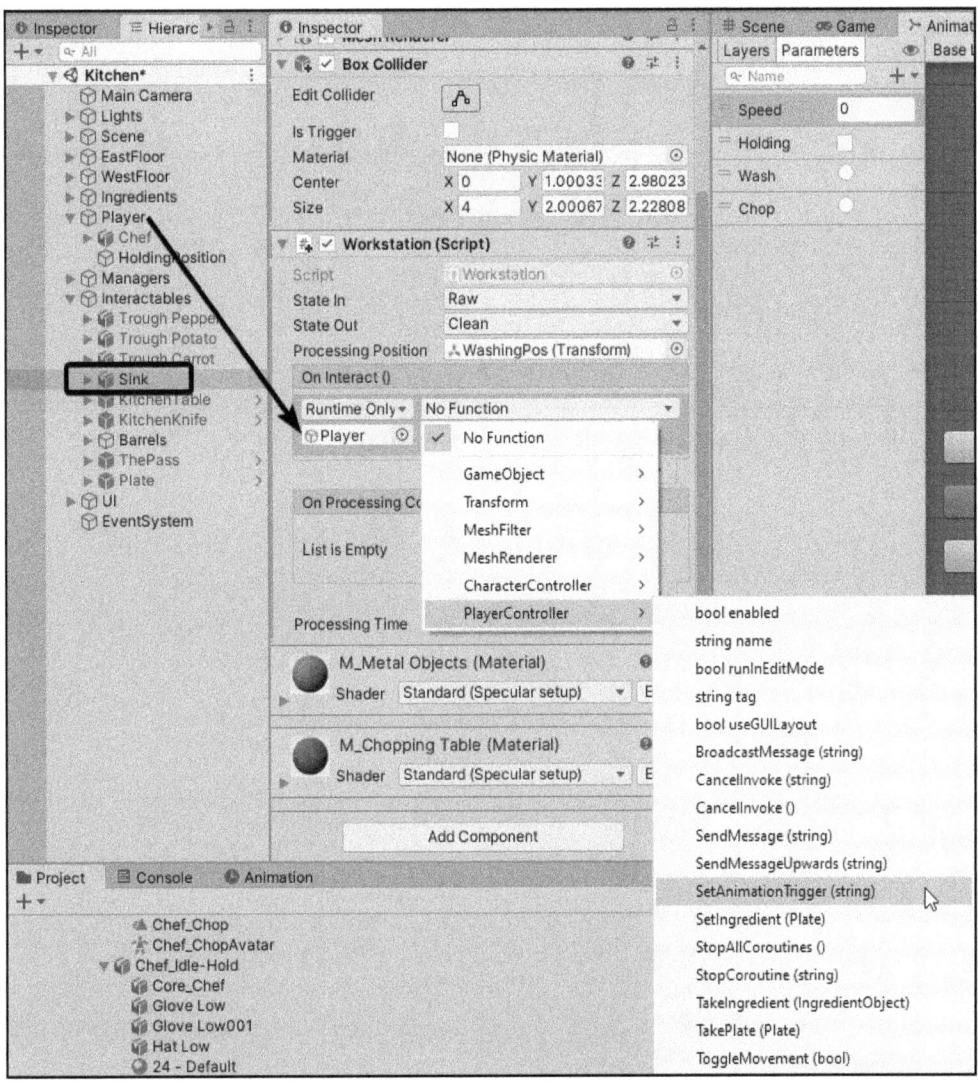

Do the same with the **Kitchen Table** GameObject, but type **Chop** into the field. Remember that the strings you pass should exactly match the parameters added in the animator controller, or they won't work as expected.

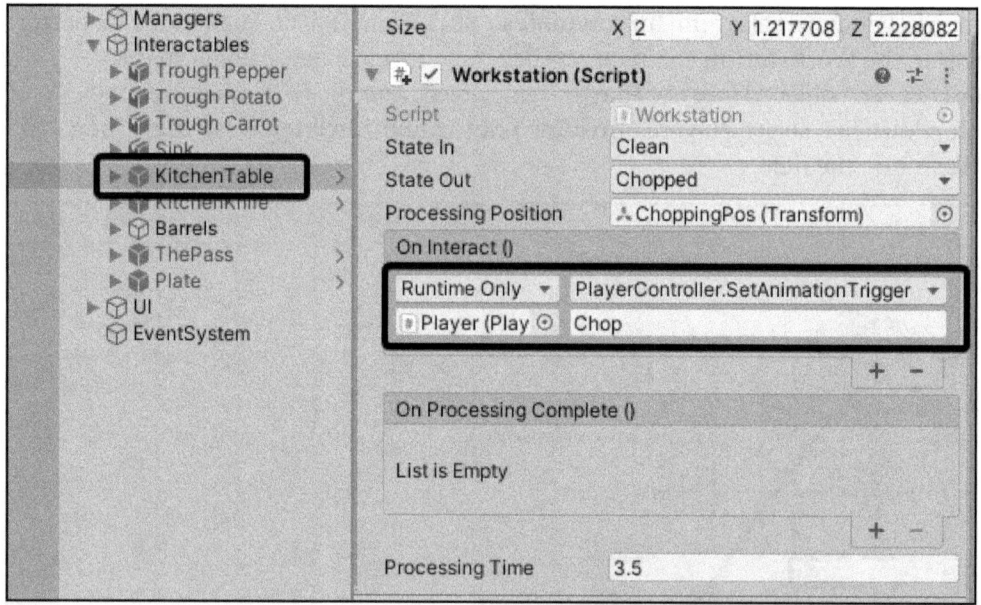

With everything in place, save the scene and click **Play**.

Take an ingredient over to that sink and get washing!

Congratulations! You've completely set up all of Chef's animations, and he's now ready to serve some much-needed sustenance to the Veggie Warriors about to head out into battle against the tank. The only thing left is to cook some delicious recipes, which you'll do in the next chapter.

Thankfully, the ingredients keep dropping in for more dishes…

Challenge

Sometimes you may have an animation that would work either in forward or reverse motion. Using the **Speed** variable on an animation state, you can vary how that animation plays in the game. For a challenge, try adding another state for **Chef_PutDown** and add it into the animator controller for when the user puts an ingredient onto the plate or puts the plate onto ThePass.

Here're a few hints:

- **Holding** will become false at these points and the animation will transition to **Chef_Idle** or **Chef_Walk**.

- Instead, make those transitions go through the new **Chef_PutDown** state and have it play the **Chef_PickUp** animation, but in reverse! Set the **Speed** variable to **-1**.

- Then, have transitions go back to the **Chef_Idle** and **Chef_Walk** states.

Now when Chef puts something down, you'll see more hand movement than before and the **Chef_PickUp** animation will play in reverse.

Key points

- **Animator controller** controls different animation states.
- **Animation States** hold animation clips.
- **Transitions** describe how you move from one state to another.
- **Parameters** can be used as **conditions** to transition between states.
- **Has Exit Time** means that a transition will trigger once an animation has finished playing.
- Parameters **Float**, **Int** and **Bool** are values that can be set from code using `animator.SetFloat`, `animator.SetInt` or `animator.SetBool` respectively. Conditions can compare these values to see if a transition should trigger.
- **Trigger** is a special parameter that describes a condition that happens immediately when you ask it to via `animator.SetTrigger`.

Chapter 14: Advanced Scriptable Objects

By Ben MacKinnon

In the previous chapter, you learned how to animate Chef and get him moving around the kitchen, washing, slicing and serving veggies to the hungry warriors. So far, you're only serving single-ingredient plates. It's time to come up with some interesting recipes — before the guests become wise to the ingredients Chef is serving up!

But how can Chef prepare a meal without a recipe? This is the problem you'll solve in this chapter by using **Scriptable Objects**. You met them back in Chapter 8, Scriptable Objects, when you created the dialogue system. In this chapter, you'll look at a few more techniques that you can use scriptable objects for. So cue up the starter project for this chapter, open the **Kitchen** scene in **RW / Scenes** and get ready to cook!

Scriptable objects as data containers

The key property about scriptable objects is that they can be created as serialized objects and stored in your project folders. Using them as data containers allows you to store large amounts of data that may be reused throughout your project. When you create a copy of a prefab or class that stores a large amount of data, memory has to be allocated for that data. Create a whole load of these objects, and you've used a lot of memory.

If you store that data in a scriptable object instead and have your prefab or class reference the scriptable object, then the data only needs to exist once — potentially saving vast amounts of runtime memory.

Beyond the potential memory-saving superpowers, scriptable objects can also help you increase your workflow - you can save data changes to them while playing in the Editor - but they can also be used to decouple your code architecture. Scriptable objects follow the Flyweight (http://www.gameprogrammingpatterns.com/flyweight.html) design pattern, which helps reduce memory usage in keeping things decoupled.

For your Chef, you'll use scriptable objects to first set up what you need to define a recipe. If you consider a game like you're creating here, in the full version, there could be many different recipes designed for the game. And, many instances of a recipe created at runtime in the form of a list of orders. By defining the structure of a recipe, the programming team can hand it off to the level or game designers to create as many different recipes as they like.

Defining the recipe scriptable object

You'll find the foundations of the recipe inside **RW / Scripts / ScriptableObjects**. Open the **Recipe** script inside your code editor.

At the top, notice the class currently inherits from `MonoBehaviour`.

```
public class Recipe : MonoBehaviour
```

The first step is to change this to a `ScriptableObject` class:

```
public class Recipe : ScriptableObject
```

In order to create new recipes, you need to add a menu item option to the class. Above the class definition, add the following line:

```
[CreateAssetMenu(fileName = "New Recipe", menuName = "Scriptable Objects/New Recipe", order = 51)]
```

This instruction allows you to create recipe assets in your project. Save the class and head back into the Unity Editor. Then, right-click the **Assets / RW / Recipes** folder and select **Create ▸ Scriptable Objects ▸ New Recipe**. Name the new recipe asset **Peas&Carrots**.

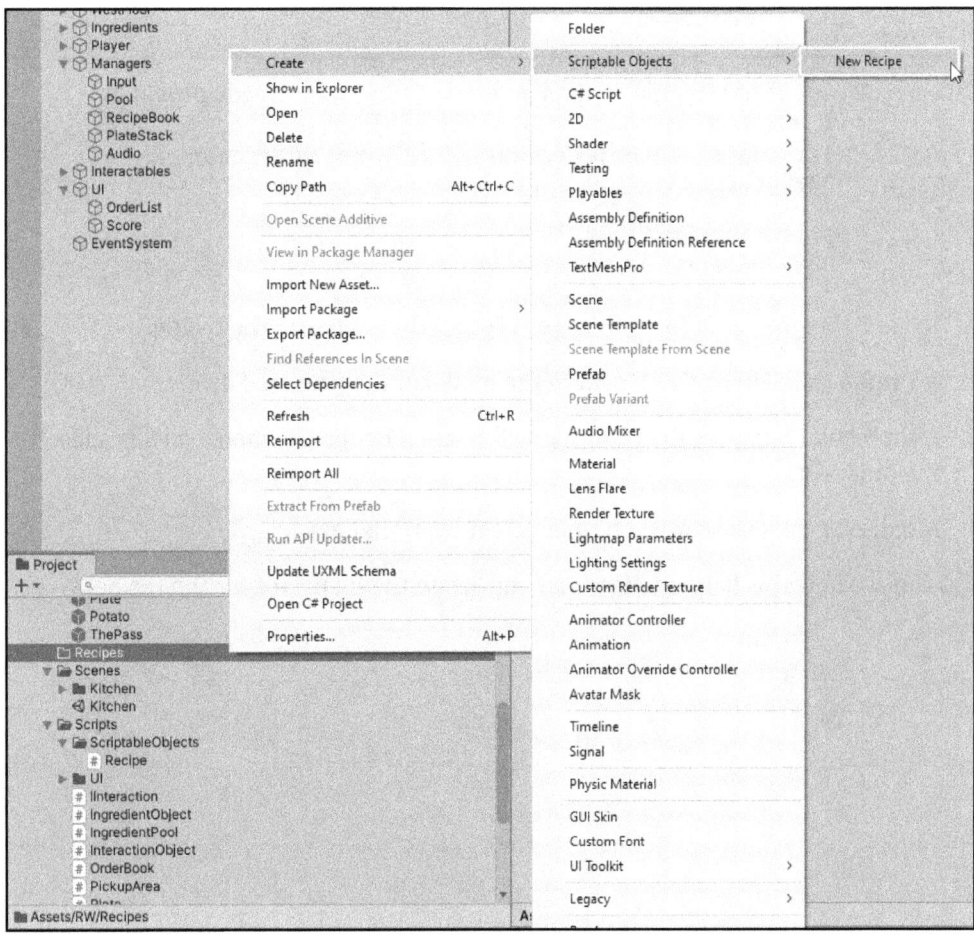

Select your newly created recipe in the Inspector and you'll see it's already expecting a few pieces of data.

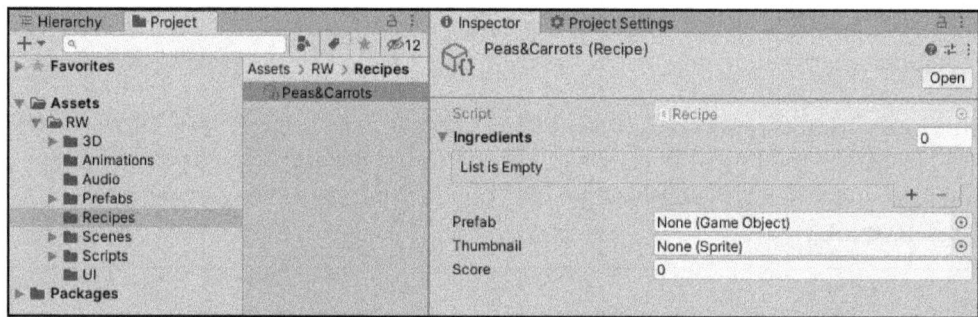

Take a look back at the **Recipe** script again to see what was already provided.

```
public List<IngredientObject.IngredientType> ingredients; // 1
public GameObject prefab; // 2

public Sprite thumbnail; // 3
public int score; // 4
```

1. A List of ingredients (or IngredientTypes) that make up the recipe.

2. A **Prefab** that will be used to store the model of the prepared dish.

3. A thumbnail image of the dish that will be used by the UI when a dish is added to the order list.

4. A score for the dish, for when Chef gets it over ThePass.

You can see how this list matches what you see in the Inspector for the recipe.

Fortunately, everything you need to set up the **Peas & Carrots** dish is already in the project.

1. Add **two** ingredients to the list. From the drop-downs, select — you guessed it — **Carrot** and **Pea**.

2. For the **Prefab**, add the **Dish_Carrot** prefab from the **Assets / RW / Prefabs / Dishes** folder.

3. For the **Thumbnail**, add the **Peas&Carrots** image from **Assets / RW / UI** folder.

4. For the score, well that's up to you! By default, the player gets **5** points for serving anything, so **20** seems like a reasonable score for a requested dish.

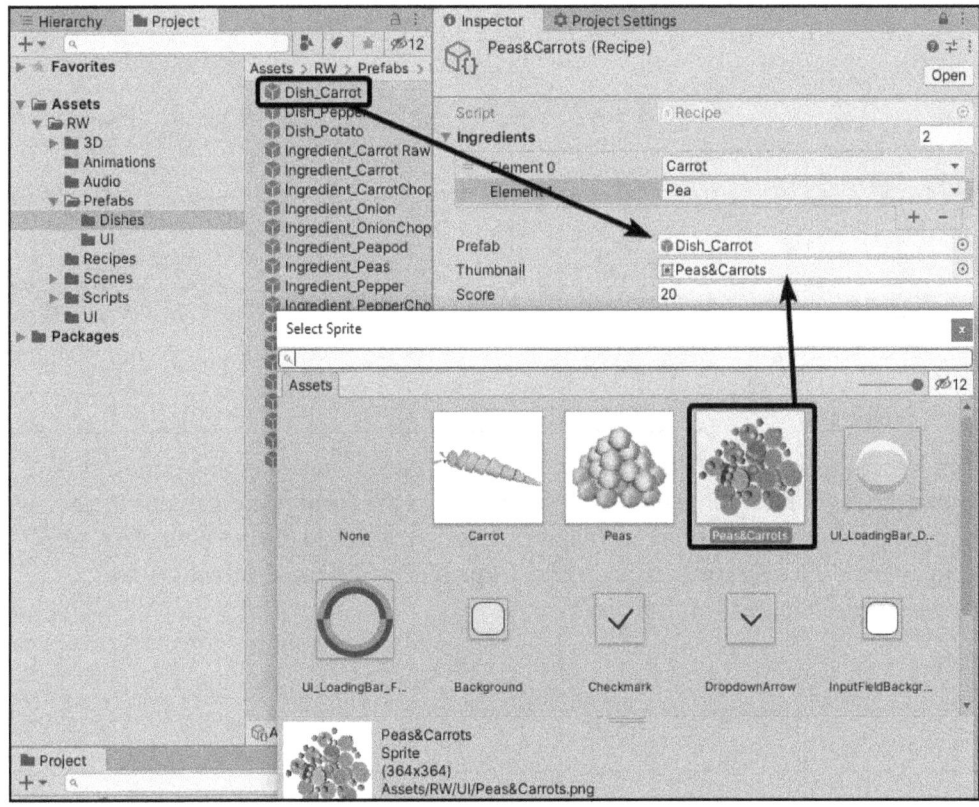

There you have it — the first recipe is in the book!

Only, it's not *in* the book yet. To start getting orders for your new dish, find the **Managers** / **RecipeBook** in the Hierarchy and add the **Peas&Carrots** recipe to the list of **Recipes** on the **Order Book** component.

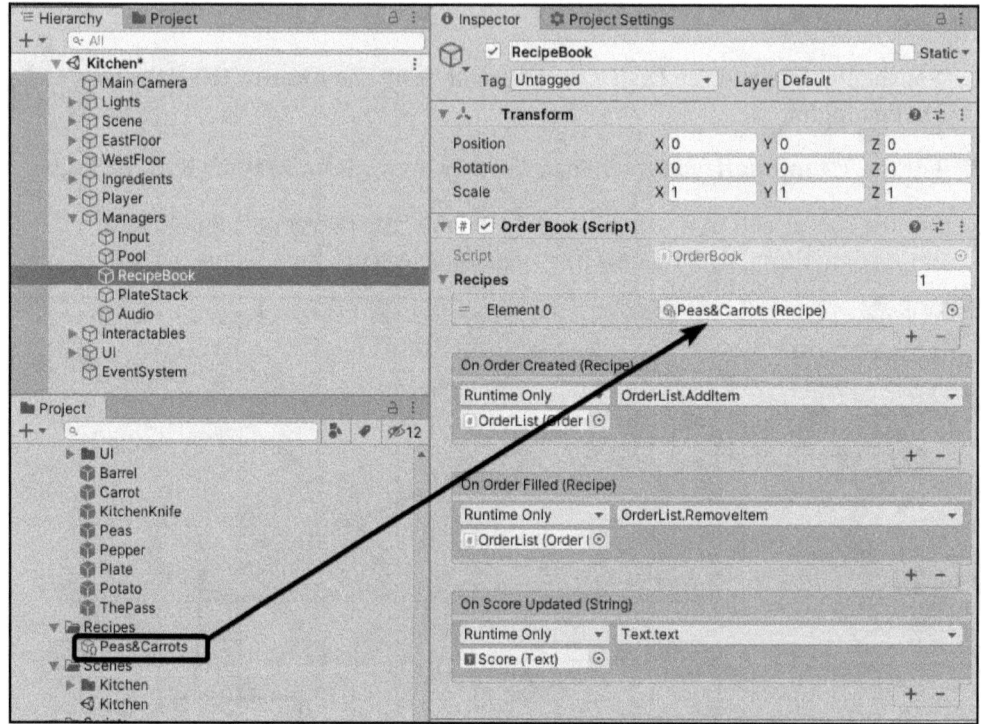

Save the scene and enter **Play** mode. Notice that orders start popping onto the screen. Grab yourself some peas from the barrel in the corner (you can put them straight onto the plate), then wash and chop a carrot to add to the same plate. As a recap, you can use **Space** to pick up and drop objects and the **Control** key for washing and chopping (in that order).

The ingredients change to the prefab you assigned earlier and can serve up that ordered dish!

But wait, **0** points? You were going to score generously for this exquisite dish of raw vegetables.

Scriptable Objects as events

The logic to handle scoring is inside the **Plate** script. Open it from **Assets / RW / Scripts** in your code editor, and navigate down to the last method: **Serve**.

```
public void Serve()
{
    // Check for a recipe
    if (Recipe != null)
    {

    }
    else
    {
        // Player served a non-recipe dish, award some points
        OrderBook.instance.Service();
    }
    // Return ingredients to the pool
    foreach (IngredientObject ingredient in transform.GetComponentsInChildren<IngredientObject>(true))
    {
        IngredientPool.Instance.Add(ingredient);
```

```
        }
        OnPlateServed?.Invoke();
        Destroy(gameObject, 1f);
}
```

As you can see, the opening `if` statement checks to see if there's a recipe on the plate (this has been worked out in the method above, **CheckRecipes**). Currently, though, it does nothing. If no match is found it calls `Service` in the `OrderBook`. That's where the **5** points are awarded for a non-recipe dish.

We need a new way to award points for when the player serves a requested dish. Not only that, but we'll also need to take that order out of the queue once it's been fulfilled.

This is the perfect opportunity to look at one of the other great uses of scriptable objects - as an event system. As you know, scriptable objects are defined objects which allow you to create multiple variants fairly easily. This is also an ideal situation for when you want to have multiple variants of a specific type of event. By using scriptable objects as an event, you can decouple your code further. In the code above, you could add a bunch of code to the inside of that `if` statement to do all the things you needed, but instead we'll create two new classes.

Scriptable event raiser

Inside the **Assets / RW / Scripts / ScriptableObjects** folder, create a new script called **ServeEvent**. Open it in your code editor.

First, make sure this class inherits from `ScriptableObject` and add the **CreateAssetMenu** attribute to it.

```
[CreateAssetMenu(fileName = "New Serve Event", menuName =
"Scriptable Objects/Serve Event", order = 52)]
public class ServeEvent : ScriptableObject
```

Now add this to the top of the class:

```
private List<ServeEventListener> listeners
    = new List<ServeEventListener>();
```

This declares a `List` of `ServeEventListener`. `ServeEventListener` doesn't exist yet, but we'll get to that next.

The ServeEvent class exists for one purpose (as most classes should!), and that is to raise an event when a recipe is served. ServeEventListener objects will serve one purpose — to listen for the serve events and pass instruction on to other parts of the code. Listeners will be able to register and unregister themselves, so that you don't try to pass an event to a listener that's not active — or worse, doesn't exist anymore!

With all that in mind, you need to create three methods. First add this in ServeEvent:

```
public void Raise()
{
    for(int i = listeners.Count -1; i>=0 ; i--)
    {
        listeners[i].OnEventRaised();
    }
}
```

The Raise method runs through the list of listeners and calls a method called OnEventRaised that you'll add later.

Now add this method under the last:

```
public void RegisterListener(ServeEventListener listener)
{
    listeners.Add(listener);
}
```

RegisterListener will add the passed listener to the list of listeners.

Finally, continue by adding this:

```
public void UnregisterListener(ServeEventListener listener)
{
    listeners.Remove(listener);
}
```

UnregisterListener will remove the passed listener from the list.

That's it for the **SeverEvent** script. Save it and head back to the Unity editor.

> **Note**: You'll see a couple of errors in the **Console** window at this point. That's OK — they relate to the fact that you haven't created the **ServeEventListener** class yet.

Event listener

Now that you have the event class, it's time to create the listener class. Create another script in the **Assets / RW / Scripts / ScriptableObjects** folder called **ServeEventListener**. You're putting it in the same folder as the event, however this class is *not* going to be a scriptable object. Instead, it stays as a `MonoBehaviour` because you'll attach it as a component to objects in the scene.

Open the **ServeEventListener** script. At the top, add the following `using` statement below the other directives already there:

```
using UnityEngine.Events;
```

This library allows us to use **UnityEvents**. This is Unity's own inbuilt event system that allows you to hook events up in the editor in the same way that you connected the animation events in the last chapter. The `ServeEventListener` will translate your own custom event into a Unity event, so that you can use it in the same way.

Now right inside the `ServeEventListener` class, add the following fields at the top of the class:

```
[SerializeField]
private ServeEvent serveEvent;
[SerializeField]
private UnityEvent response;
```

These fields are private, so they can't be accessed by code outside this class. But you also mark them as **Serialized** so you can access them as fields of the component inside the Unity editor. This will allow you to assign values to them later.

Remember what the listener class has to do?

1. Register itself as a listener.

2. Unregister itself as a listener.

3. Respond to the `OnEventRaised` call from `ServeEvent`.

For the first two items, you can make use of some `Monobehaviour` methods. `OnEnable` and `OnDisable` are called when a GameObject becomes active or inactive, respectively. The power of these methods is that they can be called from a number of different actions:

- When a GameObject is created or destroyed.
- When a GameObject is activated or deactivated (either in the editor or by calling `.SetActive(bool)`).
- When the component is enabled or disabled (again, either in the editor or by using the `.enabled` variable).

Add the following to **ServeEventListener**:

```
private void OnEnable()
{
    serveEvent.RegisterListener(this);
}
private void OnDisable()
{
    serveEvent.UnregisterListener(this);
}
```

These get your event listener to register and unregister itself in the situations noted above.

Now add the following:

```
public void OnEventRaised()
{
    response.Invoke();
}
```

As discussed, the `OnEventRaised` method is required by the **ServeEvent**. It passes the instruction through to the `UnityEvent` by calling its `Invoke` method.

Save the script and head back to the Unity editor. **Right-click** in the **Assets / RW / Scripts / ScriptableObjects** folder and select **Create ▸ Scriptable Objects ▸ Serve Event**. Name your new event **Peas&Carrots**.

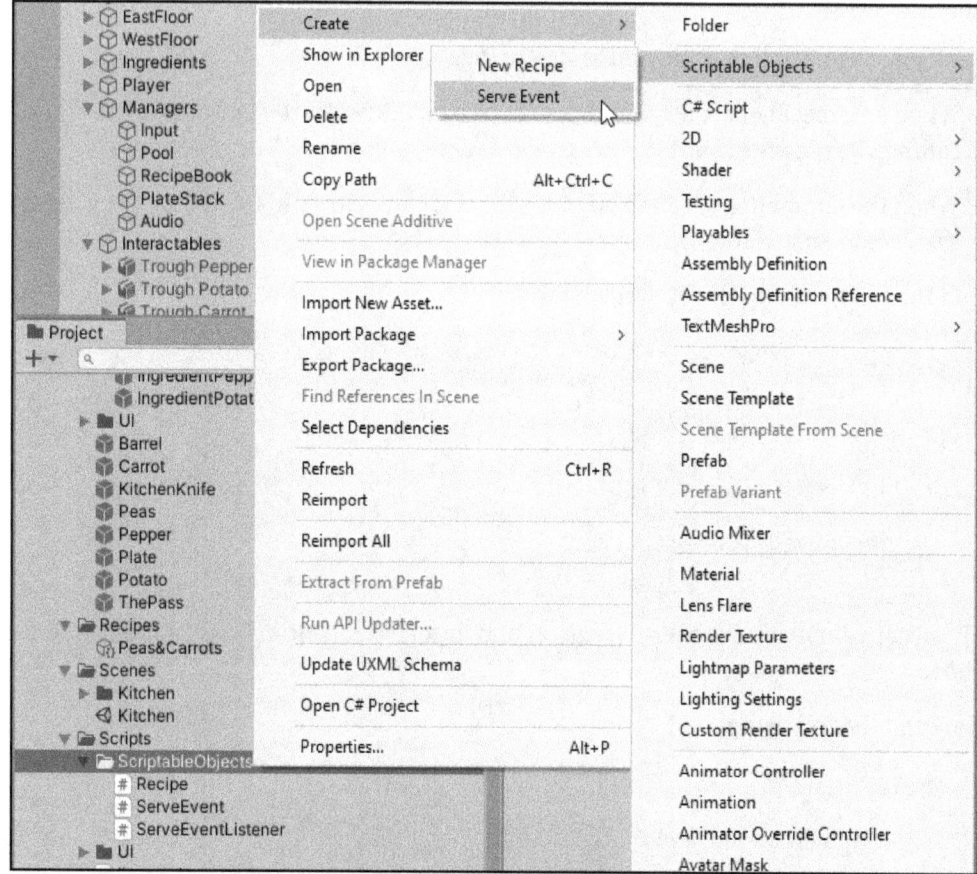

Now select the **Managers / RecipeBook** in the **Hierarchy** once more. Add a **ServeEventListener** component to it, and set it up like this:

- Add the new **Peas&Carrots** event as the **Serve Event**.

- For the **Response**, add an item, **drag** the **RecipeBook** into the **Object** field and choose **OrderBook ▸ Service (Recipe)** in the drop-down.

- Finally, add the **Peas&Carrots** recipe as the passed recipe.

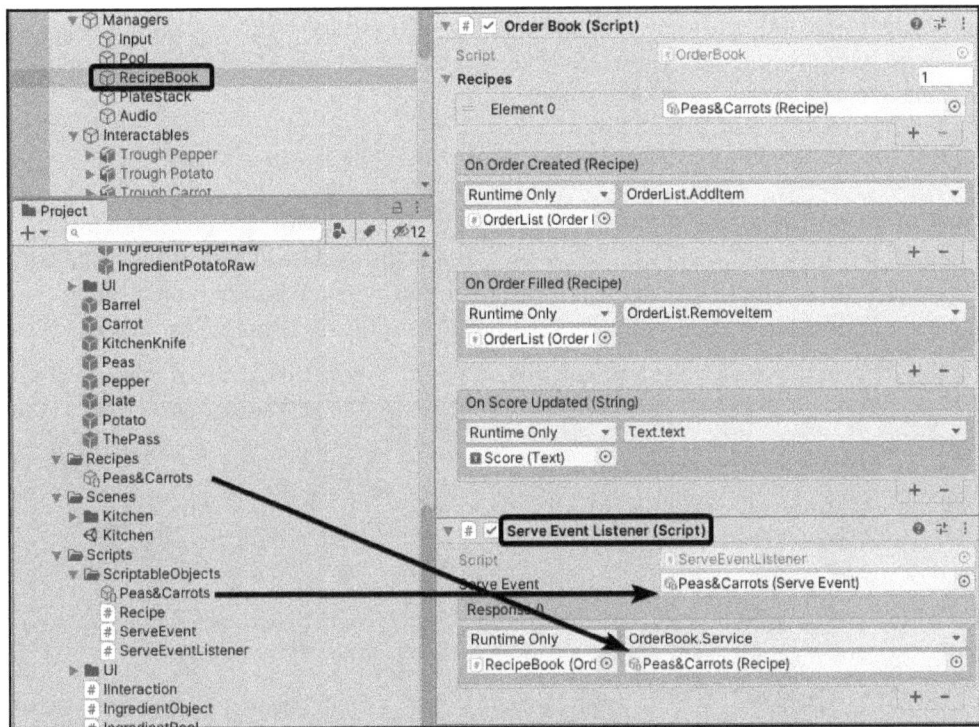

There's one final thing to set up before the new event system is working. You need to be able to raise the events when a recipe is served. Open the **Recipe** script from **RW / Scripts / ScriptableObjects**. Add a **ServeEvent** field to the scriptable object:

```
public ServeEvent serveEvent;
```

Save the script and head back to the Unity editor. Select your **Peas&Carrots** recipe in **Assets / RW / Recipes** and add the **Peas&Carrots** event to the new **Serve Event** field.

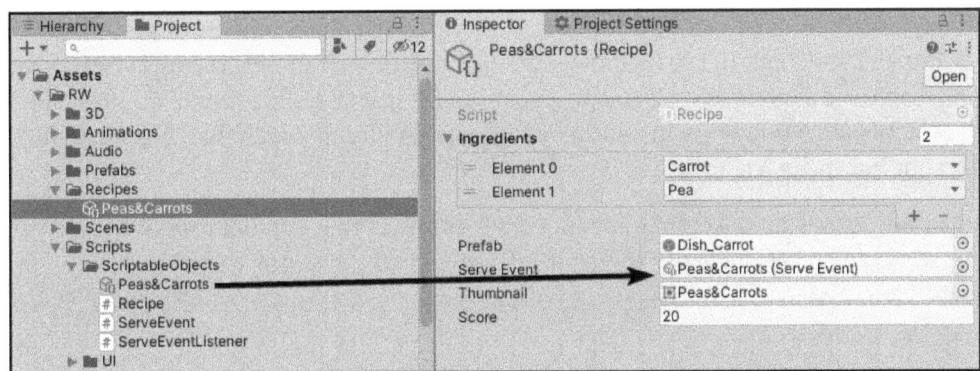

Remember where this whole thing started? Open the **Plate** script once more, and navigate back down to the **Serve** method. Inside the empty `if` statement that you saw earlier, add the following statement:

```
Recipe.serveEvent?.Raise();
```

Now, when a plate is served across ThePass, if there is a known recipe on the plate, that recipes serve event will get raised. Save the script and head back into the editor for the last time. Click **Play** and test it out! Not only will you get **20** points (or however many you defined in the recipe), but the order will come off the list of current orders.

Expanding Chef's repertoire

It may have felt like a lot of work to get the scriptable objects and event system set up, but you are about to see the power of having done so. Sure, Peas and Carrots is a fine dish to be serving, but Chef is too talented for just one signature dish! It's time to mix things up by adding in another dish — Potatoes and Zucchini. (Or Courgette for your European friends.)

However, there's no Zucchini to be found currently, so first you do need to prepare the scene and project a little. To begin with, you need a new prefab for the ingredient.

Navigate to **Assets / RW / Prefabs**, right-click and select **Create ▸ Prefab**. Name it **Zucchini**.

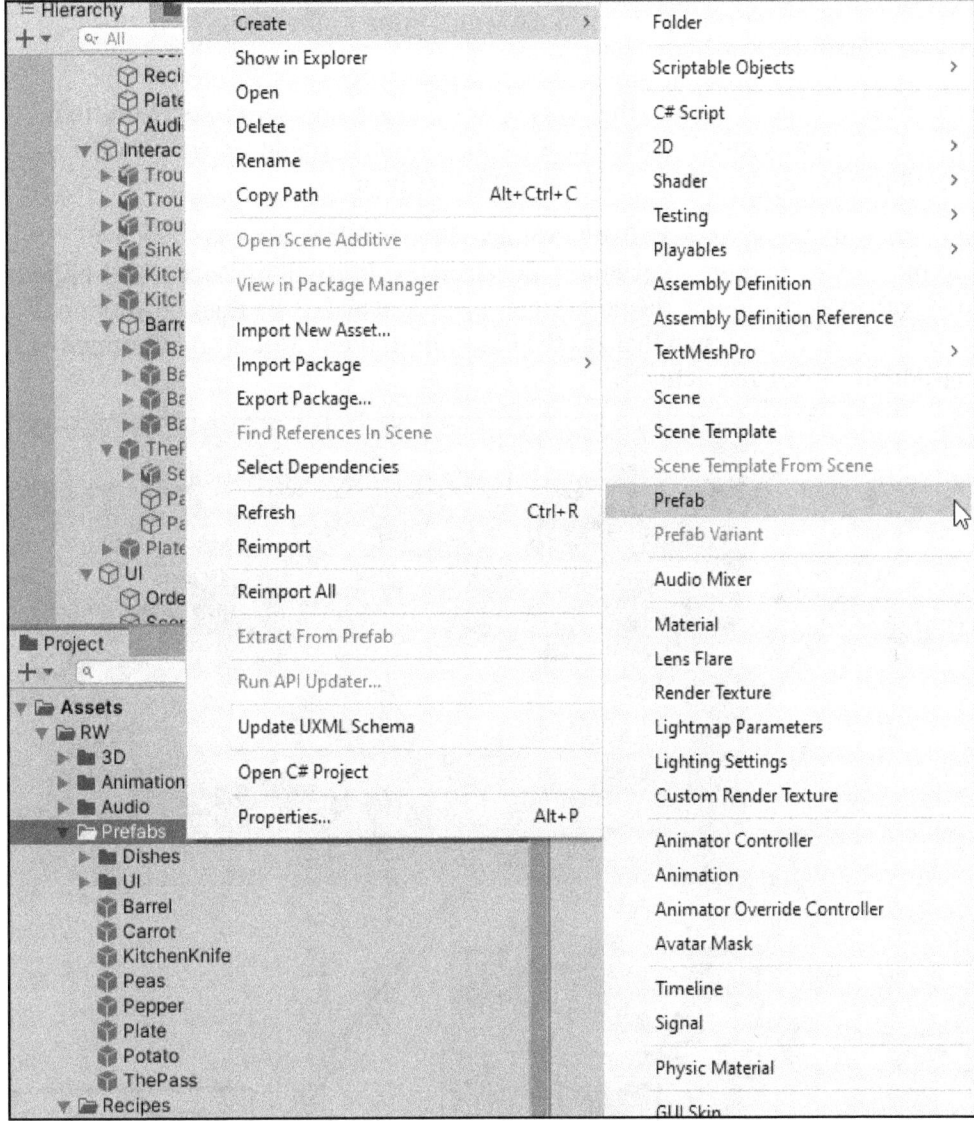

Double-click the prefab to open it in the prefab editor. You currently have an empty GameObject, so add the **IngredientObject** component to it.

IngredientObject has a type drop-down that doesn't currently have **Zucchini** on the list, so open the script and add it to the `IngredientType` enum:

```
public enum IngredientType { Carrot, Pepper, Potato, Pea, 
  Zucchini }
```

Save the script and go back to the Unity editor. You can now select **Zucchini** from the dropdown for **Type**. There are no Zucchini warriors dropping down, so Chef doesn't need to wash them. You can set **State** to **Clean**.

Next, navigate to the **Assets** / **RW** / **Prefabs** / **Dishes** folder and you'll see two Zucchini models in there: **Ingredient_Zucchini** and **Ingredient_ZucchiniChopped**. Drag both in as children of the root GameObject, and make sure their positions are set to **{0, 0, 0}**. Then, assign them as the **Clean Ingredient Model** and **Chopped Ingredient Model**, respectively.

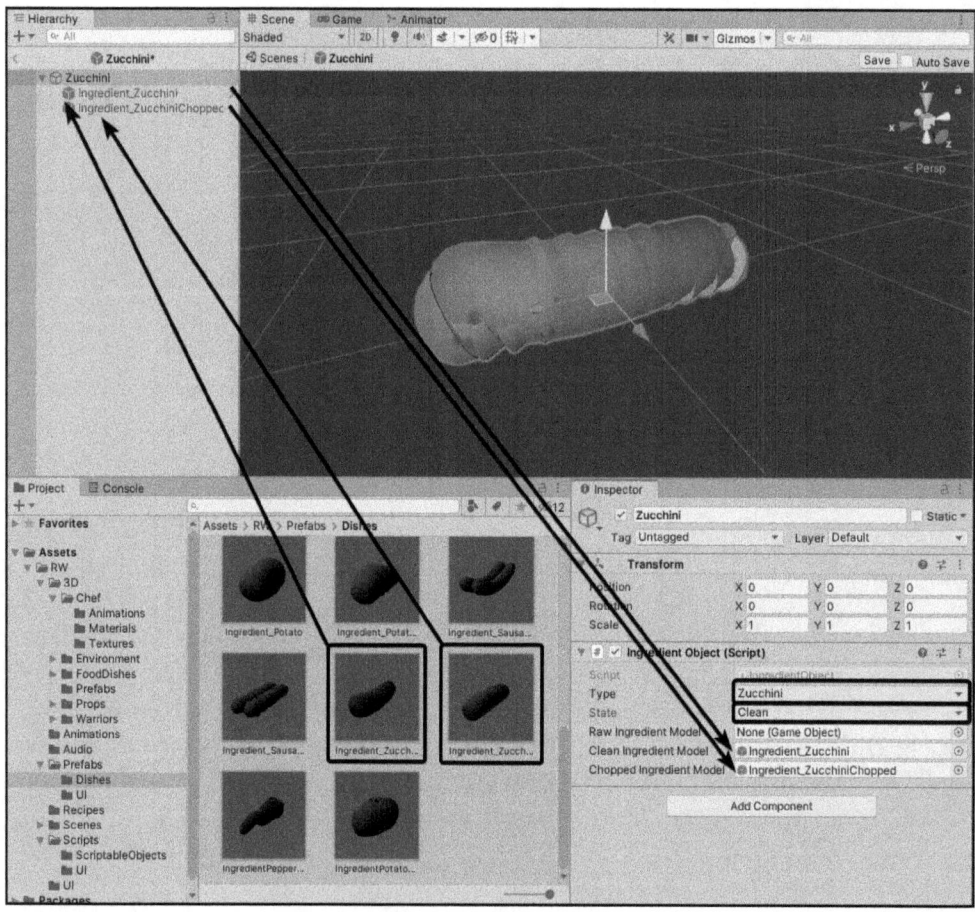

Save the prefab and go back into the scene. In the Hierarchy, find **Interactables / Barrels** and select **Barrel (3)**. Rename it to **Barrel (Zucchini)** and add the **Supply Barrel** component. Assign your new **Zucchini** prefab as the **Ingredient Prefab**.

For aesthetics, add the **Ingredient_Zucchini** model from the **Assets / RW / Prefabs / Dishes** folder (not your prefab!) as the child of the Barrels Barrel model, and set its position to **{0, 0.75, 0}**.

Finally, select the **Player** GameObject in the Hierarchy and add the new supply barrel to the list of **Pick Up Zones**.

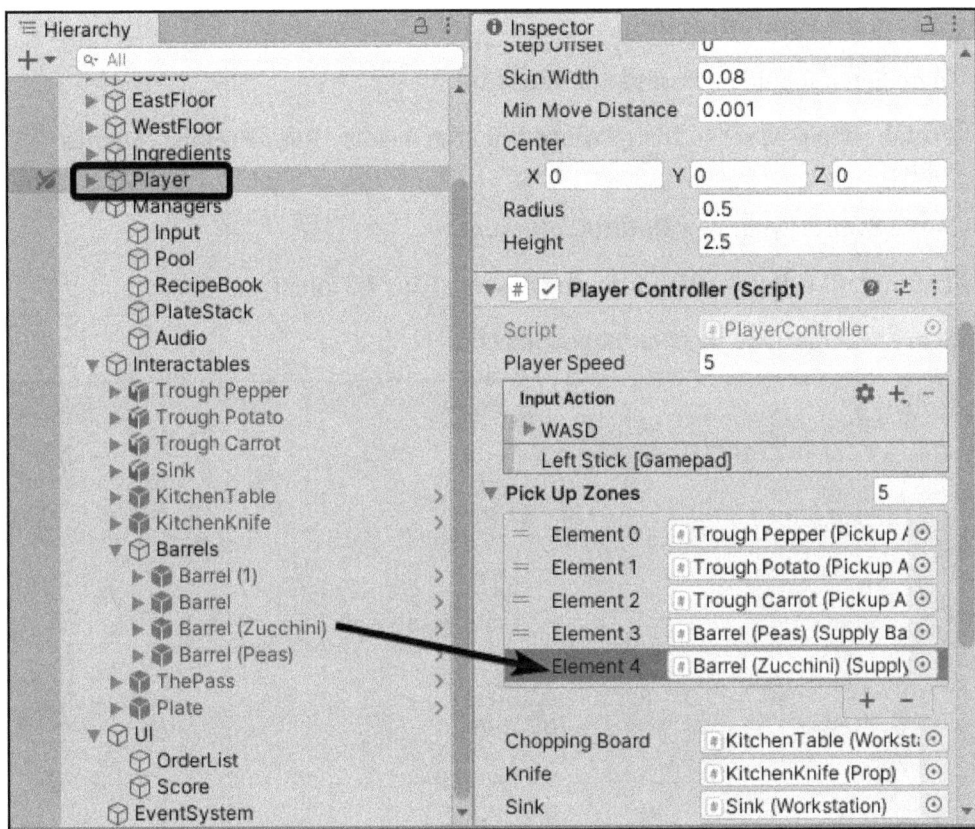

That's all the set up needed. From here on, you already know what you're doing!

1. Add a new **Recipe** (**Create ▸ Scriptable Objects ▸ New Recipe**) in the **Assets / RW / Recipes** folder called **PotatoDish** (because Zucchini is tiresome to spell).

2. Add a new **Serve Event** (**Create ▸ Scriptable Objects ▸ Serve Event**) in the **Assets / RW / Scripts / ScriptableObjects** folder called **PotatoDish**.

3. Set up the **PotatoDish** recipe:

- Ingredients should be **Potato** and **Zucchini**.
- **Prefab** should be set to **Dish_Potato** from the **Assets / RW / Prefabs / Dishes** folder.
- **Serve Event** is your new **PotatoDish** event.
- **Thumbnail** is **PotatoDish** from the **Assets / RW / UI** folder.
- **Score** again is up to you, but **20** sounds fair.

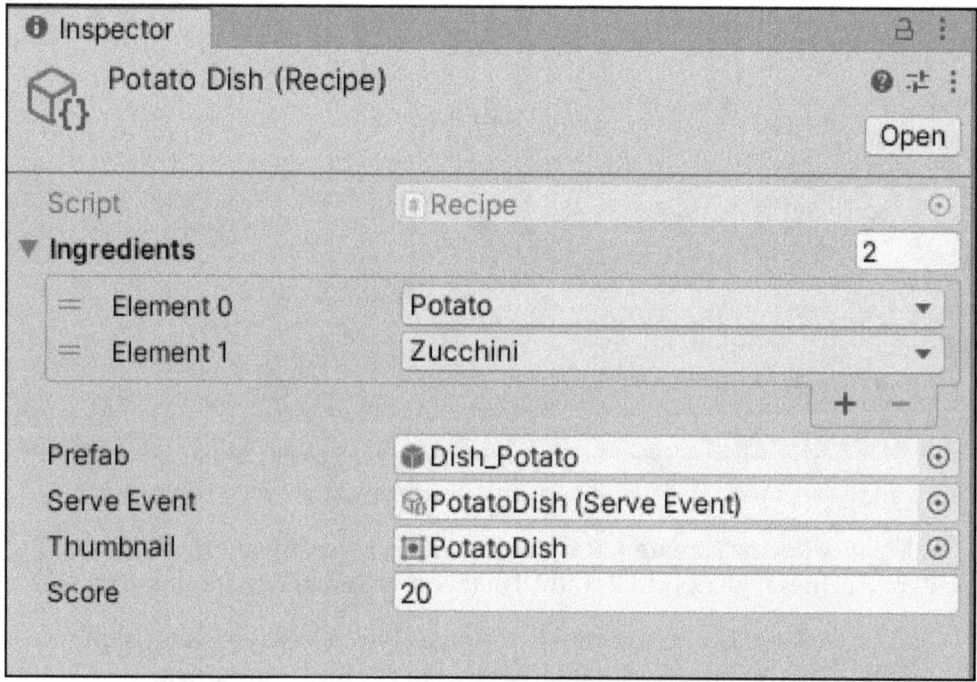

Finally, in the Hierarchy select the **Managers / RecipeBook** and add the **PotatoDish** to the list of recipes.

Add another **Serve Event Listener** component for the new event, passing the new recipe to the same method as before, `OrderBook.Service(Recipe)`.

Chapter 14: Advanced Scriptable Objects   323

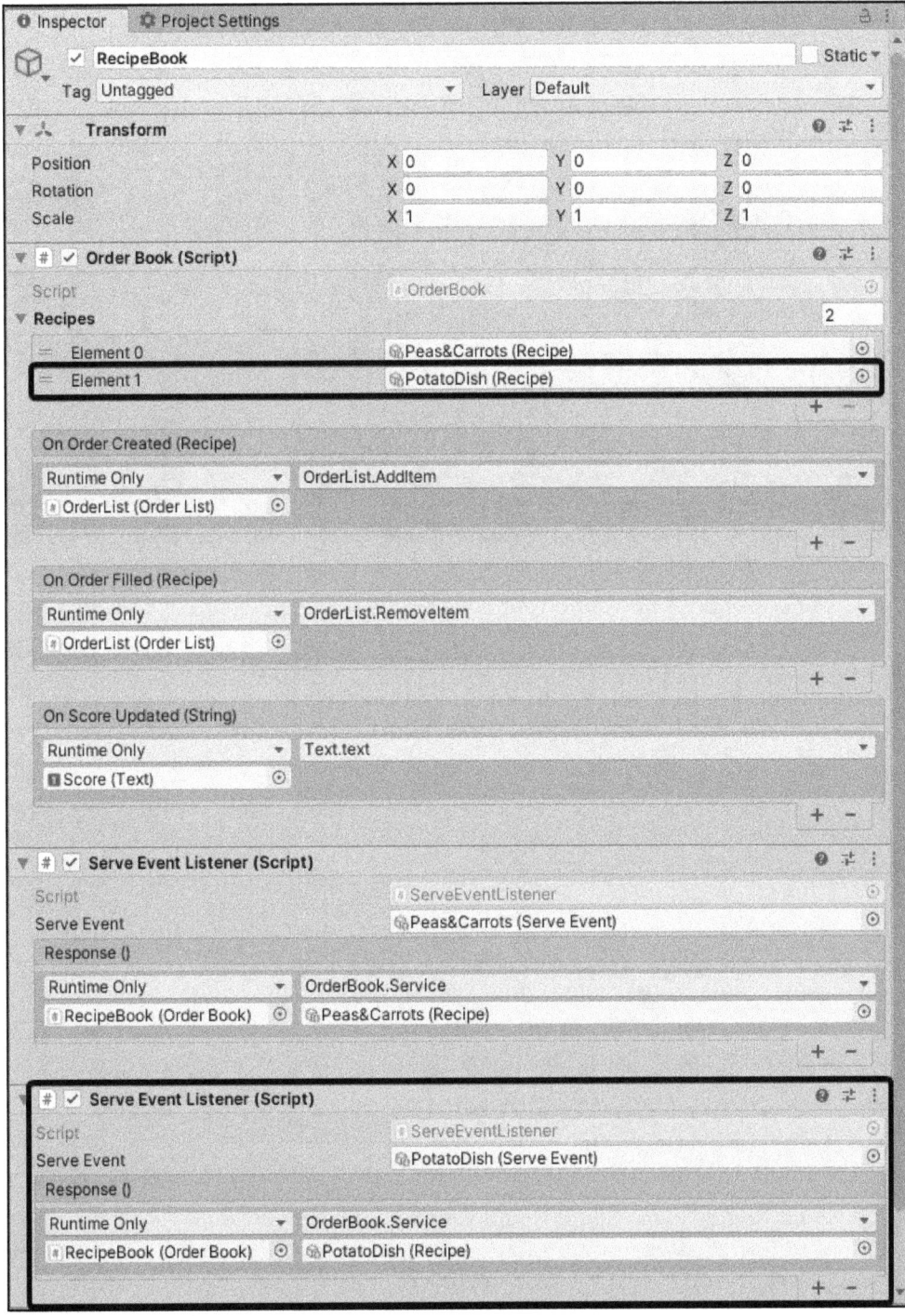

Save the scene, click **Play** and start serving some potato dishes!

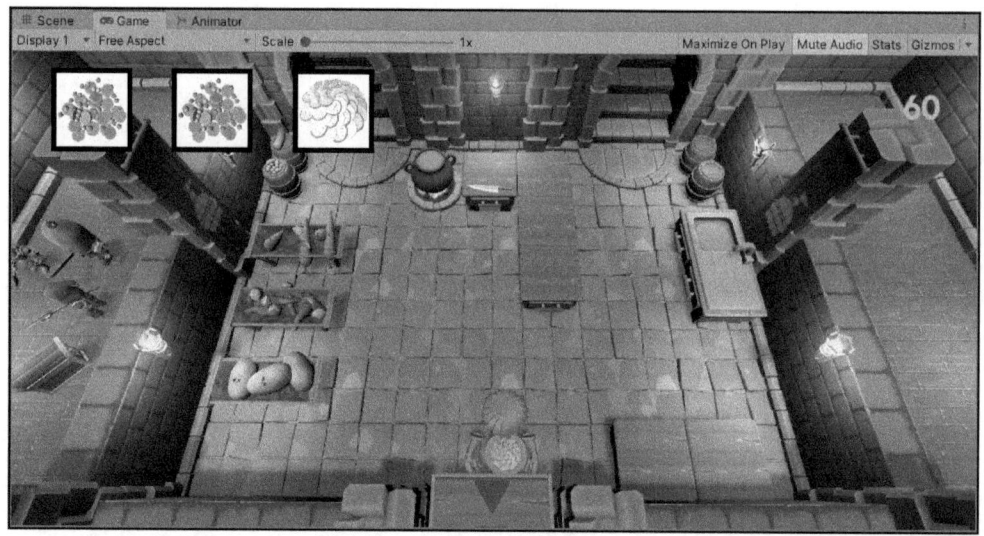

Challenge

Got one more in you? All the materials you need to create a third recipe are in the project. The final dish involves Peppers, Onion and Sausage. You've already learned everything you need to know to complete the steps for this final recipe, but the tasks you need to complete are:

1. Add **Onion** and **Sausage** to the list of ingredients in **IngredientObject**.
2. Create new **IngredientObject** prefabs for **Onion** and **Sausage**. (You can find the models you need in the **Assets** / **RW** / **Prefabs** / **Dishes** folder.)
3. Create a new **Recipe**
4. Create a new **ServeEvent**.
5. Set up **Supply Barrels** for the ingredients. There's two more barrels already in the scene, beside the sink.
6. Add the **Supply Barrels** to the **Player Controllers** list of **Pick Up Zones**.
7. Add the new **Recipe** to the list on **Managers** / **RecipeBook**.
8. Add a new **ServeEventListener** on **Managers** / **RecipeBook** to listen for your new serve event, and pass the new recipe to the same `OrderBook.Service(Recipe)` event.

And with those steps, you've added yet another recipe for Chef to serve up to the hungry warriors. Hopefully you can see now how easy it would be to continue to expand this game with new levels, new ingredients and new recipes.

Key points

- Scriptable objects can be used as data containers — allowing you to reuse data throughout instances of objects — without assigning additional memory for the data.

- Scriptable objects can also be used to represent events — allowing you to decouple your code and make a system that's easy for a level designer to come in and expand your game without extra programming.

- Scriptable objects are ideal in supporting the Flyweight (http://www.gameprogrammingpatterns.com/flyweight.html) design pattern.

Conclusion

Congratulations! What a journey it's been. If you followed along through the whole book, you learned a lot about Unity — from the basics of how to use the Unity Editor, all the way through to creating all the neat things that make a game compelling and fun.

You also learned some best-practice techniques from some seasoned Unity developers. By using these concepts in your own games, you'll be able to make them more dynamic and exciting and take them to the next (game) level. :]

We hope the ideas you've seen in this book inspire you to create great games. We'd love to hear from you about them if you do. Maybe your game will become the next must-play classic?

If you want to further your understanding of Unity game development, don't forget about the Unity articles and videos available at raywenderlich.com.

If you have any questions or comments as you work through this book, please stop by our forums at forums.raywenderlich.com and look for the particular forum category for this book.

Thanks again for purchasing this book. Your continued support is what makes the books, tutorials, videos and other things we do at raywenderlich.com possible. We truly appreciate it!

– The *Unity Apprentice* team

CPSIA information can be obtained
at www.ICGtesting.com
Printed in the USA
LVHW051330291122
734184LV00005B/364